Anthony Trotta effectively describes and analyzes E-Government in its many forms, meanings and contexts. He convinced me that E-Government is both basis and impetus for deliberative democracy – ultimately building trust – that goes beyond mere technocratic interaction between representatives and their clients and constituents. In his survey, he provides both breadth and depth and reveals a remarkable understanding of E-Government, one that will be beneficial to practitioners, students and academic researchers.

Gerald J. Miller, *Arizona State University, USA*

Advances in E-Governance

E-Governance as a field of study is relatively new when considered within the broader historical context of U.S. democracy. The advent of the modern Internet in the early 1990s yielded new technologies that began to shift citizen expectations of how government can—and in many cases should—govern. Though innovations continue to emerge at a rapid pace, these technologies may be used to reinforce long-held deliberative democracy principles, including transparency, accountability and flexibility. *Advances in E-Governance* offers a comprehensive exploration of the role that technological innovation plays in facilitating government action and citizen participation.

In this timely book, author Anthony Trotta differentiates E-Governance from E-Government and examines the increasingly important role social media and crowdsourcing have come to play in our democracy, and the interactions between technology, polling, voting and outcomes. Including practical cases ranging from DMV registration to online tax filing and markers of successful implementation, *Advances in E-Governance* carefully addresses how the adoption and expansion of electronic platforms align with new government expectations and looks to future trends in this rapidly expanding field.

Anthony Trotta holds a Ph.D. in Public Administration from the School of Public Affairs and Administration at Rutgers University–Newark and has extensive university-level teaching and course-development experience in public administration and political science (both in the traditional and virtual classroom) at the undergraduate and graduate levels.

ASPA Series in Public Administration and Public Policy

David H. Rosenbloom, Ph.D.
Editor-in-Chief

Mission: Throughout its history, ASPA has sought to be true to its founding principles of promoting scholarship and professionalism within the public service. The ASPA Book Series on Public Administration and Public Policy publishes books that increase national and international interest for public administration and which discuss practical or cutting edge topics in engaging ways of interest to practitioners, policy makers, and those concerned with bringing scholarship to the practice of public administration.

Managing Public Sector Projects
A Strategic Framework for Success in an Era of Downsized Government, Second Edition
by David S. Kassel

The Handbook of Federal Government Leadership and Administration
Transforming, Performing, and Innovating in a Complex World
Edited by David H. Rosenbloom, Patrick S. Malone, and Bill Valdez

Managing Digital Governance: Issues, Challenges, and Solutions
by Yu-Che Chen

The Future of Disaster Management in the US
Rethinking Legislation, Policy, and Finance
edited by Amy LePore

Case Studies in Disaster Response and Emergency Management, Second Edition
by Nicolas A. Valcik and Paul E. Tracy

Researcher-Policymaker Partnerships
Strategies for Launching and Sustaining Successful Collaborations
by Jenni W. Owen and Anita M. Larson

Advances in E-Governance
Theory and Application of Technological Initiatives
by Anthony Trotta

Advances in E-Governance

Theory and Application of
Technological Initiatives

Anthony Trotta

NEW YORK AND LONDON

American Society for
Public Administration
ADVANCING EXCELLENCE IN PUBLIC SERVICE

First published 2018
by Routledge
711 Third Avenue, New York, NY 10017

and by Routledge
2 Park Square, Milton Park, Abingdon, Oxon OX14 4RN

Routledge is an imprint of the Taylor & Francis Group, an informa business

© 2018 Taylor & Francis

Library of Congress Cataloging in Publication Data
Names: Trotta, Anthony M., 1974- author.
Title: Advances in E-governance : theory and application of technological initiatives / by Anthony Trotta.
Description: New York : Routledge, 2017. | Series: ASPA series in public administration & public policy | Includes bibliographical references and index.
Identifiers: LCCN 2016057296| ISBN 9781498701181 (hardback : alk. paper) | ISBN 9781315181530 (ebook)
Subjects: LCSH: Internet in public administration–United States. | Political participation–Technological innovations–United States. | Social media–Political aspects–United States. | Deliberative democracy–United States.
Classification: LCC JK468.A8 T76 2017 | DDC 352.3/802854678–dc23
LC record available at https://lccn.loc.gov/2016057296

ISBN: 978-1-498-70118-1 (hbk)
ISBN: 978-1-315-18153-0 (ebk)

Typeset in Sabon
by Taylor & Francis Books

<u>This Book is Dedicated to</u>

My Mom and Dad
Jo Anne and Alfred Trotta

Contents

List of Illustrations

Figures

Tables

Boxes

About the Author

Dr. Anthony Trotta has studied public administration and political science for over 25 years in pursuit of knowledge that would allow for him to better comprehend and appreciate the workings of governance. During that time he has earned a B.A. in political science from Rutgers University–Camden in 1996, an M.P.A. from Rutgers University–Camden in 2000 and a Ph.D. in Public Administration from the School of Public Affairs and Administration at Rutgers University–Newark in 2006. In addition, he has extensive university-level teaching and course-development experience in public administration and political science (both in the traditional and virtual classroom) at the undergraduate and graduate levels since he began his teaching career in 2002. Although primarily serving in a teaching capacity at the university level since 2002, Anthony Trotta also has experience contributing to academic works. This includes serving in the academic journal manuscript-review process and in a classroom textbook editorial-review capacity. In addition, Anthony's academic background is supplemented with real-world management experience in the public sector and the private sector. The past 25 years (and counting) serving as a student, teacher and practitioner of public administration and political science has provided him with an amalgamation of knowledge and insight, which was used to complete this book on E-Governance. He would like to thank the reader for taking the time to join him on this phase of the journey that has provided him the opportunity to continue the pursuit of his passion for better understanding governance.

1 Introduction

E-Government and E-Governance

E-Governance as a field of study is relatively new within the historical context of the United States' deliberative democracy. The advent of the Internet by the early 1990s yielded a plethora of newly emerging technologies that began shifting citizen expectations regarding how government can and should govern. The rapid development of information and communication technologies (ICTs) that continued to proliferate since then caused a steady increase in the expectations of citizens regarding the government's usage of these innovations. Modern innovations made available during the E-Governance Era reinforce many traditional deliberative democracy principles, such as transparency, accountability and flexibility. As such, the focus of this work is to better understand the role that technological innovation plays in facilitating government actions within a deliberative democracy. The technological innovations available within the E-Governance Era can greatly contribute to strengthening the deliberative democracy framework by creating meaningful opportunities for citizens to participate with government. For example, advancements in technology can create an opportunity for citizens to participate in any number of interactive events that are capable of affecting changes to the political system. The value of deliberative democracy is partly based on the development and usage of tools that facilitate meaningful participation allowing for the public to affect verifiable system changes. The power of deliberative activities to shape system change is paramount to ensure that government outcomes and processes are deemed legitimate by the citizens that participate in, and are affected by, outcomes of such interactive events.

Technology provides opportunities for government in the modern era to promote the use of innovative means to fulfill its responsibilities within the context of deliberative democracy. Newly emerging innovations can be used by the public sector to meet citizens' expectations regarding democratic governance in the E-Governance Era. A key component in this dynamic is the ability of digital deliberative means to support citizen participation. Technology expectations regarding functionality are based on a wide array of citizen concerns, such as whether the innovations will serve to reliably accomplish goals in a secure fashion while also providing a higher degree of convenience. In this sense, as technological advancements proliferate throughout the whole of society, the government is expected to utilize applicable innovations in the facilitation of governance when viable. It is important to acknowledge that there may also be impediments to participation through deliberative means that stem from the digital divide. Thus the modern deliberative democracy framework should incorporate both traditional and digital means to support the diversity of citizen preferences in participation.

The evolutionary nature of the U.S. government is reflected in part through the usage of technological innovation to ensure the fulfillment of expectations for citizen participation in a deliberative democracy. Electronic means available in the E-Governance Era can play an influential role in facilitating citizen participation within the context of the deliberative democracy framework. There are a number of innovative means available to modern government that can work to fortify deliberative expectations by providing citizens the ability to operate through digital platforms that support interactions associated with social media networks, crowdsourcing, suggestion boxes, citizen review panels, deliberative polls, types of public meetings and voting. Inherent within these deliberative expectations is that participation by citizens can be deemed most meaningful when interactions result in verifiable impacts to the political system at some point after the conclusion of the process. The E-Governance Era is representative of a time in which traditional designs are often coupled with modernized innovations to facilitate deliberative democracy that expands the scope of the participatory framework. The digital means can be utilized concurrently with traditional means to ensure that the deliberative framework can accommodate a wide variety of citizen preferences for participation. The decision to apply these means may be the result of citizen expectations demanding a change, the acceptance of a given technology on a broader societal scale, the notion that applying technology will better facilitate government fulfillment of duties or an attempt by the public sector to be innovative. Whatever the impetus, be it a societal demand based on citizen preferences or government intention to innovate, digital means can bridge classic principles of deliberative democracy with modern technology to support citizen-government interactions designed to impact the political system.

The provision of *E-Government* and *E-Governance* definitions is helpful in identifying expectations inherent within these innovative designs, which can guide the implementation of these conceptions in modern government. Both conceptual designs reflect the evolutionary nature of democracy in which government is expected to promote flexible adjustments to processes and structures based on demands stemming from the political arena. Without consistent efforts on behalf of the public sector to incrementally incorporate technological innovation though a whole-of-government approach, the deliberative democracy framework would be wholly antiquated and lacking in the diversity of participatory means that is paramount to the integrity of the system. Since the E-Governance Era began over 25 years ago in the early 1990s, there have been countless advancements in technology, showing great potential in allowing for both government and citizens to better fulfill the promise of deliberative democracy. It is important to provide some introductory discussion regarding what constitutes E-Government and E-Governance before providing an in-depth look at how these conceptualizations manifest in modern government within the context of deliberative democracy.

The available literature provides an array of definitions contributing to cultivating a rich understanding of E-Government and related functions. Those listed here serve as only a few such examples provided for illustrative purposes to help create a foundation of understanding of ICTs use in government toward this end. Carter and Bélanger (2005, p. 1) explained that "E-Government is the use of information technology to enable and improve the efficiency of government services provided to citizens, employees, business and agencies." Bannister and Connolly (2012, p. 1) defined E-Government as a "use of ICTs in and by governments and public administrations," since government began to embrace the application of the "Internet and the World-Wide-Web in the 1990s." Haque and Pathrannarakul (2013, p. 25) stated that "E-Government is the systemic use of ICTs to support the functions that a government performs for its constituents, typically the provision of information and services. E-Government is the use of ICT to transform the traditional government by making it accessible, transparent, effective, and accountable." Moon (2002, p. 426) highlighted the following strategies associated with E-Government initiatives, which activities can be based on: "(1) simple information dissemination (one-way communication); (2) two-way communication (request and response); (3) service and financial transactions; (4) integration (horizontal and vertical integration); and (5) political participation." Moon (2002) also made an important distinction regarding E-Government methods in that "the adoption of e-government practices may not follow a true linear progression." Moon (2002) adds that "it is also possible that government can pursue various components of e-government simultaneously." Here, the framework for E-Government is capable of supporting multiple types of communication flows and facilitates a wide array of expectations associated with democratic interactions ranging from service delivery to citizen participation. In addition, the application of E-Government initiatives allows for a transition that is neither mutually exclusive nor conceptually restrictive during the public sector's usage of such means. West (2004, p. 17) provided the following stages of E-Government as it relates to an agency's interactive behavior with citizens:

1   The billboard stage
2   The partial-service-delivery stage
3   The portal stage, with fully executable and integrated service delivery
4   Interactive democracy with public outreach and accountability enhancing features

Generally, E-Government is considered to include efforts on behalf of the public sector to apply ICTs for the purposes of delivering services and disseminating information to the public. However, Moon's and West's final stages of E-Government each set the foundation for conceptually deeper governance issues, which further integrates more complex attributes associated with democracy derived from participatory interactions between citizens and government. Navarra and Cornford (2012) argued that the reach of E-Government can exceed being used only to enhance the citizen-consumer service delivery transactions through the application of ICTs. Navarra and Cornford (2012, p. 37) argued that "e-government initiatives can be constitutive of new forms of governmental legitimacy, with ICT supporting new backward, forward, and lateral mechanisms to reshape political power to further democratic ideals." Navarra and Cornford (2012) explained that state efforts to utilize ICTs to deliver services to the public can be supplemented with designs focused on including citizen-consumers in dialogue activities, such the development of public policy. Navarra and Cornford (2012) noted that ICTs can be applied to E-Government for improving the facilitation of bureaucratic transactions, such as delivering services to the citizen-consumer and to accomplish E-Governance goals intended to promote a more legitimate government by providing designs that encourage citizen participation to affect changes to political system functions such as public policy development. For Marche and McNiven (2003), there is a distinction between E-Government transaction-level interactions, associated with service delivery and basic information dissemination, and E-Governance deliberations designed to promote citizen–government interactions with the intention of affecting changes to the political system. This conceptual demarcation paves the way for cultivating an understanding for E-Governance, sometimes referred to as *E-Democracy*, which is representative of public sector designs applying ICTs in accordance with broader interactive expectations associated with deliberative democracy.

Graham, Amos, and Plumptre (2003, p. 1) distinguished *government* from *governance* by noting that the latter is focused on "how governments and other social organizations interact, how they relate to citizens, and how decisions are taken in a complex world. Thus governance is a process whereby societies or organizations make their important decisions, determine whom they involve in the process and how they render account." This conceptualization is applicable to E-Governance, which is reflective of technologically based interactions between citizens and government ultimately intended to affect changes to the political system. E-Governance by its nature indicates that the public sector utilizes technological advancements associated with ICTs that are supportive of political actors' pursuit of goal achievement, including those focused on achieving change derived though participatory events. Kalsi and Kiran (2015, p. 170) explained that ICTs are "recognized as the engine for growth and a source of energy for the social and economic empowerment of any country. Today, governments are empowering masses through ICT as it can prove to be effective short-cut to higher levels of equity in the emerging global digital networked information economy." The usage of technology as a vehicle for change includes the important role that ICTs play in facilitating citizen–government interactions associated with deliberative democracy. Clearly, paramount among these technologies is the Internet. Gibson (2001, p. 562) said that "for many observers, the emergence of new information and communication technologies (ICTs) such as the World Wide Web (WWW) and e-mail has revived hopes for so-called electronic or 'e-democracy'—a polity whereby interactive media promotes a wider base of citizen participation." Kakabadse, Kakabadse, and Kouzmin (2003, p. 47) noted that E-Democracy is reflective of a "capacity of the new communications environment to enhance the degree and quality of public participation in government." They expanded on this notion by explaining that citizens with access to the Internet and applicable ICTs may utilize these in concert to participate in opportunities such as those allowing them "to vote electronically in elections, referendums, and plebiscites" (2003, p. 47). Solop (2001, p. 289) observed that "digital democracy refers to the integration of Internet technologies into the functions of government and the apparatus of democracy, i.e. making governmental information accessible through web sites; online political mobilization; and, now, Internet voting." Here, the Internet is considered to assume a primary role in E-Governance designs that are focused on enhancing the means available for citizens to participate with government in the hopes of enacting changes to the system.

Chadwick and May (2003, p. 276) discussed that E-Democracy interactions can be based on a "managerial" perspective in which ICTs are used to affect incremental change to services provided to the public to ensure delivery will be "made more 'efficient,' where 'efficiency' means increased speed of delivery combined with a reduction in costs." Chadwick and May (2003, p. 278) expanded further on this type of interaction by noting that "the state will place information in accessible forums and the onus is on the user to access it. The audience members are seen a passive recipients, rather than interlocutors." In this sense, technology is utilized to affect incremental changes to the political system largely focused on improving the means through which government performs specific tasks (i.e., delivery of public services, dissemination of information) for the citizen-recipient. Chadwick (2003) explained that E-Democracy interactions can also be categorized as "consultative" or "deliberative." Chadwick (2003, p. 449) pointed out that the former "principally stresses the vertical flows of state-citizen communication," while the latter "conceives of a more complex, horizontal, and multidirectional interactivity." Chadwick (2003, p. 448) added that consultative interactions in an E-Democracy applies ICTs to "facilitate the communication of citizen opinion to government" and the resulting knowledge gained from discourse can be used by a government to determine how "to provide better policy and administration." Chadwick (2003) recognized the role of the state in developing and facilitating E-Democracy means supporting citizen–government deliberations with the understanding that there will be a multitude of sources in the political system capable of facilitating discursive interactions from a variety of origin points. For Chadwick (2003, p. 449) the deliberative aspects of E-Democracy "contains a recognition that knowledge is discursive, contingent, and changeable; that it emerges through interaction." Here, participation between citizens and government is guided by the nature of discourse in which gaining access to information is derived through interaction. Agrawal, Sethi, and Mittal (2015) acknowledged that although the terms *E-Government* and *E-Governance* are often used interchangeably, there are subtle differences regarding the scope and nature of their application in the political system. They expanded on this idea by noting that "e-governance embraces e-democracy, e-voting, e-justice, e-education, e-healthcare and so on, whereas e-government uses ICT to promote efficient, cost-effective and convenient government services, allowing greater public access to information" (2015, p. 35). Marche and McNiven (2003) observed that various forms of "electronically mediated interaction" may affect public policy development, citizen–government participation dynamics, lobbying processes, the role of traditional power structures associated with information sharing, online efforts to promote transparency and accountability and expectations for the inclusion of online communities in a deliberative democracy. In sum, E-Government applies technology solely for providing services or disseminating information, which lacks the multidimensional purpose of the use of the ICTs associated with E-Governance. E-Governance's usage of technologies such as the Internet facilitates basic information dissemination to the public leading to more informed decision-making, but more importantly involves means to support complex, dynamic citizen–government interactions capable of affecting change to deliberative democracy.

The public sector's capacity to achieve broad expectations associated with democracy can be enhanced in the E-Governance Era by applying innovations to simultaneously provide services, disseminate information and facilitate direct participation. Innovations can be utilized to provide further means to facilitate the provision of information and services to citizens while also being able to promote more complex citizen–government interactions associated with deliberative democracy, such as online e-voting (Schaupp & Carter, 2005). Finger (2010) discussed the role that technology plays in altering infrastructures in which government provides services to citizens, but also noted that the transformative nature of the dynamic reflects inherent instability in E-Government as a model. The dynamic nature associated with the usage of technology remains an important consideration during the E-Governance Era. This relates to the mercurial quality of technology itself in which emerging technologies rapidly replace existing ones and that innovative means are applied to facilitate a continuously growing list of government-related activities. The Internet is used to facilitate information sharing between citizens and public sector agencies at all levels of government in the U.S. federal system, to raise funds for campaign contribution purposes, to provide citizens detailed access to laws passed by the legislative branch, to highlight voting records for members of a legislative branch, to support government provision of a multitude of services to the public and to further contribute to deliberative democracy framework by providing means to vote online (Solop, 2001). Schlozman, Verba, and Brady (2010) observed that the Internet can be used for a wide range of citizen participation activities, such as facilitating political discourse, providing access to higher levels of user-friendly information, encouraging political activity through online recruitment and facilitating the exchange of money to fund political campaigns. Modern-era governance processes, including voting, can utilize any number of innovations in technology designed to electronically facilitate actions (Kakabadse, Kakabadse, & Kouzmin, 2003). Here, ICTs in the U.S. political system can be used to institutionalize a deliberative democracy schema simultaneously being accommodating to participatory expectations associated with E-Government and E-Governance functions. The nature of E-Governance is dynamic in that expectations for the usage of emerging technologies and the role of governmental duties to be fulfilled through innovation are rapidly changing.

Although E-Government and E-Governance are interrelated concepts that apply ICTs to fulfill democratic expectations, there are minor functional differences that distinguish each within the context of a broader digital deliberative framework. Here, *E-Government* is a term that strictly encompasses the application of ICTs for transactions based on public sector–citizen interactions. E-Government is focused exclusively on citizen–government interactions, which facilitate functions such as the delivery of services and disseminating basic information. This is not to discount the important role that E-Government plays in disseminating basic information or providing services to the public at large through technologically innovations means. Since the creation of the Internet, various emerging technological innovations have provided a plethora of new E-Government means in which government can interact with citizens to provide services and disseminate basic information. These functions of E-Government greatly contribute to fulfilling expectations of U.S. democracy in which electronic means are capable of promoting activities supporting traditional principles such as transparency, accountability and flexibility. This dynamic is vital to contributing to the overall integrity and legitimacy of the U.S. government, which is built on the foundation of such classic democratic principles. However, ICTs can also play a role in promoting E-Governance designs supportive of participatory events that can strengthen the overall deliberative democracy framework. E-Governance, or E-Democracy, may include information-dissemination components capable of contributing to more informed decision-making on behalf of citizens, but this design is primarily focused on understanding how interested parties in a deliberative democracy interact. E-Governance is representative of a richer and more complex citizen–government dynamic in which ICT-based interactions are intended to contribute to deliberative expectations for participatory democracy. E-Governance designs can be focused on supporting the interactive nature of deliberations designed largely by the state through which the public can participate with the intention of influencing political outcomes. These E-Governance electronic interactions are constructed to support activities such as generating knowledge through citizen–government dialogue, which can be applied to improve democracy in some way and through those digital means, which can then, more immediately, affect direct changes to the political system, such as voting. It is also important to acknowledge the role that ICTs can play in affecting deliberations with interested parties through organic, non-state-initiated discursive events. There are a multitude of virtual venues that fall outside the purview of state-run deliberative means that may complement the process of gathering citizen-centric knowledge capable of improving the political system. Ultimately, the technology available in the E-Governance Era provides the opportunity for the public sector to apply innovations toward the purpose of facilitating meaningful participation with citizens. This understanding of the role of innovation in the E-Governance Era sets the foundation for later discussions regarding the application of technology in modern-era U.S. governance within the deliberative democracy framework.

There are a number of examples associated with practical applications of digital deliberative means in the U.S. political system, but it is important to first introduce some basic foundational information associated with the role of technology in government since the advent of the E-Governance Era in the early 1990s. This includes priming the discussion with an introduction as

Table 1.1 Qualities of E-Government and E-Governance

E-Government	E-Government and E-Governance	E-Governance
Online services which includes allowing citizens to:	Online information dissemination providing access to:	Online activities designed for citizen–government interaction through means such as:
− Log on to a judicial website to register for jury duty − Pay parking tickets − Renew car registration via a state DMV website − File for building permits − Obtain hunting and fishing licenses	− Full text of legislation − Federal Register publication of proposed agency rule changes − Websites for the President of the United States, members of Congress and the Supreme Court − Methods for government to relay information to the public such as websites, RSS feeds and e-mails	− Suggestion boxes − Social media networks − Crowdsourcing − Citizen review panels − Public meeting (including town hall meetings) − Voting

to how the initial development of technology may not necessarily involve its immediate wide-scale acceptance because it may take some degree of time in which influential political system factors affect the levels of proliferation and use in society. This is applicable regarding the application of technology in the E-Governance Era in which the initial use of innovations by government was representative of a gradual, incremental process over the past 25 years which has now resulted in an unprecedented level of technology use in the public sector to facilitate E-Government and E-Governance activities. The application of technological innovation in governance was far from immediate in the early 1990s and was instead a gradual process in which acceptance of use was based on a number of factors stemming from the political environment. The role of favorable or unfavorable societal impressions of technology in influencing government's decision to apply innovations toward goal achievement is recognized as playing a pivotal role in E-Governance's development. For example, the expectations of citizens regarding the role that technology should play in government activities serves as a guiding factor that often dictates acceptable use of innovations in the public sector. Once enough citizen influence is generated from within the political arena, civically oriented inertia is created, which can guide government to take actions to innovate. There are many factors that influence the process in which growing societal acceptance of technology affects government use, and this includes recognizing the influence of various technology models that guides societal belief that application of a given technology is required. It is also important to identify possible concerns to remain wary of regarding the general application of technology in the E-Governance Era. This establishes a deeper foundational understanding in which more detailed discussions regarding practical applications of digital deliberative participatory means in U.S. governance will be expanded upon.

References

Agrawal, S., Sethi, P., & Mittal, M. (2015) E-governance: An analysis of citizens' perception. *IUP Journal of Information Technology*, 11(3): 34–46.

Bannister, F., & Connolly, R. (2012) Forward to the past: Lessons for the future of e-government from the story so far. *Information Polity: The International Journal of Government & Democracy in the Information Age*, 17(3/4): 211–226.

Carter, L., & Bélanger, F. (2005) The utilization of e-government services: Citizen trust, innovation and acceptance factors. *Information Systems Journal*, 15(1): 5–25. doi: 10.1111/j.1365-2575.2005.00183.x.

Chadwick, A. (2003) Bringing e-democracy back in: Why it matters for future research on e-governance. *Social Science Computer Review*, 21(4): 443–455.

Chadwick, A., & May, C. (2003) Interaction between states and citizens in the age of the Internet: "E-government" in the United States, Britain, and the European union. *Governance*, 16(2): 271–300. doi: 10.1111/1468-0491.00216.

Finger, M. (2010) What role for government in e-government? *Journal of E-Governance*, 33(4): 197–202. doi: 10.3233/GOV20100230.

Gibson, R. (2001) Elections online: Assessing Internet voting in light of the Arizona democratic primary. *Political Science Quarterly*, 116(4): 561–583.

Graham, J., Amos, B., & Plumptre, T. (2003) Policy brief no. 15: Principles for good governance in the 21st century. Retrieved from http://unpan1.un.org/intradoc/groups/public/documents/UNPAN/UNPAN011842.pdf.

Haque, S., & Pathrannarakul, P. (2013) E-government towards good governance: A global appraisal. *Journal of E-Governance*, 36(1): 25–34.

Kakabadse, A., Kakabadse, N. K., & Kouzmin, A. (2003) Reinventing the democratic governance project through information technology? A growing agenda for debate. *Public Administration Review*, 63(1): 44–60.

Kalsi, N. S., & Kiran, R. (2015) A strategic framework for good governance through e-governance optimization. *Program: Electronic Library & Information Systems*, 49(2): 170–204. doi: 10.1108/PROG-12-2013-0067.

Marche, S., & McNiven, J. D. (2003) E-government and e-governance: The future isn't what it used to be. *Revue Canadienne Des Sciences De L'administration/ Canadian Journal of Administrative Sciences*, 20(1): 74–86.

Moon, M. J. (2002) The evolution of e-government among municipalities: Rhetoric or reality? *Public Administration Review*, 62(4): 424–433.

Navarra, D. D., & Cornford, T. (2012) The state and democracy after new public management: Exploring alternative models of e-governance. *Information Society*, 28(1): 37–45. doi: 10.1080/01972243.2012.632264.

Schaupp, L. C., & Carter, L. (2005) E-voting: From apathy to adoption. *Journal of Enterprise Information Management*, 18(5): 586–601. Retrieved from http://search.proquest.com/docview/220020269?accountid=32521.

Schlozman, K. L., Verba, S., & Brady, H. E. (2010) Weapon of the strong? Participatory inequality and the Internet. *Perspectives on Politics*, 8(2): 487–509. doi: 10.1017/S1537592710001210.

Solop, F. I. (2001) Digital democracy comes of age: Internet voting and the 2000 Arizona democratic primary election. *PS: Political Science & Politics*, 34(2): 289–293. doi: 10.1017/S104909650100052X.

West, D. M. (2004) E-Government and the transformation of service delivery and citizen attitudes. *Public Administration Review*, 64(1): 15–27. doi: 10.1111/j.1540-6210.2004.00343.x.

2 E-Governance Era

Paradigm Shifts and Megatrends, Janus Face of Technology, Digital Divide and the Hype Curve/Hype Cycle

Although the existence of ICTs such as e-mail and the Internet came about in the early 1990s, the U.S. government's usage of technology to facilitate activities related to E-Government and E-Governance was far from immediate. In order for any conceptual ideal, emerging innovation or practical technique to be applied in government toward wide-scale goal achievement, whether originating from the private sector or public sector, there needs to be an accumulation of the necessary levels of support to justify change. In relation, the support for the application of technology may be derived from multiple origin points within the political environment, which can be assessed to determine if the requisite expectation level for innovation-based change is present. However, the shift in expectations for government to apply innovation in the performance of duties is not intended to enact change that will diminish the substantive nature of U.S. democracy. There are numerous principles associated with classic democracy, including accountability, transparency and flexibility, which continue to maintain great meaning in modern U.S. governance. The significance of these principles in the E-Governance Era remains unchanged, and these principals continue to serve as unwavering pillars of democratic importance. Today, democracy in the modern era remains true to many such classic principles associated with this form of government. Therefore, modern efforts associated with E-Governance are utilized to contribute to delivering on the promise of long-established principles within the paradigm of traditional U.S. democracy. The contemporary political environment supporting E-Governance would not require a complete "paradigm change" or "paradigm shift" (Kuhn, 1962), which would ultimately yield broad, overarching changes to the means to fulfill government responsibilities and to the traditional expectations associated with principles inherent within the present form of democracy. E-Governance would not require a paradigm change regarding the form of government in the United States—only an adjustment to the participatory means within the deliberative democracy framework. For example, E-Governance would not require the United States to take extreme measures such as drafting a new constitution calling for a different type of government to be developed to support the public sector utilizing technological innovation that encourages meaningful interactions with citizens. It would be unnecessary and unfeasible to commence with a full, system-wide change to the traditional form of U.S. government, but instead, efforts to alter the means utilized to better fulfill the expected functions of democracy is a serviceable goal for E-Governance.

E-Governance initiatives require adjustments to the way people participate to accommodate the growing need for the application of technological innovations associated with modern-era deliberative democracy. This includes the development of digital means that are open to all interested parties and are cyclical in nature, allowing for continued participation at multiple points of time and from which outcomes are intended to ultimately affect changes to the political system. Therefore, changes to the modern political system associated with E-Governance are generally misaligned with the expansive focus required for full paradigm shifts and would be more reflective of what Hajkowicz, Cook, & Littleboy (2012) refer to as a "megatrend" as it relates to new technologically innovative means contributing to achieving deliberative democracy ends. Hajkowicz, Cook, and Littleboy (2012, p. 2) explained that "a megatrend is a significant shift in environmental, economic and social conditions that will play out over the coming decades." These shifts from multiple societal strata have the capacity to influence any number of government-related activities, including problem identification and goal achievement. The existence of megatrends is also an item of importance that can directly affect societal expectations related to the political environment, such as those concerning the means through which citizen–government interactions occur. Hajkowicz, Cook, and Littleboy (2012) identified megatrends that will be important within the next 20 years, including potential global issues associated with the decline in natural resources, environmental threats to wildlife, geographical shifting of strong economies to non-traditional locales throughout the world community and the recognition of the positive contributions from the demographically oriented aging public. Hajkowicz, Cook, and Littleboy (2012, p. 3) identified two additional megatrends that are most applicable to the discussion associated with E-Governance, categorized as "virtually here" (in which digital means create an enhanced level of connectivity in society between citizens, businesses and government) and "great expectations" (in which social components associated with relationships are of import). The digital means associated with E-Governance should be able to facilitate relationships between citizens and government. E-Governance digital means in the modern era are able to expand the communications structures in which relationships are fostered between citizens and government in a way that exceeds the depth and scope of past traditional, non-electronic methods of deliberative interaction. The E-Governance Era reflects megatrend qualities in the sense that, since the early 1990s, large-scale technologically based changes are continuously being implemented across all levels of U.S. government to provide virtual venues to further cultivate citizen–government interactions in which outcomes derived from participation have the capacity to influence changes to the system. The expectations for government usage of innovations to increase levels of technologically sophisticated interactions with the public contributes to framing E-Governance as a "megatrend" that will likely continue well into the foreseeable future.

The megatrend's digital and social components are related to the E-Governance Era deliberative democracy framework in which virtual interactive events can be used to achieve changes to the system. Weymouth and Hartz-Karp (2015, p. 1) discussed the role that "Deliberative Collaborative Governance (DCG)" can play in promoting "discursive politics to co-decide issues that matter" such as those megatrends related to "wicked problems" and "declining public trust." Here, the traditional problem-solving practice based on interactions through hierarchical structures of government is often insufficient to generate information capable of contributing to effective solutions to solve emerging problems in modern society (Weymouth & Hartz-Karp, 2015). Weymouth and Hartz-Karp (2015) noted that deliberative efforts can be designed to create "collective ownership" of problems and solutions between parties within the political system. Weymouth and Hartz-Karp (2015) added that effective deliberative initiatives should be facilitated on a continual basis over time, structured based on adaptive needs derived from an assessment of problems and include a deliberative framework that is diverse in means. These qualities are important elements associated with establishing a responsive deliberative government structure capable of assessing societal problems in a timely manner and developing action designed to actively address those problems identified on a continual basis. This is applicable when considering the development of means that should facilitate a diverse, and often conversational, framework for E-Governance. The concept of the "megatrend" remains more applicable to E-Governance Era usage of technological innovation than assuming this movement is representative of a full paradigm change, which would require changes to perceptions associated with basic principles of democracy. Instead, E-Governance Era actions are facilitated through constructed designs based on the application of new technological means made possible through modern innovations, which strengthens deliberative democracy principles. Deliberative activities that are adaptive, diverse, continual and dynamic remain integral to the development of means to encourage citizen–government interaction associated with E-Governance. The social and digital aspects of a megatrend are imminently relatable to modern deliberative democracy in which the overall discursive framework applies both traditional and modern (i.e., electronic) means supporting a wide range of citizen–government interactions whereby outcomes can affect system changes to address continually emerging issues.

It is important to acknowledge that technological innovation in the E-Governance Era can ultimately affect who participates and how that participation may occur. This understanding will help to set the foundation for analysis of examples of modern citizen–government interactive means available within the deliberative democracy framework. Technology advancements can occur over time which are capable of improving the ability of government to perform activities related to delivering services, sharing information with the public and engaging in meaningful dialogue with the citizen base in which they serve. A main focal point in E-Governance initiatives is the acknowledgement that advancements in technological innovation affect citizen–government interactions within a deliberative democracy. Although technological advancements may affect E-Government means in which the public sector performs tasks across a wide array of responsibilities, the scope of the analysis will remain focused largely on E-Governance communication dynamics associated with citizen–government participation within the socio-political network. In this context, technological advancements can impact the structures and processes associated with citizen–government interactions while still preserving important traditional principles associated with this form of governance. The following sections offer non-technically oriented discussions on the progression of the significant innovations that play a role in affecting citizen–government interactions associated with modern governance, how these advancements in technology can affect network participation and how this contributes to strengthening the deliberative democracy framework in the E-Governance Era.

The origin point for the E-Governance Era can be associated with the creation of the Internet and the cascade of ICT-based innovations since its development in the early 1990s. It is not uncommon that the government contributes greatly in the development of cutting-edge technological advancements that eventually become adapted and refined before the innovation proliferates the whole of society. Many of these advancements have been rooted in U.S. military research, including those government-led actions that ultimately contributed to the creation of what was to become the modern Internet. The technology that would contribute to the development of the Internet was established initially through public sector research efforts. This includes military efforts to advance technology through the Advanced Research Projects Agency (ARPA) created in 1958 (known today as the Defense Advanced Research Projects Agency, or DARPA) which led to the development of a wide range of innovations including weather satellites, personal computers, the computer mouse and the Internet (United States DARPA, 2016). According to DARPA (2016, "Highlights" section), "ARPA research played a central role in launching the Information Revolution. The agency developed and furthered much of the conceptual basis for the ARPANET-prototypical communications network launched nearly half a century ago, and invented the digital protocols that gave birth to the Internet." These initiatives served as precursors to the creation of the World Wide Web in the early 1990s, which helps to serve as the foundation of the modern Internet usage as it is known today (Zakon, 1997; Campbell-Kelly & Garcia-Swartz, 2013). The World Wide Web and Internet are related concepts, but differ significantly regarding their application. In short, the *World Wide Web* serves to provide the means in which users interact electronically (i.e., webpages, web-browsers, etc.) and the *Internet* acts as the broad connective network that facilitates various types of web interactions. The progression of technological advancements spanning the course of a little over 30 years since ARPA's creation in 1958 led to the conceptualization of Tim Berners-Lee's World Wide Web in the early 1990s and to network connections facilitating citizen–government interactions via the Internet. In the context of the scope of human history, 30 years is a proverbial blink of an eye. However, the technological advancements enabling the government to disseminate information, provide services or facilitate deliberations through a device connected to the Internet in essentially a 30-year window should not be overlooked or underestimated regarding the significance of the accomplishment. The initial government efforts in the late 1950s eventually led to the application of devices such as home computers connected to the Internet by the mid-1990s. This represents of one of the most significant advancements in technology ever.

The timeframe in which technology was developed, refined and then applied for practical usage by government within the system was, and continues to be, an impressive public sector innovation-based endeavor. This remarkable enterprise has continued to gain relevance since the early 1990s and is due in part to the expansive nature of applicable technology during the E-Governance Era. The evolution of innovations that would become germane to the initial stages of E-Governance began with development of the Internet and e-mail, which have increased in societal usage at a steady rate since their inception. Demirdjian (2016, p. 109) explained, "on August 6, 1991, the Web officially made its debut, thus bringing instantly order to the chaos that was cyberspace system of scattered, but related, documents." Demirdjian (2016) noted the "marriage" of the World Wide Web with the Internet led to the rapid proliferation of wide-scale Internet usage. Demirdjian (2016, p. 109) added that "within five years of its inception, the number of Internet users jumped from 600,000 to 40 million in 1996." A similar observation can be made regarding the development of websites. For example, according to Netcraft (2006), the number of websites grew from 18,000 in 1995 to 100 million in 2006. Since 2006, the number of websites has grown considerably, and will likely continue to do so into the foreseeable future. According to Netcraft (2016), there are presently over 1 billion websites as of June 2016. The invention of the Internet also led to the development of ICTs, such as Hotmail in 1996, which eventually contributed to wide-scale proliferation of personal e-mail accounts. Clearly, the initial usage of the Internet and related innovations in the early 1990s was minimal, and logically its role in citizen–government interactions was not yet significant. Therefore, the Internet and e-mail were used relatively sparingly by government to fulfill more basic E-Government related tasks associated with the transfer of information through websites and e-mail based communication. Then, the capacity to support wide-scale public usage of the Internet was insufficient; there was still little-to-no digital infrastructure set up to support applications, home computers were less common and the skill set of citizens had yet to develop to the point that would facilitate ease of use. The developmental actions led by government set into motion the eventual creation of various innovations supporting many E-Governance-related online, citizen-centric interactions. This succession of events resulted in creating expectations that government would be responsible for further refining these means for use in the U.S. deliberative democracy. This cyclical development-to-application process allows for innovations, like the Internet, whose creation is derived from research based on government initiatives, to permeate society as they become refined through use. Once this process occurs, it gradually leads back to government as societal expectations for increased usage of that technology to fulfill public sector responsibilities are generated. Once technological advancements become more polished through wide-scale usage and have proliferated throughout society at more substantial levels, the public sector eventually becomes expected to engage citizens through those innovations deemed capable of supporting E-Governance interactions.

The actions set forth by government that led to the development of the Internet would initially place the public sector behind the private sector in its general application of related technologies at the outset of the E-Governance Era. This gap between the public sector and private sector as it relates to the application of technology in the performance of duties was a key finding highlighted in the National Performance Review (NPR) of 1993. In short, the NPR of 1993 was an initiative enacted by President Clinton empowering Vice President Al Gore to assess how the federal government could be reinvented to improve the effectiveness and efficiency of governance. President Clinton (NPR, 1993, p. 1) announced that NPR was developed "to make the entire federal government both less expensive and more efficient, and to change the culture of our national bureaucracy away from complacency and entitlement toward initiative and empowerment. We intend to redesign, to reinvent, to reinvigorate the entire national government." In 1993, the E-Governance Era was in its preliminary stages so that neither E-Government nor E-Governance means were prevalent within the U.S. political system, and in most cases the applications of technology supporting these designs were relatively non-existent. A number of important aspects identified within the NPR helped to set the foundation for the proliferation of technological innovation in the public sector. These include identifying a general lack of application of technology by government at that time and a discussion of factors that may have initially contributed to the somewhat lethargic pace of the proliferation of innovations within the federal bureaucracy. The NPR (1993, p. 112) noted that "the history of the closing decade of this century is being written on the computer. You wouldn't know it if you worked for many federal agencies, however." The NPR (1993) continued in this regard by noting that private sector application of computer technologies had far outpaced the public sector at that time and that government efforts should be made to close the private sector–public sector technology gap. The NPR (1993, p. 113) warned that "failure to adapt to the information age threatens many aspects of government." This comment within the NPR highlights key points related to governance in a modern democracy, such as the importance of continuously adapting to the technological demands extant within society to fulfill a wide range of governmental duties. Although government entities may not share the same mandated responsibilities, they could have all benefitted from further integration of technology to accomplish their respective tasks. Another important component in this regard is the belief that the government may have the ability to close this technological gap, but has lacked the incentive to do so. The NPR (1993) report highlighted the possibility that government had yet to apply technology at the rate and effectiveness of the private sector based on the following three premises: (a) that government acted as a monopoly, which by nature is often less innovative than the private sector, conversely, private sector entities need to constantly adapt to technological demands of the time because without relevant and timely application of technology they would simply go out of business (NPR, 1993); (b) that government "employees who do want to modernize management have their hands tied with red tape–detailed budgets and cumbersome procurement procedures that deter investment;" and (c) that there is a "natural inclination, familiar to private and public managers alike, to do things as they've always been done" (p. 113). Here, the NPR report indicated that much of the public sector had yet to make significant efforts to incorporate technology into governance based on an inherent institutionalized preference to perpetuate the status quo. The identification of government's technology shortcoming would provide justification for the creation of many designs that would empower the public to apply innovations to better perform a wide array of government's expected duties. As such, there would be a number of government efforts since 1993 that focused on applying the power of technology to remedy this early stage inequity, ushering in new means to facilitate citizen–government interactions associated with modern deliberative democracy, which will be the focus of later chapters.

In the 1980s leading up the E-Governance Era, communication with citizens could be facilitated by way of any number of entrenched means that were considered traditional and acceptable at that time, including communications via mailing letters through the postal service, home-based telephone calls, fax machines and even early-stage cell phones. In the 1990s, the methods of communication began to shift somewhat to incorporate advancements in ICTs, including the creation of more universally utilized e-mail systems, cell phones and video conferencing. In the 2000s, the continued rapid advancements of communication technology led to further proliferation of these means on a broad societal level. As time progressed, the older technologies were not eliminated. The new technologies were added to the pre-existing technologies, which expanded the overall scope of communication means available to citizens. The demand for government to acquiesce to growing societal expectations to apply technological advancements toward E-Governance-related tasks was not immediate. Initially, the capacity of E-Governance developed somewhat slowly since the early 1990s; the governmental approach represented a gradual, incremental plan of action. The increased wide-scale societal applications of emerging technologies led to enhanced levels of usage of such innovations throughout society eventually required a corresponding government response. The creation of the modern Internet and subsequent related technological communications advancements, like e-mail, did not immediately proliferate throughout all levels of society, so an immediate governmental response was not required or expected. By the mid-1990s, the government had yet to begin to marshal the full power of Internet-based technologies toward the purpose of fulfilling public sector E-Government or E-Governance duties on a consistent basis. Although the initial advancements in Internet-based technology yielded limited levels of applicability for governance, the continued societal proliferation of such innovations and subsequent developments of more sophisticated communication technologies would eventually reach a saturation point in which a broad, cogent public sector response would be required. This is indicative of the function of flexibility inherent in the U.S. democratic system, which is designed to be able to address new demands developing within the political environment. An important element to consider in this dynamic is how emerging technologies within society may eventually influence the expectations of citizens regarding how government functions. In relation, advancements in communication technology can directly influence citizen–government network interactions, creating the expectations for the public sector to use innovation for deliberative goal-oriented achievement. This understanding eventually served as part of the motivational justification in which the development of digital participatory means would be used to contribute to the overall deliberative framework in the E-Governance Era.

The more commonplace advanced technology becomes in society, the broader the application potential for its usage. This includes the idea that the continued permeation of technological advancements within the public and private sectors can eventually be used to complete both complex and ordinary tasks within society and government. The technological improvements and the expanded societal existence of the Internet led to a natural progression of these innovations in private sector and public sector usage since the advent of E-Governance Era in the early 1990s. The advancement in information technologies allowed for the continued diffusion of its applicability within society on the whole and would eventually become a serious consideration in governance. The more citizens obtained home computers and Internet usage spread in the United States, the more changes in expectations regarding government usage of technology citizens had. Once technological proliferation in society became more commonplace and connecting to the Internet became a societal reality on a broad scale, the expectation of citizens for the public sector to utilize this capacity in relation to governance became a strong consideration. When there is enough of a demand and the capacity of government is able to adequately address that demand, the government can then make efforts to develop actions that addresses the conditions of the newly emerging expectation. For example, the U.S. federal government initiative in the mid-1990s entitled "THOMAS" (http://thomas.loc.gov) was an innovative conceptual website that provided citizens access to information associated with details of proposed bills, the status of those bills as they progressed through Congress and whether bills were voted into law. It also provided information associated with which member(s) of Congress initially proposed each bill and whether a bill was proposed in the House or the Senate. Today, this activity is relatively commonplace through any number of governmental websites, such the newly developed Congress.gov (https://congress.gov/). In the summer of 2016, Congress.gov officially replaced THOMAS (see Box 2.1).

Box 2.1 Congress.gov

THOMAS was launched in the mid-1990s using technology that was incapable of providing new functionality users have come to expect in a website. The new Congress.gov platform enhances access through features such as videos explaining the legislative process, compatibility with mobile devices, and a user-friendly presentation.

Congress.gov provides modern functionality, including:

– Single search across all collections and all dates
– Meaningful, persistent URLs
– Faceted search results

Located at www.congress.gov/help/faq#thomasretirement.

Congress.gov built upon the initial THOMAS website by applying more modernized technology with the intention to increase ease of access and to improve functionality for online legislative searches being conducted by the public. In addition, as many inquisitive individuals did prior to the mid-1990s, research on governance was often conducted in places like in a library by combing through countless dusty copies of the Congressional Record (now located digitally from 1995 to present at www.congress.gov/congressional-record) and the Federal Register (now located digitally from 1994 to present at www.federalregister.gov). The digital presence for government also now includes websites for an expansive list of federal agencies (www.usa.gov/federal-agencies/a), the President of the United States (www.whitehouse.gov) and the U.S. Supreme Court (www.supremecourt.gov). The U.S. government also provides websites associated with E-Government activities related to advertising federal jobs online (www.usajobs.gov). Of course, the practice of creating a digital presence for activities has also become common at the U.S. state and local levels in which E-Government information representing the three branches of government is also significantly represented. The levels of access to E-Government-oriented information and services within the U.S. federal system is unprecedented in the modern era and helps to further institutionalize important democratic principles, such as transparency and accountability. In addition, the expansion of digital means to facilitate citizen–government interactions associated with E-Governance also increased significantly since the early 1990s. These electronic changes to the overall nature of U.S. government's participatory means were not immediate and have continued to expand in scope since the introduction of the E-Governance Era.

The creation of the Internet led to corresponding advancements in communication-focused ICTs that found relevance for use within the private and public sectors. The continued developments in information technology (IT) since the early 1990s led to increasingly high levels of permeation of these means throughout society and correspondingly increased citizens' expectations for government to apply innovations toward task completion for a wide range of activities. This is applicable to E-Government and E-Governance efforts on behalf of the public sector in which a contemporary whole-of-government approach has become commonplace to accommodate societal expectations for a modern digital U.S. government. Chun *et al.* (2011, p. 233) explained that the whole-of-government approach "is increasingly seen as an imperative for delivering coherent and integrated policies, joined up and seamless services, and integrated program management in government." In general, the whole-of-government approach calls for wide-scale coordinated efforts encompassing public sector entities charged with the responsibility of implementing a given mandate to achieve a specific goal in an area of policy (i.e., national security, environmental, economy, etc.). For example, the Open Government initiative is an E-Governance Era design originally promoted during the first term of President Obama in 2009 requiring that all federal agencies develop innovative means in which to ensure a more transparent, collaborative and participatory government, for example by publishing information online. Although there may be numerous benefits to using modern innovations in governance, the application of technology is not without potential hazards. The government should be wary of the possible detriments of technology use on societal participants. This includes the possibility that the process associated with applying technology to fulfill governmental duties may result in a number of unintended and unforeseen consequences. Coughlin (2010, p. 62) noted that "despite its promise, technology has a Janus face introducing both new solutions as well as new problems." Coughlin (2010, p. 66) also noted the Janus face of technology as it relates to the duality of effects to an aging population and their potential caregivers in that the positives associated with technological advancement in care may be offset by prohibitive factors, such as cost and knowledge of use, resulting in "a problem of societal equity." Coughlin (2010, p. 66) recommended that efforts be made to overcome this social inequity associated with technologies, including "government subsidies, purchasing, tax incentives, or the provision of resources to accelerate research and development may improve lower income users' access to new technologies." Taylor (2012, p. 233) focused on the "Janus face of information-intensive government in its relations with citizens." Cousins and Robey (2015) also discussed the Janus effect of mobile technologies: "as work continues to become detached from specific times and places, the management of work-life boundaries will become increasingly important, especially for mobile workers." Here, it is important to recognize that the public sector application of technology may have significant negative consequences. The benefits associated with applying technologies in the public sector may coincide with unintended consequences that include digital divide inequities, uncertainty regarding acceptable boundaries for interactions, and technical failures. It is plausible that issues stemming from the Janus face of technology could extend to a wide array of activities related to service delivery, information dissemination and collaborative citizen–government relationships that are prevalent in the E-Governance Era. The uncertainty of outcomes derived from the Janus face of technology serves as a key factor to consider during the usage of innovations associated with E-Government- and E-Governance-related actions. Government should continue to maintain due diligence to actively determine factors that may affect the successful implementation of technological innovation in the E-Governance Era. This includes recognizing that the entirety of the populous may not be completely proficient in or have access to any number of technologies used in the E-Governance movement. The possibility of technical failure is also a key concern that a responsible government should continue to monitor. The government may allocate tax dollars to promote the wider use of technology in society by responsibly endeavoring to educate the public in the usage of available innovations and to maintain technical integrity during the implementation of public sector duties. Potential unintended issues stemming from the Janus face of technology further reinforce the importance of having a diverse deliberative framework allowing for government to use both traditional and digital means in fulfilling its duties.

The application of modern innovations in the E-Governance Era is apt to yield a number of equity-based concerns regarding the digital divide, and this serves as an example of unintended consequences associated with the Janus face of technology. Therefore, providing working definitions of the digital divide and noting key issues of concern can be helpful toward establishing a baseline of understanding of this concept going forward. The digital divide is a complex topic that can potentially affect a diverse population in the United States especially during the process of implementing innovations toward the fulfillment of E-Governance responsibilities. Rogers (2001, p. 96) stated, "the digital divide is the gap that exists between individuals advantaged by the internet and those individuals relatively disadvantaged by the internet." Schlozman, Verba, and Brady (2010, p. 489) viewed the digital divide as "a continuum ranging from, at one end, those who have no Internet access or experience" to individuals with "broadband access at home, use the Internet frequently, and are comfortable with a variety of online techniques." Howland (1998, p. 287) explains that the digital divide is representative of a technology-based rift among the general public in which some individuals are "comfortable with computers" and are privy to "adequate access to telecommunications technologies" while other individuals "neither possesses, nor has access to, these tools." In this respect, the digital divide may create a societal disjoint between the "technological haves and have-nots" (Hammond, 1997; Howland, 1998; Ali, 1999; Kenski, 2005; Jorgensen & Cable, 2002). This schism regarding access to and proficiency with technologies can have an influence on determining the role that E-Governance means can effectively play in deliberative democracy if the process of applying technology negatively affects some individuals disproportionately. Hammond (1997, p. 182) warned that "as we identify the potential of network technology to benefit society, we must be wary that it not become a tool of disenfranchisement." Jorgensen and Cable (2002) observed that "politicians, management, and citizens suggest that a lack of access to e-government technology can further economic inequities within the city and limits choice and opportunities for the poor, the elderly and historically underrepresented groups, creating a 'digital divide' in the public sector." Relatedly, in some circumstances the digital divide may disproportionately affect demographic groups based on age, ethnicity, gender, place of residence, race and socio-economic status (Hammond, 1997; Ali, 1999; Rogers, 2001; Rogers, 2003; Campos-Castillo, 2015). Campos-Castillo (2015, p. 423) explained access regarding the digital divide may reflect variances based on gender in that "women are more likely to report having Internet access than men." Campos-Castillo (2015, p. 423) added that "Blacks and Latinos are equally likely to report having Internet access, and both groups are less likely to report having Internet access than Whites." Howland (1998, p. 288) warned against "electronic redlining," which could be a contributing factor to promoting the digital divide because "access to the technological infrastructure will be weighted heavily in favor of white and affluent segments of society." In addition, the digital divide may yield finer, more nuanced considerations that may affect the role that technology plays when implemented in the public sector. Marche and McNiven (2003, p. 76) viewed the multidimensional determinants of the digital divide's presence as being associated with whether the Internet is available, whether that access is to high-speed Internet to achieve "functional richness" and if the user has the "necessary experience, training, skills, and comfort to get the maximum benefit from any form of facilities." There may be some citizens who are comfortable with using basic Internet innovations for e-mail, social media and research, but less comfortable with more sophisticated tasks, as with online voting and utilizing "protective software" to ensure the security of the process (Gibson, 2001). As such, there may be variances within the technology-savvy demographic in regard to their ability, comfort level and access to more advanced innovations that may be required to facilitate all manner of online interactions with government. The digital divide may not only be indicative of a society that is composed of technological have and have-nots but also a group classified as the "want-nots" (Gibson, 2001) in individuals that may either be overwhelmed by or have a general lack of interest in using technological innovations used in E-Governance endeavors. If the government implements a whole-of-government approach to incorporate electronic means to facilitate interactions with the public, then the entirety of the populous may not actually be able to participate. The nature of the digital divide yields complex concerns regarding individuals in society that (a) experience inequity of access to technology, (b) lack opportunity to develop the requisite skills needed to utilize technology, or (c) have a disinterest in participating through nontraditional, high-tech means. Relatedly, the application of technology toward governance activities may potentially yield significant societal implications affecting those representing the digital divide disproportionately.

The digital divide is representative of a complex social issue, and the perpetuation of technological divisiveness is capable of affecting a wide array of individuals in respect to electronic-based government endeavors. Individuals unable to access or use a given technology will be unable to fully benefit from E-Governance designs, and this issue can contribute to widening the societal disjoint of technology-based aptitudes among the public. Access to innovations may not be universal in society, which can exacerbate digital divide inequity issues during the implementation of E-Governance initiatives. Citizens may not have access to personal home computers and the local digital infrastructure may not be adequate in their community, which creates barriers to participation. The infrastructure concern is one that could extend to citizens that reside in a range of locales including an urban setting or rural setting. Therefore, the digital divide dilemma is largely focused on understanding that there may be citizens without the required levels of understanding of innovations or access to those available innovations. However, there may also be a certain level of division between those individuals from within the technically advantaged citizen base. For example, some members of the public may have extensive training in modern innovations, personal access to a high-end computer at their residence and the fastest Internet connection available for home use. The upper range of this division creates an even more technologically proficient group of citizens that are able and willing to utilize their markedly more advanced skills toward private sector– or public sector–oriented goal completion. This creates a line of further demarcation regarding skill set and access even among citizens that are classified as being among the most technologically proficient in society, as highlighted in Figure 2.1.

Due to the levels of complexity attached with understanding the digital divide, those involved with the public sector implementation of innovations should be sensitive to the existence of broad-scale implications of technology-based inequities within the political environment, which can impact the ability of various individuals to participate. The government can also take measures to lessen, or preferably eliminate, the impact of the digital divide by developing initiatives promoting higher levels of participation through E-Governance

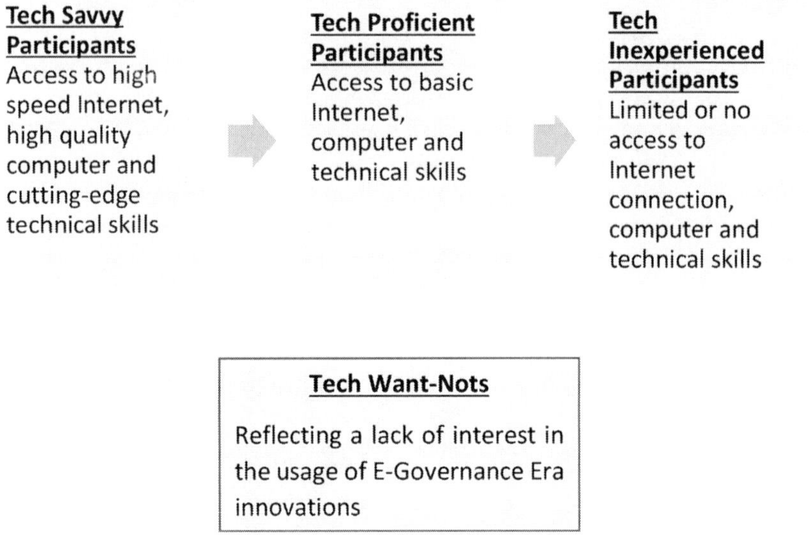

Tech Savvy Participants
Access to high speed Internet, high quality computer and cutting-edge technical skills

Tech Proficient Participants
Access to basic Internet, computer and technical skills

Tech Inexperienced Participants
Limited or no access to Internet connection, computer and technical skills

Tech Want-Nots

Reflecting a lack of interest in the usage of E-Governance Era innovations

Figure 2.1 Digital Divide Spectrum of Participants

designs. This includes allocating public funds to help overcome technological inequities in society by improving the infrastructure capable of facilitating the use of innovations (especially in rural and inner-city areas), promoting the availability of public buildings, like libraries and the development of public kiosks, to increase access, initiating training and education programs for individuals seeking to develop the skill set required to participate and cooperating with nonprofit organizations that may work within the community to help diffuse disparities stemming from the digital divide. Among the more significant lessons learned from identifying digital divide inequities is the importance that the public sector ensures that citizen–government interactions within the political system are able to simultaneously maintain both traditional and digital means for governance. At this stage in the evolution of E-Governance, the public sector must continue to avoid adopting exclusivity in electronic means, as this would not be sufficient to accommodate the whole of society due to the present state of digital divide inequities.

Although consideration for the issues stemming from the digital divide will continue to be important, there are a number of additional concerns associated with the potential application of innovation by government to facilitate electronic participatory interactions associated with E-Governance. This includes issues reflecting unintended consequences derived from the Janus face of technology, such as the societal tendency to become too reliant on technology and to prematurely adopt innovations. Howland (1998, p. 287) noted that "information technology is merely a tool." This perception of ICTs can help to guard against potential overreliance on digital technologies during the evolutionary process of E-Governance. Jin-Wook (2006, p. 69) expanded on this notion by noting that "new technology-driven civic participation" should not be utilized for enacting a wholesale change for "the traditional way of aggregating public opinion" and recommends that because of this, deliberative democracy means should ensure that "ICTs play a complementary role." Bannister and Connolly (2012, p. 211) explained that a vast array of political actors in society are inclined "to embrace the latest technological developments before older ones have been fully exploited or in some cases even fully understood." This phenomenon is sometimes referred to as the "Hype Cycle" (Fenn & Raskino, 2008; Edwards, 2015; Johnson, 2015) or the "Hype Curve" (Bannister & Connolly, 2012) in which the rush to apply the newest technological innovation outpaces the ability to determine if the application of existing technologies has been, or still will be, effective. This may cause government to apply ICTs in the public sector not based on whether technology has become outdated, but as a result of fear-based actions to avoid "being left behind in the latest technology wave" (Bannister & Connolly, 2012). The government ICT-planning efforts for the application of newly emerging technology for E-Governance should generally avoid conceding to such fear-based or pressure-based concerns. Instead, public sector ICT-planning efforts should reflect a more tempered approach in which decisions for the continued usage of innovations is based on a merit-based perspective for determining continued applicability of means. Before abandoning a current method in use in favor of newly emerging technologies, it should be determined whether this change is based on succumbing to pressures associated with technology hype or the possibility that the replacement technology will actually be better suited to accomplish government tasks. In addition, there are limits associated with the impact that various forms of information and communication technologies (ICTs) can have regarding contributing to a deliberative democracy framework. This further stresses the importance of developing and maintaining a deliberative framework that is representative of a diversity in means that are reflective of both traditional methods and digital innovations. E-Governance Era actions to apply digital means in which to facilitate citizen–government interactions would be well served by taking a calculated approach to applying technology and by accommodating diversity in participatory means. Doing so would help to guard against the perils of applying a technological innovation too prematurely in its development before it can be properly vetted for effectiveness and can help to create institutional safeguards to ensure that a diversity in means is present to accommodate citizen preferences for interactions.

References

Ali, A. J. (1999) Digital divide: A challenge that must be faced. *Advances in Competitiveness Research*, 7(1).

Bannister, F., & Connolly, R. (2012) Forward to the past: Lessons for the future of e-government from the story so far. *Information Polity: The International Journal of Government & Democracy in the Information Age*, 17(3/4): 211–226.

Campbell-Kelly, M., & Garcia-Swartz, D. (2013) The history of the Internet: The missing narratives. *Journal of Information Technology*, 28(1): 18–33. doi: 10.1057/jit.2013.4.

Campos-Castillo, C. (2015) Revisiting the first-level digital divide in the United States: Gender and race/ethnicity patterns, 2007–2012. *Social Science Computer Review*, 33(4): 423–439. doi: 10.1177/0894439314547617.

Chun, S. A., Sandoval, R., Arens, Y., Ojo, A., Janowski, T., & Estevez, E. (2011) Whole-of-government approach to information technology strategy management: Building a sustainable collaborative technology environment in government. *Information Polity: The International Journal of Government & Democracy in the Information Age*, 16(3): 233–250.

Congress.gov. (2016) Frequently asked questions: THOMAS retirement. Retrieved from www.congress.gov/help/faq#thomasretirement.

Coughlin, J. F. (2010) Understanding the Janus face of technology and ageing: Implications for older consumers, business innovation and society. *International Journal of Emerging Technologies & Society*, 8(2): 62–67.

Cousins, K., & Robey, D. (2015) Managing work-life boundaries with mobile technologies. *Information Technology & People*, 28(1): 34–71. Retrieved from http://search.proquest.com/docview/1652621905?accountid=32521.

Demirdjian, Z. S. (2016) *Challenges and opportunities in exponential times*. Bloomington, IN: Xlibris.

Edwards, C. (2015) Waiting for the drop. *Engineering & Technology*, 10(4): 32–35.

Fenn, J., & Raskino, M. (2008) *Mastering the hype cycle: How to choose the right innovation at the right time*. Boston, MA: Harvard Business Press.

Gibson, R. (2001) Elections online: Assessing Internet voting in light of the Arizona democratic primary. *Political Science Quarterly*, 4: 561–583.

Hajkowicz, S., Cook, H., & Littleboy, A. (2012) *Our future world: Global megatrends that will change the way we live: The 2012 revision*. Clayton South: CSIRO. Retrieved from https://publications.csiro.au/rpr/download?pid=csiro:EP126135&dsid=DS2.

Hammond, A. S. (1997) The telecommunications act of 1996: Codifying the digital divide. *Federal Communications Law Journal*, 50(1): 179–214. Retrieved from http://search.proquest.com/docview/213153100?accountid=32521.

Howland, J. S. (1998) The 'digital divide': Are we becoming a world of technological 'haves' and 'have-nots'? *The Electronic Library*, 16(5): 287–289.

Johnson, A. T. (2015) The technology hype cycle [state of the art]. *IEEE Pulse*, 6(2): 50. 10.1109/MPUL.2014.2386491.

Jorgensen, D. J., & Cable, S. (2002) Facing the challenges of E-Government: A case study of the city of Corpus Christi, Texas. *SAM Advanced Management Journal* (07497075), 67(3): 15.

Jin-Wook, C. (2006) Deliberative democracy, rational participation and e-voting in South Korea. *Asian Journal of Political Science*, 14(1): 64–81. doi: 10.1080/02185370600832547.

Kenski, K. (2005) To i-vote or not to i-vote?: Opinions about Internet voting from Arizona voters. *Social Science Computer Review*, 23(3): 293–303. doi: 10.1177/0894439305275851.

Kuhn, T. S. (1962) *The structure of scientific revolutions*. Chicago, IL: The University of Chicago Press.

Marche, S., & McNiven, J. D. (2003) E-government and e-governance: The future isn't what it used to be. *Revue Canadienne Des Sciences De L'administration/ Canadian Journal of Administrative Sciences*, 20(1): 74–86.

National Performance Review (NPR). (1993) *From red tape to results: Creating a government that works better and costs less.* Amsterdam: Fredonia Books.

Netcraft. (2006) Marsha Walton's 'Web reaches new milestone: 100 million sites.' Retrieved from www.cnn.com/2006/TECH/internet/11/01/100millionwebsites/.

Netcraft. (2016) Web server survey. Retrieved from http://news.netcraft.com/a rchives/2016/06/22/june-2016-web-server-survey.html.

Rogers, E. M. (2001) The digital divide. *Convergence: The Journal of Research into New Media Technologies*, 7(4): 96. 10.1177/135485650100700406.

Rogers, E. M. (1995, 2003). *Diffusion of innovations (5th ed.).* New York: Free Press.

Schlozman, K. L., Verba, S., & Brady, H. E. (2010) Weapon of the strong? Participatory inequality and the Internet. *Perspectives on Politics*, 8(2): 487–509. doi: 10.1017/S1537592710001210.

Taylor, J. A. (2012) The information polity: Towards a two-speed future? *Information Polity: The International Journal of Government & Democracy in the Information Age*, 17(3/4): 227–237.

United States Defense Advanced Research Project Agency (DARPA). (2016) History and timeline: Where the future becomes now. Retrieved from www.darpa.mil/a bout-us/darpa-history-and-timeline.

Weymouth, R., & Hartz-Karp, J. (2015) Deliberative collaborative governance as a democratic reform to resolve wicked problems and improve trust. *Journal of Economic and Social Policy*, 17(1): 1–32.

Zakon, R. (1997) Hobbes' internet timeline, network working group RFC 2235. Retrieved January 30, 2013 from www.ietf.org/rfc/rfc2235.txt.

3 Technology Models and Societal Preferences

Technology Acceptance Model (TAM), Diffusion of Innovation (DOI), and Web Trust

Before expanding on what constitutes deliberative democracy and how digital means can contribute to strengthening the overall deliberative democracy framework, some discussion will be offered regarding conceptual models that may assist in determining what types of technology are deemed prime for usage in society. As previously noted, the public sector usage of digital means to fulfill responsibilities for a vast array of governance tasks is partly based on the need to align with the growing expectations for change. There may be multiple origin points from within society calling for the usage of new technologies, stemming from either the public or private sector. Vital among these potential sources of input within the context of U.S. deliberative democracy is that governmental initiatives to enact technological changes can be rooted in the perceived amenability of the citizen base toward taking action to integrate innovation. This is especially relevant when considering the role that citizen-driven system expectations have in motivating government to apply modern technology toward the completion of expected democratic functions. These motivational concerns guide the initial generalized decision to begin to enact technologies toward governmental goal achievement and provide insight into the rationale behind public sector decisions to choose a specific form of innovation over other available technological designs. Similarly, there are a number of system considerations affecting which type of technological innovation would be preferable. Johnson and Lybecker (2011, p. 602) explained that there are important factors associated with making "demand–push technological change" decisions, such as choosing from among competing new technologies to determine what will replace the old technology. Johnson and Lybecker (2011, p. 603) added that choosing when to replace the old technology can be problematic because present technology may still be sufficient and because new technology may have "early stage technical concerns." There are arguable benefits to a wait-and-see approach for the application of emerging technologies, which can allow for others to first determine the effectiveness of front-line application of innovation before deciding to employ them (Johnson & Lybecker, 2011). The rationale bridging the initial decision to use specific E-Governance means with citizen-driven system preferences for innovation can be derived from a number of theoretical conceptualizations. There is a great deal of insightful research and discussion regarding the possible role that various formulaic calculations can play in helping to explain the rate societal diffusion of technological innovation in the modern era (Griliches, 1957; Solow, 1957; Caves, Christensen, & Swanson, 1981; Onofri & Fulginiti, 2008; Färe & Karagiannis, 2014). However, the determination for the application of specific innovations by government to achieve deliberative E-Governance ends may also be guided by conceptualizations such as the Technology Acceptance Model (Davis, 1989), Diffusion of Innovation (Rogers, 2003) and Web Trust (McKnight, Choudhury, & Kacmar, 2002). These three prominent models can contribute to understanding how citizens may perceive technologies that can affect their faith in government's usage of the innovation. These explanatory models can be used to cultivate a more diverse understanding to explain the rationale behind why the citizen-consumer becomes amenable to, and has expectation of, government adapting to apply a given technological innovation. Here, a brief introduction to the main components associated with each of the three models is established. In addition, there have been a number of conceptualizations built upon the theoretical foundations of these designs to further assess factors that contribute to technology acceptance, diffusion and persistence in society that are acknowledged.

Davis's (1989) Technology Acceptance Model (TAM) helps to determine why innovations are eventually deemed acceptable for use by members of society. TAM consists of two interrelated factors that guide individuals in determining whether to accept the application of a given technological innovation. Davis (1989, p. 320) explained that "perceived usefulness" (PU) serves as one factor in determining whether technology can affect "the degree to which a person believes that using a particular system would enhance his or her job performance." Davis (1989, p. 320) added that the second factor, "perceived ease of use" (PEOU), was capable of determining "the degree to which a person believes that using a particular system would be free of effort." This finds great relevance in helping to explain why many technological innovations have proliferated the whole of society since the early 1990s. The Technology Acceptance Model, whether in original form or reflecting any number of modifications that have continued to develop since its inception, is applicable in identifying motivating factors that determine preferences for the adoption of innovations toward goal achievement. This includes considerations of the applicability of TAM to determine how college students' perceptions can affect how they may adopt digital textbooks (Hsiao, Tang, & Lin, 2015), the ability to determine the "online game player acceptance of games" (Zhu, Lin, & Hsu, 2012), intentions for online interactive participation via social networking sites (Choi & Chung, 2013), facilitation of "online fantasy sport consumption" (Ibrahim, 2013) and to help explain acceptance by consumers of "e-tailing" online consumerism (Renko & Popovic, 2015). TAM has also been applied to topics such as understanding the impact of societal perceptions on the rate of diffusion of green technology in the field of transportation (Chen & Lu, 2016) and in gauging attitudes for technology use in universities as applied to "dropout notification and return to school system" (Chen, Liu, & Lin, 2014). Rana, Dwivedi, and Williams (2013, p. 27) observed that, although a number of information system/information technology (IS/IT) adoption models can play a significant role in assessing motivations for innovation usage, "TAM is by far the best suited model for analyzing citizen centric adoption of e-government services." Cegarra-Navarro et al. (2014, p. 15) studied the usage of ICTs to deliver online public services at the local level of government, concluding that factors associated with TAM were able to "significantly affect users' citizen engagement" and that there was "general support for citizen satisfaction as a determinant of citizen engagement in e-Government services." The role of TAM in explaining how individuals perceive whether an innovation will make participation easier and allow for them to more effectively complete goals also serves as part of the conceptual foundation in understanding the expanding societal expectations for the continued usage of digital interactive means associated with E-Governance.

TAM served as the predecessor to any number of influential conceptualizations used to determine how emerging technology is accepted and proliferates throughout society, which can be related to understanding motivations behind E-Governance Era innovation initiatives. The Diffusion of Innovation theory (Rogers, 2003) and the Web Trust model (McKnight, Choudhury, & Kacmar, 2002; Gefen, Karahanna, & Straub, 2003) provide further insight regarding how accepted innovative means proliferate throughout society and the role that trust plays in consumer–vendor online interactions. The Diffusion of Innovation (DOI) theory developed by Rogers (2003) highlights the important role that specific identifiable factors play in affecting how technology is diffused throughout society. Rogers (2003, p. 5) noted that "diffusion is the process in which an innovation is communicated through certain channels over time among the members of a social system." Rogers (2003, p. 16) explained that "relative advantage, compatibility, complexity, trialability and observability" serve as "the characteristics of innovations, as perceived by individuals, help to explain their different rates of adoption." Rogers (2003, p. 12) defined *innovation* as "an idea, practice or object" that system participants interpret as cutting-edge and unconventional when assessed against comparable matters that preceded it. Here, the communication between individuals within a society regarding the perceived benefits of applying an emerging technology contributes to the government's decision to adopt new means over existing methods. Public sector efforts to mine citizen-centric networked communication to identify positive perceptions of innovations for use in E-Government duties (such as the delivery of public services and the dissemination of information) and E-governance duties (related to constructing interactive means in which to facilitate participation) affect technology adoption in these areas. Whether citizens accept

E-Government or E-Governance initiatives can also be assessed based on components associated with The Web Trust model. The Web Trust model (McKnight, Choudhury, & Kacmar, 2002; Gefen, Karahanna, & Straub, 2003) contributes to understanding the diffusion of technological means in which there are a number of criteria affecting how innovations are accepted, and eventually utilized, by individuals. McKnight, Choudhury, and Kacmar (2002) discussed the importance of developing a multidimensional understanding of how trust is developed between vendors and consumers during online interactions, which can ultimately influence future transactions. Gefen, Karahanna, and Straub's (2003) study of Internet consumers indicates that repeated online transactions are based on attributes associated with TAM in combination with the levels of trust that is established with the vendor. Trust in the online vendor is a function of (a) perceived ease of transactions, (b) a secure website that can safely facilitate the sale, (c) faith that the vendor is unlikely to be defraud consumers, and (d) that consumer usage of the website is predictable, creating familiarity with the interaction (Gefen, Karahanna, & Straub, 2003). Here, trust in online interactions is derived from positive, familiar, secure and honest transactions that are repeated between consumers and venders. This ideal regarding the cultivation of trust can be very useful when considering the usage of technological innovation to facilitate any number of E-Governance Era interactions between citizen-consumers and government. Similarly, the levels of trust that develop between the citizen-consumer and government during interactions play a role in the decision to continue or discontinue use of a given technology. It is also important to note that developing citizen trust in innovative means is an interactive, consistently dynamic process that requires multiple transactions over an extended period of time. Here, citizens' trust in the capacity of technological means to achieve goals and in the government's ability to successful employ innovations to facilitate E-Governance tasks is cultivated over time. The belief that new technology will be better suited than existing technology to fulfill government responsibilities also contributes to the demand for public sector adoption of a given innovation. The trust levels in government and the demand from the public for the adoption of new innovation will continue to play a significant role in determining whether emerging technologies permanently become part of the public sector apparatus used to facilitate citizen–government interactions. The DOI and Web Trust models further provide insight regarding how motivating factors may guide decisions regarding the usage of digital designs to fulfill public sector responsibilities in the E-Governance Era.

The TAM, DOI and Web Trust models contributed chronologically to developing a deeper understanding of how system preferences may affect acceptance, usage and wide-scale diffusion of technology. Clearly, understanding how system preferences may be influential in technology-based judgments illuminates key factors guiding decision-making processes associated with E-Government and E-Governance. The contributions of TAM,

DOI and Web Trust provide helpful insight on the factors determining which innovations are primed for usage in the E-Governance Era and can expound on how government decisions to adopt technology have been influenced by taking cues from the environment. In relation, criteria such as ease of use and usefulness are directly associated with determining the applicability of technological innovations that have proliferated throughout the whole of society since the early 1990s to accomplish a broad array of private sector or public sector tasks. Many innovations being applied in the E-Governance Era have continued to proliferate since the early 1990s partly due to the perception that the application of technology has been useful and capable of promoting greater ease for participants to complete tasks. It is also important to note that determining whether technology will be useful toward accomplishing ends and will facilitate greater ease in achieving those ends is a malleable process subject to continued reinterpretations over time. When an innovation is created, such as e-mail, it may take time to be perceived as capable to contribute toward more easily enhancing goal achievement. In turn, continued assessment over time may alter the perceptions regarding the technology in question. Internet and computers have generally made many aspects of life easier by providing useful technological innovations to accomplish any number of tasks. For example, it is generally considered easier to send an e-mail than it is to send traditional letters through the U.S. Postal Service. This is not to say that e-mail is the only useful method in which to communicate messages in the modern era or that sending information through the U.S. Postal Service is without merit. The U.S. Postal Service continues to serve as a critical means to disseminate information, and maintaining this traditional means remains relevant in the modern era. Today, there are many people that may still not be able to send an e-mail from the comfort of home, and must travel to an alternate location, such as a public library, in order to send an e-mail. Surely, this individual may find it easier to simply go to their mailbox to send a letter through the traditional mail system than it is to travel to the public library for the purpose of sending an e-mail. This serves as further evidence that both traditional and digital means should be maintained in modern governance. It also illustrates the importance of consistently maintaining efforts to determine whether initial acceptance of technology that has diffused throughout society will continue to be used in perpetuity. The development of preferences for technology by members of society and the subsequent assessment of those preferences by decision makers remains a dynamic, not static, process, which requires sustained diligence to accommodate the continued rapid advancements in technology.

There have also been a number of subsequent analysis efforts that have built upon the conceptual foundations of TAM, DOI and Web Trust to further contribute to understanding what causes technology preferences and how these preferences may affect societal acceptance, use and continued application. Relatedly, these efforts combine applicable elements associated with

TAM, DOI and Web Trust with further descriptive dimensions to broaden the scope of the discussion to more fully understand the influence of societal preferences on the proliferation of innovations. Carter and Bélanger (2005) sought to integrate elements of all three models when discussing decision-making associated with the adoption of innovations for E-Government activities, which they broadly defined as actions ranging from e-voting to processes for online license renewals. For Carter and Bélanger (2005), the nature of trust in E-Government is dependent on whether citizens have faith in the ability of government to accomplish tasks and in the actual ICTs being utilized to facilitate activities such as service delivery. Although E-Government may be able to promote higher levels of public sector accountability, better ensure cost-effectiveness in goal achievement and increase greater access to information, the societal acceptance of E-Government designs is ultimately subject to concerns associated with "citizens' willingness to adopt this innovation" (Carter & Bélanger, 2005, p. 5). Carter and Bélanger (2005, p. 21) expound on this acceptance threshold by noting that the "perceived ease of use, compatibility and trustworthiness are significant indicators of citizens' intention to use state e-government services." Mahadeo (2009, p. 391) studied E-Government services by applying factors associated with TAM and DOI to create a "hybrid model" to determine "user's intention to adopt and continue to make use of the electronic tax system" and found that "users' 'attitude' towards the e-Tax filing and payment system has been the most powerful predictor for user interaction." Wangpipatwong, Chutimaskul, and Papasratorn (2008, p. 55), in studying how public perceptions of government websites affect usage over time, observed that "perceived usefulness and perceived ease of use of e-Government websites and citizen's computer self-efficacy directly enhanced citizen's continuance intention to use e-Government websites." Xiao and Shaobo (2014, p. 44) studied web portals in China by combining traditional considerations of the TAM innovation adoption model with Continuance Intent (CI) measures to determine the contextual influence on future intended usage and found that "due to differences in citizen's intended use of e-government portals, there are differences in user's requirements in terms of service types and service quality." Yoon and Rolland (2015, p. 1) assessed contextual components associated with the Information System Continuance Model (ISCM) to, "explore the role of enjoyment and subjective norms in continuance use of social networking services." Consider also contextual elements that affect individuals' initial acceptance and intentions for continued usage of technology by applying methods such as the Unified Theory of Acceptance and Use of Technology (UTAUT) model, which assesses the role of "users' post adoption behavior" to determine future use of innovations (Venkatesh et al., 2003; Venkatesh et al., 2011). Bhattacherjee (2001, p. 351) adapted the consumer-oriented Expectation-Confirmation Theory (ECT) model to analyze the "cognitive beliefs and affect influencing one's intention to continue using (continuance) information systems (IS)" and observed that "users' continuance intention is determined by their satisfaction with IS use and perceived usefulness of continued IS use." Bhattacherjee's (2001) usage of ECT contributed to developing a richer understanding of contextual factors that may affect future usage of a given innovation and helps to identify reasons why initially accepted technologies may be subject to the "acceptance-discontinuance anomaly," which results in future disuse. There were a number of subsequent efforts that built on the initial ECT model analysis to further explore a wide range of contextual factors that may affect initial acceptance and the possibility of continued future use of technology (Bhattacherjee & Premkumar, 2004; Bhattacherjee & Lin, 2015). Alsaghier et al. (2009, p. 297) developed a conceptual model based on nine factors: "intention to engage in E-Government, perceived risk, trust in government, PU, PEOU, website quality, institution-based trust, familiarity, disposition to trust" to gauge the role of various contextual factors in affecting the levels of trust in E-Government delivery of services to citizens. Here, the means in which to measure the potential of citizen trust in E-Government service delivery means is influenced by a wide range of technical and societal factors that may affect initial adoption and continued intended use in future online service transactions. This ideal is applicable to E-Government and E-Governance alike as it remains important to acknowledge the role that many factors play in affecting perceptions associated with the capacity of technologies employed and the levels of trust in the government's ability to utilize innovation toward the fulfillment of duties.

Theoretical models such as TAM, DOI, Web Trust, ISCM, UTAUT and ECT continue to be applicable in the modern era as they relate to contributing to better understanding of the motivating factors behind preferences and the choices for technological innovations ultimately being utilized by government. This includes that the perceptions that specific innovations may be capable of creating more convenient digital means to conduct various citizen–government interactions may affect implementation efforts. In relation, recognizing the influence of preferences of network participants plays a role in determining whether initially accepted technology will continue to be used. All of these conceptual designs built on the premise that preferences can affect innovation-based decision-making, and provide further evidence regarding the importance of remaining aware of the affect of system preferences on E-Governance actions. These key models, among many others, illustrate the importance of acknowledging the role that technology preferences stemming from participants from within the political system may have on the application of innovation. Preferences may affect the initial acceptance, wide-scale diffusion and continued usage of technology. The usage of technology in the E-Governance Era was not a spontaneous event that occurred in a value vacuum without having some factors contributing to the development of precedence regarding preferences for innovation-based changes. Preferences identified from participants from within society have the capacity to affect the timing of the decision to apply innovation and the decision to select specific innovation(s) in order to accomplish governmental goals. Here, there is an understanding that acceptance and diffusion are parts of the equation associated with the role that preferences have on the process of technology adoption. It is recognized that initial acceptance and diffusion of technology is not a guarantee that future preferences will sustain continued usage. Similarly, the development of preferences based on personal experiences utilizing a given technology to participate with government is also an important consideration that may affect future continued use, or eventual discontinuance, of innovations. There are many contextual factors that may affect citizen perceptions and potentially play a key role in determining initial permeance and future permanence of innovations being utilized by government to fulfill duties. This includes the role that contextual factors associated with cultivating trust may play in affecting preferences for the usage of technology. It is important to consider the effect of trust in a specific technology—trust in the general importance of the role of technology in society and the trust in capacity of government to effectively use such innovations. This relates in part to trust derived from the belief that an individual can apply technological means to engage with government through digital means, and whether there is belief that government is capable of employing such means to adequately achieve intended results. Preferences are shaped by the context in which technology is utilized and the nature of experiences associated with using an innovation to interact with government. Positive or negative experiences in this regard can ultimately shift the expectations associated with how government should endeavor toward continued usage, or discontinuance, of innovations. TAM, DOI, Web Trust, ISCM, UTAUT and ECT are models to remain aware of when considering the application of a given digital technology for use in E-Government and E-Governance activities. These conceptualizations can provide insight regarding factors that influence citizen perceptions of technology, which play a pivotal role in dictating public sector efforts to utilize innovations in the performance of duties.

References

Alsaghier, H., Ford, M., Nguyen, A., & Hexel, R. (2009) Conceptualising citizen's trust in e-government: Application of Q methodology. *Electronic Journal of E-Government*, 7(4): 295–309.

Bhattacherjee, A. (2001) Understanding information systems continuance: An expectation-confirmation model. *MIS Quarterly*, 25(3): 351–370.

Bhattacherjee, A., & Lin, C. (2015) A unified model of IT continuance: Three complementary perspectives and crossover effects. *European Journal of Information Systems*, 24(4): 364–373. doi: 10.1057/ejis.2013.36.

Bhattacherjee, A., & Premkumar, G. (2004) Understanding changes in belief and attitude toward information technology usage: A theoretical model and longitudinal test. *MIS Quarterly*, 28(2): 229–254. Retrieved from www.jstor.org/stable/25148634.

Carter, L., & Bélanger, F. (2005) The utilization of e-government services: Citizen trust, innovation and acceptance factors. *Information Systems Journal*, 15(1): 5–25. doi: 10.1111/j.1365-2575.2005.00183.x.

Caves, D. W., Christensen, L. W., & Swanson, J. A. (1981) Productivity growth, scale economies, and capacity utilization in U.S. railroads, 1955–1974. *American Economic Review*, 71(5): 994–1002.

Cegarra-Navarro, J., Eldridge, S., Martinez-Caro, E., Teresa, M., & Polo, S. (2014) The value of extended framework of TAM in the electronic government services. *Electronic Journal of Knowledge Management*, 12(1): 15–25.

Chen, S., & Lu, C. (2016) Exploring the relationships of green perceived value, the diffusion of innovations, and the technology acceptance model of green transportation. *Transportation Journal*, 55(1): 51–77.

Chen, T., Liu, H., & Lin, S. A. (2014) Construct of educational information system's using willingness model: An extended application of technology acceptance model. *International Journal of Organizational Innovation*, 6(4): 60–71. Retrieved from http://search.proquest.com/docview/1517634932?accountid=32521.

Choi, G., & Chung, H. (2013) Applying the technology acceptance model to social networking sites (SNS): Impact of subjective norm and social capital on the acceptance of SNS. *International Journal of Human-Computer Interaction*, 29(10): 619–628. doi: 10.1080/10447318.2012.756333.

Davis, F. D. (1989) Perceived usefulness, perceived ease of use, and user acceptance of information technology. *MIS Quarterly*, 13(3): 319–340.

Färe, R., & Karagiannis, G. (2014) Radial and directional measures of the rate of technical change. *Journal of Economics*, 112(2): 183–199. doi: 10.1007/s00712-013-0344-6.

Gefen, D., Karahanna, E., & Straub, D. W. (2003) Trust and TAM in online shopping: An integrated model. *MIS Quarterly*, 27(1): 51–90.

Griliches, Z. (1957) Hybrid corn: An exploration in the economics of technological change. *Econometrica*, 25(4): 501–522.

Hsiao, C., Tang, K., & Lin, C. (2015) Exploring college students' intention to adopt e-textbooks: A modified technology acceptance model. *Libri: International Journal of Libraries & Information Services*, 65(2): 119–128. doi: 10.1515/libri-2014-0155.

Ibrahim, H. (2013) Technology acceptance model: Extension to sport consumption. *Annals of DAAAM & Proceedings*, 24(1): 1534–1540. doi: 10.1016/j. proeng.2014.03.152.

Johnson, D. N., & Lybecker, K. M. (2011) Does HAVA (Help America Vote Act) help the have-nots? U.S. adoption of new election equipment, 1980–2008. *Growth and Change*, 42(4): 601–627.

Mahadeo, J. D. (2009) Towards an understanding of the factors influencing the acceptance and diffusion of e-government services. *Electronic Journal of E-Government*, 7(4): 391–402.

McKnight, D. H., Choudhury, V., & Kacmar, C. (2002) Developing and validating trust measures for e-commerce: An integrative typology. *Information Systems Research*, 13(3): 334–359.

Onofri, A., & Fulginiti, L. E. (2008) The context of discovery: An experiment in modeling R&D in agriculture: Rejoinder. *Journal of Productivity Analysis*, 30(1): 81–85. http://dx.doi.org.proxy-library.ashford.edu/10.1007/s11123-008-0094-6.

Rana, N. P., Dwivedi, Y. K., & Williams, M. D. (2013) Evaluating alternative theoretical models for examining citizen centric adoption of e-government. *Transforming Government: People, Process and Policy*, 7(1): 27–49. doi: 10.1108/17506161311308151.

Renko, S., & Popovic, D. (2015) Exploring the consumers' acceptance of electronic retailing using technology acceptance model. *Poslovna Izvrsnost/Business Excellence*, 9(1): 29–41.

Rogers, E. M. (2003) *Diffusion of innovations (5th ed.)*. New York: Free Press.

Solow, R. M. (1957) Technical change and the aggregate production function. *The Review of Economics and Statistics*, 39(3): 312–320.

Venkatesh, V., Morris, M. G., Davis, G. B., & Davis, F. D. (2003) User acceptance of information technology: Toward a unified view. *MIS Quarterly*, 27(3): 425–478.

Venkatesh, V., Thong, J. L., Chan, F. Y., Hu, P. J., & Brown, S. A. (2011) Extending the two-stage information systems continuance model: Incorporating UTAUT predictors and the role of context. *Information Systems Journal*, 21(6): 527–555. doi: 10.1111/j.1365-2575.2011.00373.x.

Wangpipatwong, S., Chutimaskul, W., & Papasratorn, B. (2008) Understanding citizens' continuance intention to use e-government website: A composite view of technology acceptance model and computer self-efficacy. *Electronic Journal of E-Government*, 6(1): 55–64.

Xiao, J., & Shaobo, J. (2014) E-government web portal adoption: The effects of service quality. *E-Service Journal*, 9(3): 43–62.

Yoon, C., & Rolland, E. (2015) Understanding continuance use in social networking services. *The Journal of Computer Information Systems*, 55(2): 1–8. Retrieved from http://search.proquest.com/docview/1647821314?accountid=32521.

Zhu, D., Lin, T. C., & Hsu, Y. (2012) Using the technology acceptance model to evaluate user attitude and intention of use for online games. *Total Quality Management & Business Excellence*, 23(7/8): 965–980. doi: 10.1080/14783363.2012.704269.

4 Scientific Knowledge, Technocrats and the Role of the Expert

In many ways, the modern era of governance has been greatly affected by increased levels of complexity associated with technology advancements. Scientific knowledge is recognized as being important in the modern era to provide decision makers with necessary levels of technical information that can greatly contribute to ensuring that government actions are better able to address complex contemporary issues. As modern society became more complex, the rise of the influence of the technocrat coincided to meet the growing belief that expertise was needed to fully address the challenges provided by increasingly intricate issues on a global level. Thus, it is important to briefly define a technocrat and explain the role that technocratic perspectives have on affecting the political system within a modern democracy. Wickman (2011, para. 2) stated that a *technocrat* is "an expert" and that "technocrats make decisions based on specialized information rather than public opinion." Merriam-Webster's dictionary defines a *technocrat* as "a scientist or technical expert who has a lot of power in politics or industry." The usage of expert knowledge plays an important role in modern democracy, and government can use this source of information during the development of actions to address modern, technically complex problems. The benefit of the use of scientific information in governance is partly linked to Simon's (1955) Theory of Bounded Rationality in that any individual is limited in resources such as time, fiscal means, human capital and personal knowledge. Therefore, referencing specialists with technical knowledge can be beneficial for government undertakings for crafting actions to address complex societal issues like those involving environmental policy issues. A technocratic approach to governance is one that relies heavily on expert knowledge to help guide actions intended to address issues of importance that affect society on the whole. Fischer (1995, pp. 11–12) explained that "technocratic policy analysis is thus a matter of uniformly applying empirically based technical methodologies, such as cost-benefit analysis and risk assessment, to the technical aspects of all policy problems." Anderson (1994, p. 286) highlighted the expanded role that expert knowledge plays in modern era public policy development where the "growing 'technocratization' of the policy process" may sometimes render "meaningful participation by ordinary persons or average citizens more difficult." There are also variances in the degree to which technocracy manifests within governments, which essentially ranges from high use to low use (McDonnell & Valbruzzi, 2014; Wickman, 2011). *The Economist* ("Minds like machines," 2011) noted that modern-era governance may create an environment in which societal deference to the "wisdom and expertise of a technocrat" during policy making may be common. There are a number of individuals that recognized government's usage of scientific knowledge by technocrats has contributed to government's ability to govern as it relates to public policy development (Yankelovich, 1991; Anderson, 1994; Fischer, 2000; Craig, 2014; McDonnell & Valbruzzi, 2014). DeSario and Langton (1984, p. 224) explained that "technocracy, for our purposes, is the application of technical knowledge, expertise, techniques, and methods to problem solving, while democracy is used to refer to citizen involvement in government planning and policymaking." It is important to note that the belief that technocratic decisions are fully de-politicized is a fallacy. Completely value-free governance is an unrealistic expectation. Additionally, given that there is often very little consensus regarding the merits of adopting a technocratic approach and the fact that technocracy does not equal infallibility, overreliance on experts to solve all problems should not be the status quo.

Here, a technocrat is an individual that is an expert in a given field whose specialized knowledge is used by governmental decision makers when crafting public sector actions. The members of the U.S. Congress cannot possibly be expected to personally have all of the required levels of expertise needed to craft legislation related to every issue of societal importance. It is therefore beneficial for Congress to defer to experts with specific types of knowledge during the process of crafting various types of public policy, for example societal concerns that reflect complexity such as those associated with national security, transportation and education. Technocratic expertise is sourced during governance to assist in a wide range of problem-solving endeavors. Regarding issues related to the hard sciences, technocratic knowledge would prove advantageous in assisting policy makers with the creation of environmental legislation, because scientific expertise in this respect is not considered to be common knowledge. For example, experts within the Environmental Protection Agency (EPA) should be consulted by members of Congress who are drafting legislation to address issues associated with water or air quality. Representatives should rely on scientific expertise regarding what constitutes "acceptable" levels of carbon monoxide in various settings to help address air quality concerns with pollution. Therefore, expert sources of information are utilized to ensure that crafting legislation is reflective of the application of knowledge needed to adequately address a policy concern that is complex in nature. Government should also use these expert knowledge sources to assist in the review of existing policy to determine if the intended goals inherent within a legislative mandate were successfully being addressed during implementation. Expert knowledge in a modernized democracy represents a meaningful source of information capable of making a significant contribution across a vast number of technically based problems. These types of complex information are not generally categorized as common knowledge, and require some form of expertise to be sourced by government to help ensure more informed decision-making. A modern society is reflective of a vast array of complex modern problems. Here, knowledge furnished by experts can serve as a significant source of information for government to be able to better construct actions more capable of addressing modernized problems that are of a specialized nature.

However, the usage (or is some cases, the overusage) of scientific knowledge in the public sector may create a whole subset of issues for democratic governance in the modern era. Dahl (1989) noted that there are dangers associated with the application of "specialized knowledge" in circumstances in which the value of alternate sources of information are discounted or ignored. Here, programmed deference to experts may result in government actions that have failed to consider supplementary sources of input capable of contributing valuable perspectives to problem solving endeavours. Failing to consider supplementary sources may negatively affect levels of trust in government if subsequent actions are not able to adequately address societal problems or are not reflective of citizen preferences. Dahl (1989, p. 69) discussed a number of critiques associated with technocrats, including noting that "the specialization required in order to acquire a high degree of expert knowledge is today inherently limiting: one becomes a specialist in *something*, that is, in *one* thing, and by necessity remains ignorant of other things." In this case, the specialization of knowledge in the narrowest sense may be developed at the expense of an individual cultivating a broad and diverse understanding of topics of societal importance. Doing so limits the levels of personalized knowledge, which remain narrow in scope. This can be especially detrimental toward efforts in fostering connectivity of knowledge among related ideas within the political system. Dahl (1989, p. 69) also critiqued technocrats' roles in policy making on the basis that "on a great many questions of policy, instrumental judgements depend on assumptions that are not strictly technical, scientific, or even rigorous." Here, it is important to acknowledge that experts may provide technical acumen that may contribute to solving identified problems. However, it is also imperative to avoid overlooking the role that non-technical based values such as equity could play in determining whether public sector actions are required or in affecting public sector designs to address complex issues. Craig (2014) discussed a dilemma associated with granting increased levels of authority to experts that wield technical knowledge related to the effect on citizen–government participatory dynamics. Craig (2014, p. 32) noted that the growing societal trend of deferring to a "technocratic elite encourages apathy and depoliticization in the citizenry." Craig (2014, p. 32) posited that this lack of interest could result in a system in which "the once proudly self-governing citizen, vigilant and prickly in defense of his right to decide for himself, becomes the timid and deferential client of an ever-growing state, dominated by a small cadre of elites armed with special knowledge." In this sense, citizens may too often defer to the expert knowledge of technocrats to the point where an individual's interest in being involved with civic participation activities is minimal at best. Therefore, the willingness to pursue an interest in knowledge may be replaced with voluntary acceptance of, and preference for, the facts set forth by experts. Yankelovich (1991, p. 242) expanded on this dynamic by noting that "for decades now, a vicious cycle has been unfolding: as the experts usurp more and more of the nation's decision making, the public slumps ever more into mass opinion." Yankelovich (1991, p. 11) referred to a "culture of technical control" that contributes to a "trend that elevates the specialized knowledge of the expert" and at the same time "denigrating the value of the public's potentially most important contribution— a high level of thoughtful and responsible public judgement." Here, citizen input is viewed as somehow less meaningful simply because it lacks the technical proficiency of knowledge held by experts. Whereas expertise can be a crucial specialized source of information, acknowledging this does not imply that technocratic knowledge should always be the default reference when government considers taking actions to address problems—citizen preferences should also be considered. Craig (2014) observed a certain level of disbelief has developed on behalf of citizens in the power of scientific information and in the technocrats that wield the information in which facts are considered to have been "cherry-picked" or "fabricated." This in itself creates some skepticism associated with technical information across a wide array of policy areas and may negatively contribute to the overall degradation of the fabric of democracy. If there is a lack of confidence in those responsible for cultivating scientific knowledge and a crisis of credibility as to whether that information is unbiased, then it is likely that the application of this information toward government action will provide outcomes that fail to fully hold the faith of the public.

An overreliance on technocratic knowledge, coupled with failure to seek alternate sources of information, such as those associated with citizen preferences, can render government outcomes as indifferent, unresponsive or incapable of addressing the spectrum of legitimate demands present within the political system. In relation, it is also important to further consider the impact that deference to experts can have on reducing the dialectic skill set required for citizens to actively participate in meaningful interactions with government. There are also possible negative effects on the nature of democracy, which is conceptually dependent on a certain level of interaction between interested parties seeking to affect change to the political system. A lack of available participatory events between citizens and government may result in what Norris (2011) referred to as a *democratic deficit*. A number of factors can conceivably contribute to a democratic deficit, including "some combination of growing public expectations, negative news, and/or failing government performance" (Norris, 2011, p. 5). Norris (2011, p. 125) explained that "*democratic* 'aspirations' are measured by importance that is attached to living in a democracy, while democratic '*satisfaction*' refers to evaluations of the perceived performance of democracy." Norris (2011) continued by noting, "the '*deficit*' represents the difference when satisfaction is subtracted from aspirations." In this sense, a democratic deficit may be generated if the realities of existing participatory means fall short of public expectations. Nabatchi (2010) observed that it is plausible that a "citizen deficit" and a "democratic deficit" may simultaneously negatively impact levels of civic engagement and traditional expectations of the influential factors guiding government outcomes in a democracy. This includes that "citizen deficits" may result in a diminishing level of participation skills combined with an overall reduction of a willingness to actively be engaged in civic involvement (Nabatchi, 2010). Relatedly, the "democratic deficits" may yield correspondingly higher levels of government outcomes that fail to fully reflect societal preferences, and therefore may lack a certain degree of legitimacy because results were not determined through deliberative democracy means to ascertain citizen preferences (Nabatchi, 2010). Nabatchi (2010, p. 379) explained that the two system shortfalls are interrelated in that "as more policy decisions poorly manifest public preferences, citizens further withdraw from political activity." Deliberation is a skill like any other, and without practicing this skill, through engaging consistently in active dialogue, the likelihood of cultivating dialectic proficiency may be diminished somewhat. Citizens who actively engage in discursive events with government on a consistent basis can better hone applicable skills to use in situations that support citizen participation. In this sense, automatic deference to the technical knowledge of experts may diminish the development of requisite dialectic, research and inquiry skills that would have otherwise been shaped through experience in participating in discourse. In addition to these micro-level, individual dialectic skill sets that are typically developed through experiencing deliberations with government, there is also a possible macro effect on the whole of democracy that results from a lack of consistently active participation due to the entrenchment of voluntary deference to expert knowledge. Government actions taken without any explicit link to citizen-based input derived from participating in dialogue processes may not reflect the collective will of the people. Government actions that are far removed from the actual expectations and needs of the people may contribute to the erosion of the legitimacy of democracy. Without some interactive efforts on behalf of citizens to affect governance-based change, there may be individual and systemic concerns associated with accountability and legitimacy of subsequent governmental actions. This further highlights the importance of maintaining interactive deliberative means within the political system to strengthen principles associated with democratic expectations for citizen participation on both the micro and macro levels. The tendency of citizens in the modern era to defer to technical information from experts may devolve into a cycle of deference and apathy that runs counter to democratic principles associated with deliberative participation. This speaks to the importance of developing and maintaining collaborative means that are supportive of dialogue to facilitate authentic citizen participation. Experts and citizens are among the multitude of policy actors that can contribute insight to assist policy makers in making more informed decisions during the development of policy solutions. In this limited scenario, expert knowledge from technocrats and citizen-centric knowledge should both be used by policy makers toward the development of government actions (see Figure 4.1).

Scientific information used in government decision making can be undeniably important, but there are a number of dangers associated with overreliance on this source of knowledge if by default it becomes entrenched at the expense of exposure to input from complimentary sources from within the political arena. Here, overreliance on technocrats can pose certain challenges to democracy, one being the reduced perception that government outcomes are legitimate. In addition, there are a multitude of sources of information (i.e., citizens, elected officials, media, etc.) from within the political system that can contribute to informed decision-making other than technocratic expertise. In relation, multiple sources of input can be referred to so that a solution is derived from discourse between a variety of policy actors.

The wide-scale deference to technocratic knowledge during governmental decision-making without seeking alternate sources of input may yield outcomes that are technically sound, but somewhat disjointed from actual the will of public. Technocratic should not wholly replace democratic as the participatory means in which political system outcomes are determined. The habitual and automatic deference to experts is seen as a critical detriment to the fabric of democracy, which is intended to include, not exclude, citizen perspectives on governance. Fischer (1993, p. 165) recognized the importance of cooperative problem solving for "intractable" problems by noting that "citizen–expert inquiry may well hold the key to solving a specific category of contemporary policy problems." Wilson (2006, p. 519) explained that classic technocracy inequities for policy development can be offset by contemporary perspectives focused on citizen–expert cooperative efforts to develop solutions to problems by creating "learning spaces," which can ensure that "the

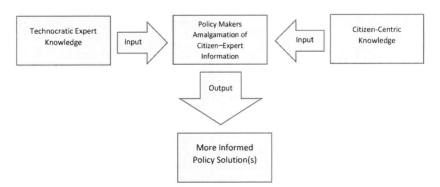

Figure 4.1 Policy Solutions Based on Citizen–Expert Knowledge

very process of engaging in joint practice can develop trust." Experts' contributions have a place within the deliberative framework in aiding governmental problem-solving endeavors, however technical expertise is not automatically a cure-all for society's problems. Expert knowledge serves as one of many key sources of information that can help to contribute to good decision making in a democracy. DeSario and Langton (1984) claimed that perspectives focused on both a technocratic approach and democratic approach to problem solving are often considered to be at odds with one another, but there is room within the modern policy arena for both types of contributions. DeSario and Langton (1984) explained that promoting "heightened citizen participation" and "citizen activism" can contribute to diffusing levels of societal deference to expertise by creating a more inclusive political environment. Craig (2014) noted that the "specter of technocracy" is a key motivation on which the foundation of many deliberative means to promote civic engagement has been built. Such participatory means are intended to encourage civic engagement in an effort to add citizen input to other sources of information during public sector decision-making. The expertise of technocrats may be helpful in contributing toward the pool of collective knowledge used for government problem solving, but consistent efforts should also be made to strongly consider citizen insight when applicable. Yankelovich (1991, p. 242) noted that "if our democracy is to remain vital, no goal is more important than bringing the expert–public relationship into better balance." In addition, Yankelovich (1991) provided an important foundational component associated with democracy: There is a subtle distinction between the interrelated concepts of "an informed public" and "public judgement." The existence of a plethora of information being made available to the public is important in a democracy, but insufficient as a stand-alone measure to promote informed actions (Yankelovich, 1991). However, information is important toward contributing to transitional conditions allowing for "public opinion" to evolve into "public judgement" (Yankelovich, 1991). Yankelovich (1991, p. 6) explained, "public judgement is the state of highly developed public opinion that exists once people have engaged an issue, considered it from all sides, understood the choice it leads to, and accepted the full consequences of the choices they make." For Yankelovich (1991), an "informed public" is quantified as a public that has access to information that can be used to make decisions and can contribute to citizens engaging in dialogue with government to actively create "public judgement." Therefore, access to information is of great importance in a democracy, because it can be used to promote more informed citizen participation. For the influence of expert knowledge to be reduced and for the role of citizen knowledge to be enhanced (Yankelovich, 1991), action must be taken to facilitate this balancing-out process. This relates to many modern mechanisms of deliberative democracy, which are designed to facilitate dialogue between citizens and government to achieve consensus based on collective intelligence. The balancing-out process represents an active, purposeful design. It is systemic in nature and involves the creation of multiple deliberative means by government and a citizen base willing to consistently engage in thoughtful dialogue in thoughtful dialogue capable of creating public judgement on issues of importance. Here, a deliberative democracy framework includes traditional and digital means that encourage meaningful dialogue in which well-informed citizens can help identify societal problems and can contribute toward generating consensus on viable solutions based on public judgement. The transitory process from public opinion to public judgement can be significantly impeded without the creation of appropriate interactive means in which citizens can actively gather information which can be synthesized into judicious ideas capable of affecting change in accordance with deliberative democracy expectations. There is a certain degree of mutual responsibility on behalf of government and citizens that must be maintained in order for this process to become effectively integrated into the deliberative democracy framework. Government and the public must be willing partners. While deliberative means are to be provided by government, the public is responsible for making efforts to consistently participate in dialogue through manufactured designs, and those informed decisions that result from discourse maintain relevance when visibly incorporated into political actions. This helps to preserve legitimacy in the deliberative process and can promote future dialogue with citizens who believe authentic participation yields results. Doing so may also contribute to the reduction in levels of apathy on behalf of citizens regarding participating in deliberative democracy by promoting increased levels of access and can help to maintain a more favorable balance between citizen–expert knowledge being used to affect change in the public sector. For E-Governance, citizen input through a wide range of digital participatory events is an integral supplemental source of knowledge to guide government actions within a deliberative democracy.

The expertise of technocrats can provide access to influential knowledge allowing government to develop actions based on considerations of a key source of information within the political environment. Expert knowledge is one of many sources of information that can play an influential role during decision-making in a modern democracy, and serves as a key building block within this action–resolution framework. Again, the usefulness of technocratic knowledge in contributing to informed governmental decision-making, especially regarding issues of technical complexity, is not to imply its universal acceptance in all situations without consultation of other perspectives. Overreliance on technical information wielded by experts may undermine democratic ideals by creating a lack of interest in the self-pursuit of knowledge by citizens, promoting citizen apathy over engagement and strengthening distrust for a government. Technocratic expertise represents one of many important sources of perspectives from within the political environment. Democracy requires input from a large representation of ideas to fully and accurately reflect a broad array of system interests. The idea here is to further develop means in which government can tap into a wide assortment of perspectives. These interactive means can give voice to an increased number of sources from within the political system for the purposes of more adequately identifying issues of significance, generating solutions for identified policy problems or obtaining feedback associated with public policy development. In relation, the provision of interactive means can augment the legitimacy associated with democratic processes when public sector outcomes are derived from subsequent authentic citizen participation that contributes to creating consensus derived from public judgement. Creating direct means that can yield visible public sector outcomes based on feedback provided by citizens during interactive sessions can also increase levels of public ownership in government actions, enhance faith in the power of authentic citizen participation and encourage enhanced levels of participation. Here, the way is further paved for a discussion of conceptual considerations and practical applications of E-Governance designs in which to facilitate meaningful interactions with citizens. Meaningful interactions can denote any number of matters in the context of citizen participation, and are expanded on in greater detail in the following sections. In short, facilitating meaningful citizen participation will encompass a wide range of technologically innovative means in which E-Governance interaction occurs. This includes events focused on meaningful citizen–government dialogue, which requires openness and cyclical components associated with deliberative democracy. These events allow for all interested citizens to continuously participate through means focused on generating solutions to policy problems and enacting changes to the political system. This is not to imply a return to direct democracy is preferred or even feasible in the modern era. Simply it means that further efforts to provide voice through electronic structural means to those interested in participating can generate enhanced levels of access to sources of information for an increasingly enormous chorus of interests within the U.S. democracy.

The question then becomes what types of digital means can be developed by government through which increased levels of citizen participation can be encouraged, cultivated, promoted and further institutionalized into the existing representative deliberative democracy framework. There are a number technologically innovative means that are capable of facilitating higher levels of civic engagement with government, including digital town hall meetings and crowdsourcing, that will be discussed in subsequent sections. However, it is first helpful to further discuss additional conceptual components which contributes to the foundation in which a deliberative democracy framework is built upon as it relates to the opportunity provided through digital citizen participation. This includes recognizing the influence that a traditionally private sector–oriented ideal referred to as *open innovation* plays in influencing E-Governance Era digital dialogue events between citizens and government. In addition, advancements in technological innovation during the E-Governance Era have provided increased opportunity for deliberative means that were not possible previously. These technological advancements can affect network dynamics within the political environment as it relates to determining who is involved in interactions within the modern deliberative democracy framework. This is based partly on the effect that the creation of new avenues of communication supporting interactions can have on potentially expanding the scope of those participating through digital events. The increased presence of technological advancements and the consideration of the applicability of open innovation can influence the means supporting citizen–government interactions in the modern E-Governance Era. As such, an introductory discussion on open innovation and the influence of technology on network theory are highlighted. This will help to further set the foundation for the subsequent discussion regarding citizen participation through technologically advanced communications means within the deliberative democracy framework associated with E-Governance.

References

Anderson, J. E. (1994) *Public policy making (2nd ed.).* New York: Houghton Mifflen Company.

Craig, T. (2014) Citizen forums against technocracy? The challenge of science to democratic decision making. *Perspectives on Political Science*, 43(1): 31–40. doi: 10.1080/10457097.2012.720836.

Dahl, R. (1989) *Democracy and its critics.* New Haven, CT: Yale University Press.

DeSario, J., & Langton, S. (1984) Citizen participation and technocracy. *Policy Studies Review*, 3(2): 223–233.

Fischer, F. (1993) Citizen participation and the democratization of policy expertise: From theoretical inquiry to practical cases. *Policy Sciences*, 26(3): 165–187.

Fischer, F. (1995) *Evaluating public policy.* Nashville, TN: Nelson-Hall.

Fischer, F. (2000) *Citizens, experts and the environment: The politics of local knowledge.* Durham, NC and London: Duke University Press.

McDonnell, D., & Valbruzzi, M. (2014) Defining and classifying technocrat-led and technocratic governments. *European Journal of Political Research*, 53(4): 654–671. doi: 10.1111/1475-6765.12054.

The Economist. (2011) Minds like machines, 401(8760): 63.

Nabatchi, T. (2010) Addressing the citizenship and democratic deficits: The potential of deliberative democracy for public administration. *American Review of Public Administration*, 40(4): 376–399. doi: 10.1177/0275074009356467.

Norris, P. (2011) *Democratic deficit: Critical citizens revisited.* New York: Cambridge University Press.

Simon, H. (1955) A behavioral model of rational choice. *The Quarterly Journal of Economics*, 69(1): 99–118.

Technocrat [Def. 2]. (n.d.). *Merriam-Webster Online.* In Merriam-Webster. Retrieved from www.merriam-webster.com/dictionary/technocrat.

Wickman, F. (2011) What's a technocrat? Have they ever really been in charge? *Slate.* Retrieved from www.slate.com/articles/news_and_politics/explainer/2011/11/technocrats_and_the_european_debt_crisis_what_s_a_technocrat_.html.

Wilson, G. (2006) Beyond the technocrat? The professional expert in development practice. *Development & Change*, 37(3): 501–523. doi: 10.1111/j.0012-155X.2006.00488.x.

Yankelovich, D. (1991) *Coming to public judgement: Making democracy work in a complex world.* Syracuse, NY: Syracuse University Press.

5 Open Innovation, Advancements in Technological Innovation and the Impact of Modern Networks on Participation

The application of private sector ideals contributing to the completion of public sector activities has an established and rich history in United States governance. This is indicated by a number of examples over time that focused on incorporating business-oriented perspectives into government, such as those attributed to Wilson's (2003) politics–administration dichotomy and the rise of the privatization movement in the 1990s. As time progresses and changes within the political environment occur, there is a continued stream of plausibly applicable ideas derived from any number of points of origin, public or private, that may enhance government's capacity to achieve democratically oriented goals. Such ideals, regardless of origin point, may be helpful in further strengthening the relationship between government and the populace while working toward improving public sector task performance in the fulfillment of duties within the E-Governance Era. Although there are clear differences between the two sectors, there have still been a number of times in U.S. history in which private sector techniques have been applied in the public sector with various degrees of success. Recognition of the differences between the private sector and public sector is not automatically a justification for excluding application of successful innovations through a cross-pollination of means. Therefore, it is helpful to briefly introduce a few key examples in which the public sector has sought to apply private sector conceptualizations to set the foundation for later discussion of applicable contemporary circumstances associated with E-Governance Era deliberative democracy.

The U.S. political system is reflective of multiple efforts over time in which private sector techniques and principles have been applied in the public sector to address issues of concern associated with performance of duties. In general, the responsive nature of the democratic system provides opportunity for government to pursue the application of private sector techniques and principles to try to correct perceived failures associated with status quo problem-solving endeavors. In part, government is expected to respond to consensus-driven perceptions that private sector techniques and principles would somehow enhance the public sector's ability to perform tasks, such as those associated with the provision of services. These past scenarios were intended to provide means that were perceived to have the capacity to allow government to pursue goal achievement in addressing issues of societal importance. The deliberative democracy context indicates that government made an effort to adjust actions to respond to expectations that the public sector could evolve to fulfill duties more effectively, efficiently and equitably. The precedent for the application of private sector techniques in the public sector stems in part from historical examples, such as the politics–administration dichotomy posited by Wilson (2003, p. 20), which was rooted in the belief that "the field of administration is a field of business. It is removed from the hurry and strife of politics." Here, Wilson (2003) introduced the possibility that administrative actions should be conducted in a manner that would be less susceptible to political influences, which, when left unfettered, had the capacity to negatively affect bureaucratic competence and to diminish trust in government. The politics–administration dichotomy was a pioneering conceptualization guiding bureaucratic actions at the time, but is argued to be insufficient as a stand-alone principle in contemporary politics, as there are real-world considerations associated with bureaucratic implementation of policy, including the fact that bureaucratic actions are completed by human beings who are themselves imperfect and subject to personal bias. In addition, Lipsky (2003) noted that "street level bureaucrats" may exercise a certain degree of power when choosing to implement public policy. Although government goes to great lengths to ensure that public services are delivered in an equitable fashion and without any bias in the performance of duties, the human element inherent within the bureaucracy requires minimization to diffuse personal influences during the fulfilment of obligations. There have also been modern efforts to apply private sector techniques and principles, such as those associated with performance-measurement endeavors, designed to further entrench accountability while promoting effectiveness, efficiency and equity in government programming (Holzer & Halachmi, 1996; de Lancer Julnes & Holzer, 2001; Hatry, 2006; Holzer & Halachmi, 2010). This movement resulted in a slew of corresponding government actions designed to enhance government performance, including the 1993 Government Performance Results Act (GPRA), which sought to ensure that federal agencies develop, publish and enforce performance plans to guide the bureaucracy in achieving greater levels of transparency and accountability. The privatization movement in the United States that rose to prominence in the 1990s also sought to incorporate private sector methods to improve the effectiveness and efficiency in the performance of governmental duties. In this respect, Savas (2002, p. 82) observed that "privatization is intended to improve public services by introducing competition and choice." Here, it was believed that encouraging better governance can be facilitated in part by introducing private sector ideals associated with competition. This includes the focus on introducing concepts such as competition into the bidding process to offer services to citizens and in completion of governmental duties (Savas, 2000). Privatization can be used to address perceived weaknesses associated with specific tasks within a public sector entity, like payroll services, or can be utilized in an attempt to improve all mandated responsibilities assigned to said entity (Savas, 2000). Privatization advocates believe that overall government performance can be improved by allowing private sector and public sector entities to compete for the opportunity to provide any number of services, from prison privatization to private sector provision of K–12 education though charter school competition. Competition is believed to drive entities to take necessary measures to significantly improve performance and to provide a higher quality of service for the fear of losing the opportunity to provide service delivery. Privatization opponents believe that competition does not necessarily equal success given that private sector entities fail frequently and that some public services, like national defense, are appropriate only for government to fulfill. As indicated in this brief historical recap, government commonly applies private sector techniques to complete public sector tasks within the context of democratic expectations. The precedent for the complementary application of private sector techniques in the public sector has a rich tradition in the U.S. democratic system, setting the groundwork for further efforts to consider conceptual intersections between private and public sector ideals applicable in the E-Governance Era.

The historical precedent for the application of traditionally private sector techniques and ideals in the public sector exists in part due to the evolutionary nature of democracy in which government continuously seeks to adapt to shifting demands for change. In relation, the possibility of utilizing applicable combinations of private and public sector techniques can still be an important consideration associated with enhancing governmental capacity to fulfill duties. Therefore, those that are responsible for developing governmental actions in the modern era should not automatically exclude a potentially useful technique or ideal based solely on the point of origin. With this in mind, it is helpful to further explore elements of a private sector–oriented ideal termed *open innovation* that are applicable in E-Governance. The following introduction to open innovation's applicability in public sector deliberative endeavors is not intended to be exhaustive, but is designed to highlight several components that may contribute to the effective promotion of technological innovation in governance. Many ideals and techniques that have a private sector point of origin may find relevancy in impacting public sector activities associated with E-Governance. Private sector–oriented initiatives such as open innovation maintain a certain level of practical malleability lending applicability to public sector goal achievement, and play an important role in fostering a clearer understanding of the situational dynamics behind the relevant technological innovations. The conceptual elasticity inherent within private sector initiatives such as open innovation provide the opportunity for a plausible extension of such theory toward public sector goal achievement. Consideration of the nature of elasticity and malleability of private sector conceptualizations is of great assistance toward the achievement of important public sector goals. In relation, open innovation is sufficiently elastic and malleable proving capable in assisting with E-Governance related goal achievement within the context of deliberative democracy.

The applicability of private sector ideals in the E-Governance Era focuses in part on Open Innovation theory (Chesbrough, 2011; Mergel, 2011; Mergel & Desouza, 2013), which serves as a construct allowing for the integration of technologically innovative means designed to sustain activities such as those related to citizen participation. The first step is to explicate the key foundational elements that constitute Open Innovation theory and to highlight how Open Innovation theory is capable of serving as a guide for the construction of technologically innovative means. Then, it is imperative to further expand on the benefits of the continued application of these ideals in specific areas as it relates to E-Governance. In contemporary governance, many components of open innovation have become increasingly relevant in the fulfillment of public sector duties. Here, open innovation partly serves as a conceptual foundation used to explain the development of electronic means geared toward accessing pertinent knowledge from a wide array of societal sources, which get synthesized into actions for the purpose of better performing public sector tasks. Chesbrough (2011) identified four service-oriented principles associated with open innovation that facilitate innovation and growth within an organization. These are summarized as followed in Table 5.1.

Chesbrough (2011, p. 4) explained that these principles contribute to a "framework for innovation." This framework provides insight relatable to both E-Government and E-Governance. For example, basic E-Government duties can be improved through open innovation components focused on improving service delivery and enhancing available choices through the development of sustainable digital means based on determining preferences of citizens. Similarly, E-Governance calls for development of digital means in which to facilitate richer, more complex citizen–government interactions intended to affect changes to the political system. Here, internal and external perspectives help guide the public sector's development of innovative means capable of supporting cooperative governance. There are a number of additional open innovation parallels that contribute to establishing an overarching framework applicable in the promotion of citizen participation. Mergel and Desouza (2013, p. 882) contributed to the applicability of this idea by noting, "Open innovation

Table 5.1 Four Service Oriented Principles of Open Innovation

Focus on the service aspect of business to achieve sustainable growth and profits.
Develop a cooperative approach with customers to effectively determine wants.
Promote innovation and growth through advancements of specialization of multiple actors involved in the production of goods toward the purpose of enhancing choices for consumers.
Facilitate internal and external sources of innovation.

Source: Chesbrough, 2011.

encourages organizations to search for solutions outside their organizational boundaries to address core management problems." In this sense, E-Governance participatory means can be developed to obtain external input from the citizen-consumer who will ultimately interact with government to impact the political system. Alford (2002, p. 337) discussed that an underlying factor associated with private sector markets is "the notion of exchange." Public sector exchanges with citizen-consumers attributed to E-Government can be based on monetary transactions, such as those supporting localized online permit purchases, but interactions can also include a wider array of participatory components focused on "information, cooperation, compliance and co-production, which are crucial for effective organizational performance" (Alford, 2002, p. 338). As such, public sector exchanges involving engagement with an "active citizenship" are based on a multidimensional focus across a broader range of considerations than generally found in private sector–exchange relationships, which are largely focused on satisfying expectations with monetary transactions for goods/services (Alford, 2002). In this sense, it is important to recognize the pivotal role of addressing diverse expectations from a wider scope of considerations in determining successful exchanges between citizen-consumers and government. It is also necessary to reiterate the importance of acknowledging the dynamic, continuous nature of shifting expectations that are capable of affecting relationships between the citizen-consumer and government. Here, understanding that citizen-consumers become actively engaged in various types of exchanges within a political marketplace helps to further cement the applicability of the cross-pollination of private sector conceptualizations into the public domain in some instances. Open innovation elements applicable toward E-Governance focuses on the consideration that citizens can be viewed as consumers actively operating in a constantly changing political market in which activities, such as electronic participation, are facilitated to determine wants and provide guidance for actions to affect changes.

In sum, a number of aforementioned open innovation elements can help in understanding how this private sector conceptualization can be useful in affecting participation dynamics. This includes that E-Governance promotes the usage of modern digital designs that encourage cooperative participation in an effort to continuously identify citizen preferences. There is also applicability for open innovation with E-Governance in providing abundant choices to citizen-consumers regarding the types of innovative means available and by remembering that exchanges can stem from multiple focal points within the political environment. It is also important to note that open innovation can be utilized by government to access external ideas from citizen-consumers, and the process may include suggestions for implementation of solutions derived from open innovation participation. These ideals associated with open innovation can be used in many E-Governance initiatives, including those focused on facilitating citizen participation. Before discussing such E-Governance initiatives, it will be helpful to first illustrate the effects of technology on the communication networks in which digital participation occurs.

The application of technological innovation associated with E-Governance Era activities has the potential to affect the U.S. deliberative democratic system in a variety of ways. This is often the case with public sector efforts to incorporate means to match growing citizen demands, which can result in significant systemic changes. Once newly emerging technological advancements are expected to more frequently become part of daily government routines and the government technological capacity is able to meet these expectations, actions can be facilitated to accommodate the emerging demand. Government efforts to apply modern-era technological advancements can affect how network participants complete daily routines and activities. This includes that applying technological innovation can affect democratic network interactions by influencing how government delivers services, disseminates information and facilitates dialogue with the public. For example, the application of technological innovation could alter the available interactive means in which participation occurs and can affect who participates though such means within a network. There are a number of specific circumstances in which technological innovation can directly affect network participation, but it is first important to briefly explain what constitutes a network. A network could be viewed on the broadest macro level taking an international perspective that considers each possible individual seeking to participate through an endless web of interactive means from countless smaller social, business and political networks. Here, the term *network* refers to an amalgamation of available domestic social, business and government networks available to eligible participants within the U.S. deliberative democracy. In relation, E-Governance network participants will generally be considered on the basis of a specific subset of individuals active only within the system. As such, the main considerations associated with the application of E-Governance technology means focus mainly on citizens and the federal government as the key network participants. This is not to indicate that various other network participants are somehow nonessential or, even less accurate, nonexistent. In reality, network participation can accommodate a seemingly endless array of input from political actors representing interests from the private sector (i.e., corporate interests, interest groups, media, etc.), non-governmental organizations (NGOs) and representatives from various levels of the public sector employed in all branches of government. However, considering plausible implications associated with the application of electronic-based innovation on network participation will largely be focused on those affecting citizen–government interactions which can contribute to developing a better understanding of U.S. E-Governance Era deliberative democracy.

How technology can affect democratically oriented network interactions between citizens and the public sector is an important consideration associated with E-Governance. It is beneficial to first define what constitutes a network in the modern political environment, to note the influence of context on networks and to consider how technological advancements may alter structural means associated with how interested parties communicate. At the heart of this network discussion is the acknowledgement that people interact with one another through available communication constructs. In turn, innovation-based structural changes to communication means may affect who participates in citizen–government interactions. The application of modern innovations is added to the already existing traditional means facilitating citizen–government interactions present within the deliberative democracy framework. The sum total of network communication means available in this respect can affect who participates, when participation occurs and how participation is facilitated. The resulting union of traditional and digital communication means serves to create the structural overlay in which network relationships are cultivated in modern governance. Here, the availability of communication means that fosters relationships plays a critical role in developing an understanding of network participation. This is especially important as it relates to understanding the interactive capacity of modern networks, which are a combination of both traditional and digital means available to participants within a deliberative democracy framework.

There are a number of significant considerations associated with the study of network theory including the recognition of the importance of understanding the nature of relationships between actors participating in a given network and the role that context may have on impacting structural elements of networks. Granovetter (1973, p. 1361) explained that "the strength of a tie is a (probably linear) combination of the amount of time, the emotional intensity, the intimacy (mutual confiding), and the reciprocal services which characterize the tie." Granovetter (1983, p. 225) added that network relationships can reflect weak ties that are "loosely knit," representing low-density interactions and strong ties that constitute communication between actors within a "dense network." The relationship dynamics between participants within networks can also be affected by the "contexts and structures" in which communication is facilitated (Granovetter, 1999, p. 162). Communication "bridges" within a network can be conducted through individually oriented channels and organizationally oriented channels (Granovetter, 1973). Huckfeldt (2014, p. 44) commented on communication dynamics in which the "network models of socially interdependent actors are directed at bridging the divide between the macro and the micro." Lee (2013, p. 90) explained that "knowledge networks refer to the web of direct and indirect ties through which key e-government actors mutually exchange knowledge for organizational activities." Many of these important components associated with understanding networks on a broad conceptual scale correspond with the dynamics guiding E-Governance participation. E-Governance can facilitate the use of technological means to create digital bridges promoting various types of exchanges between participants within a given network. Technologically innovative means can be utilized by mutually dependent actors within a network to support various types of participation. In relation, technology can be utilized to create digital bridges designed to connect network participants, diffusing impediments to interaction based on limits to access that are geographically or temporally oriented. It is also important to consider the influence of contextual factors in providing impetus for changing the structure of communications means capable of affecting relationships between participants.

There are considerations with how the application of technology may alter traditional relationship interactions associated with network participation. Generally, the advancements in technology have affected communications dynamics by altering the scope of eligible participants within networks in a number of ways, on both a national and global scale. However, this discussion focuses on citizen–government network participation within the U.S. political system in relation to E-Governance interactions associated with deliberative democracy. Relatedly, examples of how technologically engaging political networks serve to facilitate citizen–government participation in activities such as dialogue events is expanded on in further detail in later sections. As such, it will be helpful to offer some descriptive information associated with the potential pool of eligible participants in the U.S. political system that may be directly affected by technical augmentations to existing political networks. According to the U.S. Census Bureau's Population Clock (2016), the nation's population is estimated to be 325 million people. Beato (2015, para. 2) observed that the approximately 325 million people in the United States serve as a vast network of individuals, "all with different interests, aptitudes, skills, and experience." In the broadest sense, this pool of potential network participants in the U.S. is clearly on the rise each year. However, the discussion will be limited to considerations associated with eligible participants in existing networks. A total citizen base that consists of about 325 million people is not to imply that each person would be eligible or willing to participate with the intentions of affecting meaningful changes to the political system. For example, persons in the United States may be excluded from activities such as voting based on their status as being non-voting-age individuals, nonregistered voters or convicted felons. This general understanding of the status of willing and eligible participants in society is applicable to various forms of political participation via modern networks focused on facilitating citizen–government interactions. Interactions through specific digital designs that augment communications means for modern networks are further expanded on in later sections dedicated to discussing what constitutes E-Governance Era citizen participation in the deliberative democracy framework.

The recognition of the role that technological innovation may play in affecting how government actions are carried out and in its ability to expand the scope of eligible participants communicating within political networks is a relatively unique dynamic associated with modern democracy. Understanding the role of technology in affecting how and when participation occurs in political networks in a modern deliberative democracy can be of great importance in the E-Governance Era. The evolution of modern digital designs reflects structural alterations to the traditional deliberative framework shaping communication expectations associated with E-Governance network participation. Huckfeldt (2014, p. 43) explained that "democratic politics inevitably stimulates a socially imbedded process of communication among citizens, and thus individuals experience politics by way of ongoing forms of social interaction and communication with others." De Cindio (2000, p. 222) noted that "forms of democracy have been evolving, through the centuries, in close connection to the forms of communication available at each historical turn." Nabatchi (2010, p. 377) added to this by noting, "relatively recent shifts to network and collaborative government structures require new processes that better engage citizens in the work of government." In relation, Beato (2015) recognized the potential associated with applying innovation in "using technology to help people become more engaged and productive citizens, in ways that truly harness the full range of their skills and expertise." The evolution of modern networks to include digital means for citizen–government interaction did not occur within a political vacuum, but instead is reflective to some degree of government's dynamic response to the natural progression of technological advancements.

The evolutionary nature of the U.S. democratic government has deep historical precedent focused on ensuring flexible and dynamic action to address political-environment demands stemming from the political environment. However, the evolution of U.S. democracy is presently faced with applying technological innovation consistent with E-Governance that is unique in comparison to other points in time. In this sense, citizen participation in modern collaborative governance endeavors is subject to a combination of contemporary and classical network considerations. Modern collaborative government requires evolutionary considerations that accommodate the construction of technologically advanced means being added to existing traditional means, yielding a communication network that sustains citizen participation in a diverse deliberative democracy framework. Relatedly, continued advancements in communication technologies have a direct impact on the structural means in which citizen participation is facilitated through networks. The shifts in expectations regarding the development of means to facilitate modern collaborative government are related to the continued advancements in technological capacity, which affects network participation. There are a number of modern efforts in the E-Governance Era that seek to utilize technological innovation to create a more inclusive democratic environment promoting digital civic engagement. This includes digital civic-engagement efforts designed to develop an understanding of citizen insight regarding the identification of problems (i.e., virtual town hall meeting) and to provide voice toward policy development that addresses those problems (i.e., crowdsourcing). Technological advancements being applied in the E-Governance Era are capable of altering relationship dynamics between network contributors in part by increasing the number of access points to communication means. The modern political network structure has evolved to support traditional means and digital means reflective of a more complex and diverse democratic construct capable of facilitating a wider range of citizen–government interaction. This is an essential component associated with E-Governance network considerations.

Putnam (2000, p. 171) noted, "telecommunication in general and the Internet in particular substantially enhance our ability to communicate; thus it seems reasonable to assume that their net effect will be to enhance community, perhaps even dramatically. Social capital is about networks, and the Net is the network to end all networks." There are a number of potential benefits that may be derived from network participation occurring through the Internet, including the ability of digital means to "remove barriers of time and distance" (Putnam, 2000, p. 171). Putnam (2000, p. 174) stated, "the Internet offers a low-cost and in many respects egalitarian way of connecting with millions of one's fellow citizens, particularly those with whom one shares interests, but not space and time." Putnam (2000, p. 173) expanded on possible benefits derived from Internet-participation dynamics by noting, "in workplace networks, experiments have shown, computer-mediated communication is less hierarchical, more participatory, more candid, and less biased by status differences." Putnam further explained that "the high speed, low cost, and broad scope of mobilization that is possible on the Internet can be an advantage for political organizers, by reducing transaction costs, particularly for widely scattered groups of like-minded citizens" (p. 173). Internet-based interactions may be able to provide more cost-effective, convenient and equitable means of connecting network participants when compared to the limits posed by traditional in-person communication dynamics. Putnam (2000) also recognized that there are a number of potential difficulties associated with "computer-mediated communication" that may have an effect on the interactive dynamics between participants within a given network. There are concerns associated with the negative impact of Internet communication that may diminish levels of representativeness among network participants rooted in digital divide inequities, that reflects a lack, or in some cases absence, of nonverbal cues that plays a large part in traditional in-person communication dynamics and that limits the focus of participation by facilitating interactions between individuals reflecting homogenous interests, which runs counter to the important role that diversity plays in deliberative democracy (Putnam, 2000). Putnam (2000) also raised the possibility that computer-mediated communications through the Internet may potentially "become predominantly a means of active, social communication or a means of passive, private entertainment." Here, the deliberative power of communication between network participants is weakened by limiting its functionality for personal and entertainment purposes. The allure of benefits and the propensity for challenges are not uncommon in any form of communication means, digital or traditional. This rings true when considering the role of the Internet to facilitate interaction between network participants within the context of modern deliberative democracy.

Exposure to the influence that structural boundaries play in shaping network participation contributes to a better understanding of how digital interactions have altered deliberative expectations for communication. It is also important to recognize the role that technology plays in affecting the methodology and composition of participant communities interacting via E-Governance-oriented virtual venues. Hopkins et al. (2004, p. 374) remarked that "cyberspace does allow users to overcome place-based limitations to communication." Hopkins et al. (2004, p. 370) also recognized difficulties associated with achieving consensus on what constitutes a community are further compounded in that "talking about electronic communities or online communities merely adds another layer of complexity to the issue." Zuppo (2012, p. 17) observed, "from the organizational perspective, the workplace has evolved from a discrete time-bound and defined place to a limitless, wall-less and sometimes virtual existence." Frederickson (1999, p. 702) explained, "the revolution in telecommunications has forever altered the meaning of physical space and thereby forever altered the importance of borders and boundaries, a primary element of the idea of jurisdiction." Agranoff and McGuire (2004, p. 498) noted that in the modern era of governance, "the borders of jurisdictions increasingly are porous, so the problems that citizens want addressed are seldom contained in a single municipality." Agranoff and McGuire (2004, p. 498) added that "jurisdictional borders and influences are certainly intergovernmentally permeated, but they remain real." Agranoff and McGuire (2004) discussed the importance of recognizing how continued shifts in jurisdictional boundaries affect public sector actions, such as bargaining over which policy to implement, funding levels allocated for implemented policy and the administration of policy. If modern-era governmental jurisdictions are less restricted due to increased levels of general permeability, then the usage of innovation can further contribute to this dynamic as it relates to E-Governance. This speaks to the fact that political networks are in a constant state of flux and the scope of actors participating within a network is not static in the U.S. democratic system. Changes within the political system may affect the expectations of government responsibilities, which, in turn, may call into question the usefulness of sole reliance on what now may be means to accommodate limited network relationships. As such, the scope of E-Governance is expanded to include a wider array of participants that are actively seeking to affect change within the broader political network. Adaption, either expansive or reductive in nature, is a required element associated with maintaining networks that serve to guide relationships between deliberating parties. Stagnation can be the enemy in this regard, as this may contribute to a failure to recognize the need to change and to identify a slew of available digital change possibilities, the application of which would better support a network more representative of the constantly changing array of participants seeking to interact with government electronically. The electronic means expands the conceptualizations of modern communities to include digital participation through expanded network structures. In relation, the usage of digital communication means alters the structure in which network participation occurs, while diffusing geographical and timeframe limitations associated with more traditional citizen–government interactions.

A network allows for communication between interested parties, and this participatory structure can be impacted through the application of technology. This includes the ability of technological innovation to affect modern network participation by expanding venue considerations for interactions that have now become supportive of digital means. Technological advancements have contributed considerably to the maturation of networks in modern governance and have yielded considerations that traditional participatory boundaries are diminished somewhat by the existence of virtual venues created through innovation. The impact of technology on network participation is of great importance and relates to the traditional considerations attributed with the thoughts of Habermas (1962) regarding citizen–government interactions occurring through the "public sphere." Habermas (1962, p. 141) observed that wide-scale societal changes caused corresponding modifications to the structural means supporting communication so that the "public sphere evolved in the tension-charged field between state and society." As society progressed, barriers to participation were reduced, or removed completely in some cases. The subsequent structural changes to the means facilitating private–public interactions allowed for the "public sphere" to become a more viable venue supporting interactions focused on affecting political change (Habermas, 1962). This ideal is applicable to modern-era E-Governance efforts that employ technology to facilitate citizen–government interactions capable of producing modifications to the political system. The modern designs associated with E-Governance are capable of altering network structures allowing for the "public sphere" to be expanded by applying technology capable of facilitating citizen-government interactions through virtual venues. Hauser and Benoit-Barne (2002, p. 267) noted that, functionally, "civil society highlights the public sphere's ability to authorize action through public opinion." Hauser and Benoit-Barne (2002, p. 267) added that "because civil society itself is a network of associations, each bonded internally and externally in a web of mutual dependencies, it fosters conceptualizing the public sphere as also marked by a plurality of publics and discursive arenas." Jin-Wook (2006) linked the concept of the public sphere posited by Habermas with elements associated with contemporary digital deliberative democracy by which the "E-Sphere" is created through the application of modern technology altering the venue in which discursive events occur. Jin-Wook (2006, p. 70) highlighted the possibility that "the Internet and other ICTs enhance the deliberative space for citizens to engage in a high level of exchange of ideas and opinions." The interactive nature of the modern public sphere encourages and supports the development of a multitude of electronic deliberative means in which interested parties participate to accomplish societal transformation. This understanding lends further credence to the role E-Governance Era citizen–government interactions play when deliberative outcomes are used for the purposes of guiding systemic alterations.

The understanding that ICTs can affect participation in modern networks by including digital applications will be of great significance as it relates to understanding collaborative expectations associated with E-Governance.

These conceptualizations highlight the role that the application of innovation plays in altering the structure of E-Governance networks by expanding the means of participation to include considerations of modern-technology virtual venues. Given that electronic components of modern society are relatively new when analyzed from a historical perspective, there may be proverbial growing pains associated with applications of E-Governance for both the public sector and the citizenry. Going forward, it is important that technological innovation can affect traditional considerations associated with network participation previously based on the use of physical space. The reality is that network participation that once occurred largely, if not completely, through traditional on-site physical space now also may occur via virtual space. For example, a traditional town hall meeting requires citizens to attend in-person to participate in dialogue events with government. The traditional network communication between citizens and government in this case was limited to those in attendance at designated physical locations at a specified time. The modern network structure is reflective of participatory means capable of holding town hall meetings at physical on-site locations *and* through technologically created virtual space. This affects community-based realities in that interested parties may be able to impact the political system by participating in a modern network that supports both traditional and digital means. A network in the E-Governance Era may be reflective of a wider range of potential contributors in which the concept of community is expanded to some degree to include virtual and traditional participants. Modern network structures that simultaneously support interactions through digital means and traditional means can potentially attract a more diverse set of citizens seeking to participate. Doing so can further institutionalize the deliberative goal of representativeness in that citizen–government interactions facilitated through increased access points within the network potentially allow for escalated levels of participation by creating greater choices of available means. In addition, technology may affect how jurisdictional boundaries associated with network participation are perceived. This is evidenced by the ability of government to readily expand what would otherwise be a localized, contained network to include insight from participants virtually anywhere in a state, nation or even the world. E-Governance expands traditional jurisdictional limitations for generating solutions to problems by using technology to expand the range of participatory activities to include digital citizen–government interactions focused on resolving societal concerns. For example, a small technologically savvy local government municipality may utilize virtual space to add an extra layer of insight to the existing indigenous network by supporting activities such as crowdsourcing, which can welcome participation from anyone with an Internet connection. E-Governance may better facilitate cooperative efforts between local government entities while potentially utilizing technology to reduce costs associated task performance. This is similar to when a number of small municipal government entities cooperate to share physical resources, such as fire trucks or snow removal vehicles, to reduce overall budget expenditures for each locality. E-Governance in this sense could include providing technologically innovative means to promote networking among cooperating local government entities that would be capable of enhancing the communication of ideas, facilitating information gathering processes and data sharing. The influence of the virtual venue of E-Governance deliberative democracy framework, which allows for citizen–government network participation, will be discussed at greater length with illustrative examples in the following sections. However, further discussion of the impact of technology on altering participation through modern network structures and in contributing to affecting the course of interactions is required.

There are also important considerations associated with how modern networks applying technology can impact traditional power dynamics associated with citizen–government relationships. In this sense, advancements in communication technology have the potential to alter traditional power dynamics between participants in networks in a number of ways, including those related to information acquisition and sharing. Seo and Thorson (2012, p. 345) noted that "information communication technologies (ICTs) such as the internet have enabled citizens to create and share information and content without having to rely on traditional intermediaries such as government and the press." In relation, De Cindio (2000, p. 224) discussed a multitude of benefits associated with ICT as it relates to promoting citizen participation, including that "in a society broadly dominated by mass media that simply broadcast to a passive audience (particularly, television networks), network communication, as an intrinsically interactive medium, pushes for *active involvement*." The virtual component resulting from the application of modern technologies can broaden the network structure supporting an actively involved citizenry seeking increased access to online information and can enhance the communication means in which information is shared among network participants. Benkler (2011, p. 723) explained that the increased application of technological innovation in modern-era governance has created an environment in which "computer-mediated networks of information and communications" allowed for the structure of networks "to realign in fairly substantial ways the organization of production, power and meaning making in contemporary society." Benkler (2011, p. 722) highlighted an example of the newly emerging Internet power dynamic related to actions such as the recent U.S. military leaks in 2010 published via WikiLeaks, which was made possible partly through newly emerging modern technology creating a "new context" in which participation within networks is altered and through which "new forms and pathways for discovering and disseminating information" get created. The variable influence of shifting context resulting from technological innovation can serve to expand the scope of participants contributing to democratic functions within existing networks and also allows for participants to "construct their own systems" (Benkler, 2011). Benkler (2011, p. 722) added that "the Internet has created new kinds of freedom and power," which can be an influential component when considering digital effects on modern networks. The ability of ICTs to create increased levels of access to information and to expand the role of citizens in information dissemination is something of importance; it can affect power dynamics within modern networks. If information is a tenet of power, then ICTs may contribute to creating a less inequitable playing field between government, media and citizens in this arena. Similarly, the capacity of modern technology to impact power dynamics associated with information sharing between network participants is quite unprecedented. The proliferation of ICTs utilized throughout modern networks provides new structural means capable of empowering individuals by increasing the avenues in which information is accessed and shared. It may even allow for citizens to compete with, or even circumvent in some cases, traditional power sources, such as the government and media, when it comes to the role that information plays in network participation. In turn, this may empower nontraditional actors to become more influential in the acquisition and dissemination of information that may be capable of eventually stimulating changes to the political system. At present, a lack of consensus remains regarding what constitutes "responsible" behavior regarding when, or if, the dissemination of information online should be considered. This consideration is a time-honored one as it relates to the accumulation of information that may be deemed classified for national security reasons, but the digital component adds an unprecedented dimension to the dilemma of releasing sensitive data to the public online. In relation, a key difference is that the digital age allows for anyone that obtains information, classified or otherwise, to immediately publish their findings online to share with the world. No longer does an individual need to own a major newspaper or convince someone from the media to publish information. ICTs empower individuals by providing a readily available, relatively low-cost means by which to share virtually anything that can be digitized on a global level. This is evidenced in a number of recent examples with the modern political system, such as those associated with leaked national military-oriented security information that was released via WikiLeaks in 2010. It also relates to the release of other types of sensitive data, such as those derived from the hacking of the Democratic National Committee and the Democratic Congressional Campaign Committee released by WikiLeaks during the summer of 2016 in which information disseminated through the Internet had the potential to shift public opinion enough to affect the presidential election later that year. The determination of the source of the hack as a state actor, specifically the government of Russia, or an individual acting of their own accord, was a key focal point of debate among those within the intelligence community charged with the responsibility of investigating the breach.

Technological innovation applied for E-Governance can affect power dynamics to some degree, and can impact the environmental context shaping the development of means used for network participation. As noted, the advancements in information and communication technology (ICT) have expanded the available means within a given network in which citizens may actively participate. This potentially affects power dynamics by broadening the network layers in which individuals can actively participate via information acquisition and sharing. It also includes the possible effects that utilizing new technological advancements may have on expectations regarding the immediacy of access. The dynamics regarding active network participation are somewhat altered in this sense as citizens have grown to expect greater levels of immediate interactions with government through advanced technological means. This generally seems to be a rapidly growing expectation in modern society—the expectation of instant gratification through technology-based activities. This expectation has begun to extend to citizen–government network participation in many respects, and is evidenced in countless modern governance examples that apply technology to facilitate immediate interaction, such as means supporting citizens sending an e-mail directly to elected representatives. It also includes the efforts by the public sector to fulfill the expectation for immediate interactions by creating social network means allowing participants to follow a government agency on Facebook and to interact directly with government through Twitter. Here, technology can facilitate quicker information sharing between network participants. As a note, it is helpful to observe that quicker information sharing within a network is not always better. Consider the perils and pitfalls with various forms of social networking as it relates to failing to consider the content of information before hitting the "send" or "post" button in this regard. There is a growing societal expectation for active and immediate participation associated with advanced technological means that affects citizen–government relationships that deserves continued recognition during the E-Governance Era.

There are many contextual factors that are present in a democratic system that may affect the nature of political relationships inherent within networks. Before continuing, it is helpful to briefly expand on what is meant by *context* for the purposes of the discussion associated with network participation through E-Governance means in a deliberative democracy. Here, *context* refers to the environmental circumstances that are generated from within the deliberative system that dictates actions affecting network participation. In turn, context shapes the environment in which government decision-making is completed, and can affect subsequent action in many ways. Contextual cues are derived from various private and public sector sources within the political environment, and are related to a wide array of democratic concerns. In relation, network relationships in a democracy are dependent to a certain degree on the contexts guiding how interaction occurs. Understanding the role of contextual issues in affecting communication means and relationship dynamics between participants can contribute to network analysis associated with E-Governance. Johnson (2014, p. 502) explained, "institutional context must provide as few barriers as possible to citizen involvement and citizens themselves must strive to make their voices heard in government." For example, there may be contextual cues from the political environment guiding government to take actions capable of better facilitating more open communication between participants. Here, context relates to the expectations for government to construct means to better facilitate open dialogue and for citizens to utilize those means designed to reduce communication barriers. The contextual interpretations of values in a given political system contribute to shaping the framework within which deliberation occurs and affect outcomes regarding the application of technology designed to better facilitate dialogue between network participants. Kim (2014, pp. 661, 683) noted that "political contexts influence the way in which individuals form their opinion" and "individuals' political predispositions condition the way that external events are interpreted in making judgements on values." Kim (2014) added that there are considerations associated with the communication means within a democracy that may affect understanding of events. Contextual cues are subject to value interpretation from network actors, and may affect the expectations for government actions in a given field, such as E-Governance. Noordhoff et al. (2011, p. 45) explored the potential positive and negative impacts on innovation derived from studying the embedded relationship associated with supplier–customer dynamics. Innovation within an organization could be affected by "certain relational and governance conditions" that consider formal interactions and situational components in which decisions occur (Noordhoff et al. 2011). They also noted that "an embedded relationship with the customer also gives the supplier an opportunity to test its ideas early in the innovation process" (p. 37). The consideration of the role of context in which government technology decisions are conducted, the existence of formal/informal relationships and the impact of citizen-consumer knowledge on technology preferences can play a role in decision-making associated with E-Governance innovation used to facilitate interactions within networks. The rapid advancements in technology applicable to E-Governance can directly affect a number of expectations associated with network participation in a deliberative democracy. Marland, Giasson, and Lees-Marshment (2012, p. 3) explained that "worldwide and over time, technological advancements change the practice of politics, governance and electioneering." Seo and Thorson (2012) posited that "communication infrastructure and political processes evolve together." In relation, there are temporal implications associated with advancements in technology that can influence the participatory means utilized within political networks on a broad scale.

There are contextual components in a deliberative democracy that are capable of affecting the structure of networks in the E-Governance Era. A network structure in a democracy can support discourse between political participants and contextual dynamics can guide interaction based on expectations for communication associated with the nature of deliberative democracy. Here, contextual power is associated in part when actions are guided by the expectations of the public for government to incorporate technologically advanced means capable of affecting citizen–government relationships. Expectations from actors within the political environment can guide decisions to apply technological means that can ultimately affect who participates within a network and how that participation is facilitated. In this sense, reading contextual cues within the political environment may lead to actions that promote changes to the structural means network participation occurs through. Being flexible to newly emerging citizen expectations is a key contextual element associated with understanding the responsibility of government efforts to apply technological innovation associated with E-Governance. The contextual aspect within the U.S. political environment includes understanding when to fulfill the responsibility to respond to perceptions of citizens. The motivation to respond falls within the overall framework of democracy in which government is expected to acquiesce to expectations when consensus for change is reached. There are also contextual considerations guided by the expectations for how government should take action to apply technology while promoting principles of democracy. The value-based contextual guidelines for the U.S. deliberative system are rooted partly in the expectation that network participation reflects classic democratic principles, such as responsiveness, transparency and flexibility. These principles often serve as contextual markers associated with democracy that can influence the development of communication structures, which ultimately affect network participants within the U.S. democracy. For example, transparency and accountability may be mandated by government across a broad spectrum of categories, creating relationship expectations between participants within the network in question. This could include federal legislation that requires government to publish information associated with proposed agency rule changes and to allow for feedback from citizens prior to rules being implemented. In the E-Governance Era, the publishing of proposed agency rule changes occurs in both traditional hard copy and through digital means. Also, the means supporting citizen–government interactions to develop feedback prior to rules being implemented can also be facilitated through traditional and digital means. Individuals can review proposed agency rule changes through the Federal Register, providing information via traditional print format and digitally (www.federalregister.gov). In addition, an individual can provide comments prior to an agency rule change within the established timeframe by traditional means (e.g., fax, mail) or through digital means (e.g., e-mail). In relation, the website Regulations.gov (www. regulations.gov) also provides individuals with the opportunity to review and provide feedback on proposed agency rules through traditional and digital means. In this sense, contextual markers affect the structural components that coexist, reinforcing each other through efforts deemed appropriate for government actions. The contextual and structural dynamics work in concert to affect how participants are empowered to act within the network while supporting principles of democracy expected within E-Governance.

Context in the E-Governance Era is formed in part by the expectations for government to make efforts to develop digital institutional means that reduce barriers to participation, further promoting accountability and transparency within a more open network. Contextual cues from the political environment may guide institutional efforts to ensure a more open, transparent and accountable system in which government becomes less insulated from citizen influence. Actions designed to facilitate greater levels of access are conceivably better able to hold government accountable only to the extent in which citizens make the efforts to do so by becoming actively involved. This includes efforts in modern government that applies technological innovation to develop means capable of further facilitating meaningful citizen–government interactions. Again, it is vital to highlight the importance of dual citizen–government responsibility as it relates to network participation in a deliberative democracy. Once network access is expanded and barriers to communication are reduced by the public sector, the expectations shift to citizens to make efforts to participate with government through the new means created. This is part of the participatory equation in which institutional designs to ensure openness within a network are largely ineffective without the required efforts by citizens to take full advantage of these available interactive means to impact the democratic system. The assessment of context can guide institutional responses that promote values of importance within a modern network; participants have the responsibility to make efforts to use subsequent means to ensure those identified principles manifest. Contextual cues may vary dependent on values inherent within the political environment at a given time, and institutional responses may benefit from being tailored to address shifting expectations within the network. Institutional efforts to apply technological innovation affecting network relationships between participants should be done so based partly on the results of actively assessing contextually oriented, value-based expectations for citizen–government interactions within the U.S. democratic system. Here, institutional change associated with E-Governance is based on an assessment of contextual cues, which highlight value expectancies as to how interactions between network participants should occur. In turn, citizens must maintain some degree of responsibility by making efforts to interact with government through innovation designs supporting modern network participation.

The contextual components present within a political system provide conceptual guidelines for the development of action affecting the framework of a network in which interested parties participate and may naturally limit participatory choices based on assessments of what may be societally preferable. In this sense, E-Governance context helps to frame decisions on government innovation depending upon interpretation of values. E-Governance-related expectations may play an influential role in contributing to the construction of means available for participants to disseminate information and in which to construct persuasive arguments. The development of E-Governance means are subject to contextual system expectations regarding subjects such as available technologies, technologies perceived to be effective and technologies that are in high demand. For U.S. deliberative democracy, the interpretation of contextual, value-based cues in the U.S. political system can guide the creation of technological means intended to provide the opportunity to better facilitate network participation among all interested parties. This includes the contextual values guiding participation in the U.S. deliberative democracy, which is expected to promote a network with frequent opportunities for interested parties seeking to affect change. In relation, contextual guidelines associated with deliberative democracy also calls for consistent availability of cyclical opportunities to participate within a network over time. The success of network participants operating through E-Governance means may provide the opportunity to affect outcomes associated with crafting legislation, government budget allocations and bureaucratic standard operating procedures.

There may be any number of sources of ancillary contextual cues originating from the political environment that could affect decisions associated with the development of innovation by government. These considerations extend to contextual factors created by fiscal limitations that may affect spending decisions regarding innovation, potential perceived political fallout associated with success/failure of innovation efforts capable of affecting re-election campaigns and concerns associated with bureaucratic technical capacity to implement innovations as intended. Cultivating embedded relationships between government entities and the citizen consumer may contribute to a better understanding of dynamics determining innovation decisions. Proactive communication efforts between government—that ultimately chooses the innovative means to facilitate democratic interactions—and citizens—who are the consumers within this dynamic that participate through available technologically innovative means—may play an important role in this process. Well-informed E-Governance decisions on the application of innovation are based partly on the recognition of the influence of the informal and formal embedded relationships. These relationships play a role in determining stakeholder preferences regarding a number of technological implications. E-Governance innovation decisions will benefit from efforts to develop an understanding of contextual limitations of situations stemming from within the political environment and to determine citizen-consumer preferences associated how interactions should occur through innovative means utilized during network participation.

Government's increased efforts to make digital tools available for citizens to participate in interactive opportunities are capable of yielding a unique network externality that is temporally based. This relates to the possibility that the application of technology for E-Governance purposes may create a newly emerging, and continuously expanding, tech-savvy demographic of digital participants. The overall structure of a network can be altered by applying innovative means to be utilized by the tech-savvy participants, which adds a new layer of voice to consider when facilitating citizen–government discourse. The de facto creation of the emerging tech-savvy demographic of citizens has continued to expand as the public sector has increasingly applied innovation in the E-Governance Era to keep pace with societal expectations for the use of technology. In the short term, this may exacerbate problems associated with the digital divide by drawing an even deeper wedge between traditional and digital participants. This possibility further stresses the importance of government making efforts to include traditional participants into the proverbial digital fold by developing educational efforts and creating the necessary electronic infrastructure to encourage broader use of innovation associated with E-Governance interactions. These efforts can help to mitigate some of the negative effects that are attributed to the digital divide regarding a citizen having a possible lack of technical know-how or suffering from inadequate opportunity to access technology, which may hinder participation through E-Governance means. An example in which government can play a role in closing the digital divide related to infrastructure is to create higher levels of access to citizens through venues such as public libraries or public kiosks. Public sector educational programs regarding how to use technology applicable to E-Governance may also be held at venues such as public libraries, town halls or schools. Such efforts may help to contribute to reducing digital divide inequities.

The role that diversity in means plays in affecting network participation in the E-Governance Era should not be undersold. This is reflected in efforts to incorporate technologically innovative means that allow for layers of online participants to be added to existing pools of traditional participants within the network. The number of citizens participating through technological innovation since the early 1990s has been increased through corresponding relevant means, such as publication of government information online, government e-mails and even any number of interactive platforms that facilitate citizen–government participation. In relation, citizens' usage of traditional and digital means are not necessarily mutually exclusive when it comes to E-Government and E-Governance interactions. For example, a tech-savvy citizen may complete E-Government tasks, such as renewing their car registration at the state DMV website the same week they go to the DMV in their locality to renew their driver's license in person. In this case, the citizen utilizes technologically innovation means to achieve an ends (i.e., renewal of car registration online) and traditional means (i.e., in-person renewal of driver's license with the DMV on site) within the same few days. Similarly, a citizen may interact directly with government on site by attending traditional town hall meetings and may also choose to participate in an array of E-Governance interactions including electronic town hall meetings and crowdsourcing. Technological innovation can expand the field of participants within a deliberative democracy and may ultimately alter the structure in which network participation occurs. Citizen–government transactions that are facilitated online further highlight the role that digital bridges may play in networks connecting citizens with government.

Granovetter's (1973) observation that a network may include organizational and personal communication means that serve as "bridges" between participants is applicable to E-Governance to some extent. In addition, "bridges" in communication between participants in modern networks can be facilitated through traditional means and electronic means. The construction of any such participatory means in a deliberative democracy is not enough to guarantee that communication will occur regardless of the nature of those bridges. In this sense, digital bridges are not unlike bridges built across a body of water connecting two states, such as the Outerbridge Crossing linking New York and New Jersey (www.panynj.gov/bridges-tunnels/outerbridge-crossing-history.html). Individuals have to utilize constructed bridges, digital or otherwise, in order to connect potential participants within a network. A basic visual representation of the ability of a digital bridge to allow an interested party to traverse from Point A to Point B within the context of deliberation is highlighted in Figure 5.1. Here, an interested party at Point A is unable to connect to Point B without the provision of a digital bridge that would be required to support participation.

Intent and means have a symbiotic relationship when it comes to meaningful network participation across digital bridges in the modern era. The construction of means and those network actors willing to participate through those means form a symbiotic relationship in which one cannot exist without the other if meaningful interactions are to be expected. This further reinforces the importance of recognizing that dual responsibility exists between those constructing the means and those expected to use them. It also highlights the notion that there must be some level of initiative among participants within a network to become engaged in communication through digital bridges. Conceptually, this stands in equal measure associated with digital bridges with an origin point that is constructed institutionally or individually. Essentially, the means created to serve as a citizen–public sector bridge are rendered useless if network participants don't communicate with one another. A lack of participation may simply be due to the

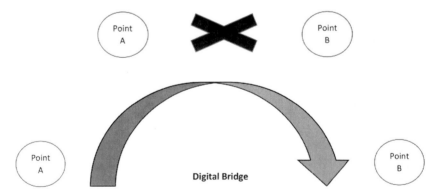

Figure 5.1 Digital Bridge Structure Allowing for Point A–to–Point B Participation

fact that these digital means are unknown to network actors. Here, the will to participate and the means to participate are available without the knowledge of where digital bridges are located. This is where initiatives associated with political marketing techniques may prove beneficial in facilitating network communication between participants. Digital bridges, with an institutional or individual origin point, may also lack the capacity to connect with all participants within the network due to limitations associated with the digital divide. Again, to account for this, modern-era governance should coordinate a diverse communication structure that is reflective of digital means and traditional means.

Electronic means of communication creates digital bridges that can facilitate network participation between interested parties. These digital bridges can accommodate multi-directional communication between network participants for any number of E-Government related activities, such as those promoting reciprocity of information and those supporting the provision of government services to the citizen base. Here, citizens contact government digitally to communicate a need and to receive a service online. Digital bridges can also be utilized as a vehicle for communication between citizens and government by providing means through which discourse can be facilitated. The origin point of digital communication bridges can be located organizationally or individually, and may ultimately sustain various types of information flows. Government organizational-based initiatives to construct digital bridges linking citizens and the public sector are seemingly endless in the modern era. For example, citizens may communicate with government representatives though electronic means such as e-mail or social networks. This also includes any number of modern-era communication bridges that are capable of facilitating one-way communication (like traditional citizen surveys) and two-way communication (like town hall meetings) between political actors within the network. In this sense, the individual may utilize digital communication means capable of bridging the gap with various public sector representatives, such as elected officials or members of the bureaucracy toward the purpose enabling meaningful citizen–government interactions. Digital bridges can allow for various types of information to be transferred electronically between E-Governance network partners including those associated with identifying citizen preferences regarding public sector actions. In relation, digital bridges may facilitate the communication of citizen opinions indicative of strong positive or negative emotions regarding the perceived performance associated with governance. If citizens can be viewed as consumers of government services within a public sector network, then the ability to determine perceptions associated with related performance can be an important component. The idea of communication means serving as a digital bridge between network participants will arguably continue to remain applicable in the E-Governance Era, as presently there seems to be no stemming the tide of the application of innovation on a broad societal level. For these digital bridges to be useful in affecting changes to the overarching political system, it is necessary that consistently significant efforts are put forth by interested parties to engage in communication with other network participants. Further evidence of the role that E-Governance digital bridges plays in facilitating participation through specific interactive events associated with deliberative democracy are discussed a greater length in later sections.

There are also grander conceptual considerations of importance regarding the potential impact of network participation through E-Governance that can affect citizens' trust in deliberative democracy and are related to broader social concerns regarding perceptions associated with responsible governance. Lawrence and Brodman (2000, p. 471) noted that "the glitter of cybertechnology tends to divert us from addressing broader problems of inequities in social and economic development, and their associated ecological consequences." The usage of advanced technology in government carries the ability to facilitate network communication capable of affecting meaningful change in democratic systems the world over, and as such there lies a certain level of responsibility with this reality. E-Governance application of technological innovation simply for superficial purposes without having the intention or capacity to promote change derived from meaningful participation should be minimized. There is a certain level of responsibility that should be considered to ensure that governmental application of technology exceeds serving merely as a promotional tool that is vacant of power. The advancement of E-Governance means within a network should not distract from, or supersede, the responsibility that the public sector carries to take actions that directly contribute to the betterment of society in other ways. The means utilized should provide an opportunity to interested parties from diverse backgrounds to truly make a meaningful contribution on issues of socio-political importance. In relation, technology can create a digital bridge between government and citizens, who previously may not have had a comparable level of access to the deliberation process. This can be helpful to engender trust that E-Governance means are intended to and are capable of providing the opportunity for network participation that has the capacity to effect real changes. Trust between citizens and government is essential if relationships in a network are expected to valued, nurtured and strengthened through use. Trust is nurtured within relationships partly "to safeguard future transactions" and because of the "expectation of good behavior that inheres in a personal relationship" (Granovetter, 1999, p. 160). In this sense, trust can be diminished, if not eliminated, without the presence of the expectation that network participation through E-Governance means are capable of resulting in real changes. A reduction in trust may negatively affect future levels of participation by citizens who have lost some degree of faith if the E-Governance means were perceived to be solely for the sake of appearance. The "glitter" of developing E-Governance means in the modern era should avoid replacing the expectations for substance associated with responsible government actions in a deliberative democracy.

References

Agranoff, R., & McGuire, M. (2004) Another look at bargaining and negotiating in intergovernmental management. *Journal of Public Administration Research and Theory*, 14(4): 495–512.

Alford, J. (2002) Defining the client in the public sector: A social-exchange perspective. *Public Administration Review*, 62(3): 337–346. Retrieved from http://search. proquest.com/docview/197171465?accountid=32521.

Beato, G. (2015) Better government through crowdsourcing. *Reason*, 47(3): 78–79.

Benkler, Y. (2011) Networks of power, degrees of freedom. *International Journal of Communication*, 5: 721–755.

Chesbrough, H. W. (2011) *Open services innovation: Rethinking your business to grow and compete in a new era.* San Francisco, CA: Jossey-Bass.

De Cindio, F. (2000) Community networks for reinventing citizenship and democracy. In M. Gurstein (ed.), *Community informatics: Enabling communities with information and communications technologies* (pp. 213–231). Hershey, PA: IGI Global.

De Lancer Julnes, P., & Holzer, M. (2001) Promoting the utilization of performance measures in public organizations: An empirical study of factors affecting adoption and implementation. *Public Administration Review*, 61(6): 693–708.

Frederickson, H. G. (1999) The repositioning of American public administration. *PS, Political Science & Politics*, 32(4): 701–711. Retrieved from http://search.proquest. com/docview/224954424?accountid=32521.

Granovetter, M. (1973) The strength of weak ties. *American Journal of Sociology*, 78(6): 1360–1380. Retrieved from www.jstor.org/stable/2776392.

Granovetter, M. (1983) The strength of weak ties: A network theory revisited. *Sociological Theory*, 1: 201–233.

Granovetter, M. (1999) Close encounters and formal models: Taking gibbons seriously. *Administrative Science Quarterly*, 44(1): 158–162.

Habermas, J. (1962) *The structural transformation of the public sphere: An inquiry into a category of bourgeois society* (T. Burger & F. Lawrence, Trans.). Cambridge, MA: The MIT Press.

Hatry, H. (2006) *Performance measurement: Getting results (2nd ed.).* Lanham, MD: Rowman and Littlefield.

Hauser, G. A., & Benoit-Barne, C. (2002) Reflections on rhetoric, deliberative democracy, civil society and trust. *Rhetoric & Public Affairs*, 5(2): 261–275.

Holzer, M., & Halachmi, A. (1996) Measurement as a means of accountability. *International Journal of Public Administration*, 19(11/12): 1921–1943.

Holzer, M., & Halachmi, A. (2010) Citizen participation and performance measurement: Operationalizing democracy through better accountability. *Public Administration Quarterly*, 34(3): 378–399.

Hopkins, L., Thomas, J., Meredyth, D., & Ewing, S. (2004) Social capital and community building through an electronic network. *Australian Journal of Social Issues (Australian Council of Social Service)*, 39(4): 369–379

Huckfeldt, R. (2014) Networks, contexts, and the combinatorial dynamics of democratic politics. *Political Psychology*, 35: 43–68. doi: 10.1111/pops.12161.

Jin-Wook, C. (2006) Deliberative democracy, rational participation and e-voting in South Korea. *Asian Journal Of Political Science*, 14(1): 64–81. doi: 10.1080/02185370600832547.

Johnson, A. A. (2014) Ambivalence, political engagement, and context. *Political Studies*, 62(3): 502–521. doi: 10.1111/1467-9248.12063.

Kim, D. (2014) The effect of partisanship, sophistication, and political contexts on belief in democracy promotion. *Politics & Policy*, 42(5): 658–692.

Lawrence, J., & Brodman, J. (2000) Linking communities to global policymaking: A new electronic window on the United Nations. In M. Gurstein (ed.), *Community informatics: Enabling communities with information and communications technologies* (pp. 470–493). Hershey, PA: IGI Global.

Lee, J. (2013) Exploring the role of knowledge networks in perceived e-government: A comparative case study of two local governments in Korea. *The American Review of Public Administration*, 43(1): 89–108. doi: 10.1177/0275074011429716.

Lipsky, M. (2003) Street level bureaucracy: Dilemmas of the individual in public service. In J. M. Shafritz, A. C. Hyde, & S. J. Parkes (eds), *Classics of public administration* (5th ed., 402–408). Nashville, TN: Thomson Wadsworth.

Marland, A., Giasson, T., & Lees-Marshment, J. (eds). (2012) *Political marketing in Canada*. Vancouver, BC: UBC Press. Retrieved from www.ebrary.com.

Mergel, I. (2011) Crowdsourced ideas make participating in government cool again. *PA Times*, 34(4): 4–6.

Mergel, I., & Desouza, K. C. (2013) Implementing open innovation in the public sector: The case of Challenge.gov. *Public Administration Review*, 73(6): 882–890.

Nabatchi, T. (2010) Addressing the citizenship and democratic deficits: The potential of deliberative democracy for public administration. *American Review of Public Administration*, 40(4): 376–399. doi: 10.1177/0275074009356467.

Noordhoff, C. S., Kyriakopoulos, K., Moorman, C., Pauwels, P., & Dellaert, B. G. (2011) The bright side and dark side of embedded ties in business-to-business innovation. *Journal of Marketing*, 75(5): 34–52. doi: 10.1509/jmkg75.5.34.

Putnam, R. D. (2000) *Bowling alone: The collapse and revival of American community*. New York: Simon & Schuster.

Savas, E. S. (2000) *Privatization and public-private partnerships*. New York: Seven Bridges Press.

Savas, E. S. (2002) Competition and choice in New York city social services. *Public Administration Review*, 62(1): 83–91.

Seo, H., & Thorson, S. J. (2012) Networks of networks: Changing Patterns in country bandwidth and centrality in global information infrastructure, 2002–2010. *Journal of Communication*, 62(2): 345–358. doi: 10.1111/j.1460-2466.2012.01631.x.

United States Census Bureau. (2016) U.S. and world population clock. Retrieved from www.census.gov/popclock/.

Wilson, W. (2003) The study of administration. In J. M. Shafritz, A. C. Hyde, & S. J. Parkes (eds), *Classics of public administration* (5th ed., 35–46). Nashville, TN: Thomson Wadsworth.

Zuppo, C. M. (2012) Defining ICT in a boundaryless world: The development of a working hierarchy. *International Journal of Information Technology*, 4(3): 13–22.

6　Deliberative Democracy and Citizen Participation

There are a number of criteria on which a deliberative democracy framework is based, and these contribute to the development of E-Governance means associated with facilitating digital interactions for authentic citizen participation (discussed in later sections). It is important to highlight several of these key deliberative democracy criteria and expand on how they relate to the development of E-Governance means which support various types of citizen-government interactions. Roberts (1997, p. 131) explained, "deliberation is a sophisticated form of social interaction. Success may depend on the developmental mix of participants in the process." The interactive nature among a diverse group of individuals contributes to understanding the essence of deliberation as it relates to a democracy. A deliberative democracy requires the existence of a number of basic participatory requirements serving as guidelines to the interactive process. Cohen (1997) noted that legitimacy for deliberative democracy is partly rooted in the framework in which citizen dialogue is cyclical and open to all interested parties. Trotta (2006, p. 14) explained that "effective deliberation of values results from the government's efforts to promote the inclusion of multiple ideologies competing in the political arena (i.e., keeping the deliberative process open to all interested parties)." In relation, an effective deliberative system partly "depends of the stability of the system" allowing for the "perpetuation of continuous value debates" (Trotta, 2006, p. 14). Estlund (1997, p. 190) noted that deliberative democracy reflects a procedural condition in that "every adult in the society is permitted to participate." Here, eligible individuals will serve as a foundational element for establishing conditions associated with openness to participate within a deliberative democracy with the understanding that eligibility could be based on a number of components dependent on the nature of the interaction in question. For example, there may be different age-based eligibility requirements permitting citizens to participate in interactions, as with voting. In addition, citizenship is a required element for an individual to participate in an official deliberative event such as voting. Developing an open framework in which all eligible interested parties can participate on a continual basis and ensuring that this structure facilitates interactions in a consistently cyclical fashion to continuously create multiple points of contact are two foundational components associated with a deliberative democracy.

Once the open and cyclical components of a deliberative democracy are present, the legitimacy of this framework is further cemented by the ability of interactions to play a role in affecting changes within the political system. Raisio and Carson (2014) contributed to the discussion toward characteristics of a deliberative democracy by noting the importance of the existence of factors reflecting "inclusiveness, deliberativeness and influence." Modern deliberative democracy is geared to functionally include perspectives from among a wide array of interests to ensure that meaningful interactions occur between participants which has the capacity to affect government actions going forward. Cohen (1997, p. 407) explained that a "fundamental idea of democratic legitimacy is that the authorization to exercise state power must arise from the collective decisions of the members of society who are governed by that power." Macedo (1999) echoed the importance of the ability of deliberations to generate collective will that is capable of affecting change as it relates to perceptions associated with legitimacy of government actions. Here, legitimacy for government decision-making in a deliberative democracy is partly based on whether the outcomes are associated with consensus derived from political negotiations. Cohen (1997, p. 73) expanded on applicable system essentials by noting the preferential importance for the existence of "institutions in which the connections between deliberation and outcomes are evident to ones in which the connections are less clear." According to Trotta (2006, p. 15), "in order for deliberative democracy to remain credible, the manifestation of values in government (i.e., legislation, policies, agencies, budgets) must accurately reflect the 'winners' of ideological debate within the political arena." Handley and Howell-Moroney (2010, p. 603) noted that "deliberative responsiveness recognizes that while making public policy decisions is complicated, administrators are seeking a consensus among their stakeholders." Roberts (1997, p. 131) explained that for results associated with deliberative process the "potential is there for gridlock as well as consensus" and that "the use of deliberation rests not on technology, but on will." In this regard, simply providing digital means does not guarantee participation if the desire to interact is missing. Similarly, participation in deliberative events does not guarantee universal agreement on all matters. Opening the deliberative system to all eligible interested parties may increase the complexity of value-based debates, enhancing the degree of difficulty associated with achieving consensus required to avoid stalemate, which result in government inaction. In addition, an important component associated with deliberative democracy is that stakeholder consensus achieved through interaction is expected to then dictate government action across a wide array of concerns, including those related to legislative action, budget allocations and administrative decision-making. Citizen dialogue can play a role in a broad scope of deliberative processes in society, which contributes to achieving overall system consensus on a line-item basis capable of providing motivation for government action. Means facilitating citizen deliberation serves as one, of many, sources of interests to consider when consensus-driven government actions are taken. It is important not only that deliberations can affect change across a wide array of governmental actions but also that evidence that participation can affect change is available. Just as consensus during deliberations is not achieved without effort and compromise, highlighting when events involving citizen dialogue with government resulted in affecting real change can benefit from some degree of active political marketing. As a note, it is important to acknowledge that there are factors other than consensus derived from citizen–government interactions that can affect government changes within the political system. For example, changes to the system could be the result of Supreme Court rulings, legislative mandates or executive orders from the president. However, this deliberative democracy framework discussion focuses on tools to facilitate interactions to generate input associated with authentic citizen participation that is used to affect identifiable changes to the political system.

Citizens may participate through available means to work toward governmental change. A deliberative democracy should remain open; there are multiple levels of communication that may occur across diverse interested parties originating from both within and outside of government. For example, public administrators deliberate with multiple stakeholders (e.g., citizens, government officials, special interest groups, etc.) and there may be a hierarchy of influence associated with which stakeholders can influence governmental outcomes in this administrative–stakeholder relationship dynamic (Handley & Howell-Moroney, 2010). Deliberation could occur between members of government across a wide range of activities, such as those that occur during agenda setting, budgeting outlays or public policy development, or between government and businesses. However, the processes that facilitate dialogue between citizens and government will remain in the forefront on this discussion on deliberative democracy. For Raisio and Carson (2014), deliberative democracy is synonymous with citizen participation or civic engagement with the understanding that deliberative democracy relates in part to realizing that citizen participation includes a number of means used to facilitate different types of interactions between the public and government. This idea that deliberative democracy and citizen participation are interrelated contributes to the discussion on how both relate to E-Governance. Nabatchi (2010) observed that there are contributions associated with deliberative democracy that are normative in nature that furthers the overall understanding of why it is important for a wide range of dialectic communication means to exist within a given network. Nabatchi (2010, p. 385) stated that deliberative democracy serves as an "umbrella term for a wide variety of processes." This relates directly to the belief that a deliberative democracy is reflective of the usage of numerous means in which participation can be facilitated. Citizen–government interactions, in which participation addresses a wide range of activities, can be reflective of a combination of both traditional and technological means. The construction of diverse techniques reflecting a combination of the traditional and digital can contribute to a more comprehensive framework that is more representative of the expectations associated with participation in a deliberative democracy. Here, a diverse deliberative framework can sustain interactions between citizens and government, linking those who seek to engage in dialogue across a broad spectrum of means. The modern deliberative democracy framework supporting citizen participation differs somewhat from past points in the history of U.S. government in that dialogue events occur through traditional means as well as through technological means unique to the E-Governance Era (i.e., virtual town hall meetings, crowdsourcing, etc.). In this sense, E-Governance can strengthen the modern deliberative democracy framework. The creation of a deliberative democracy framework that is reflective of diversity in means provides greater opportunity for citizens to be actively involved in dialogue within the political system regarding items of societal importance. It is important that digital deliberative means facilitate communication between network participants in a continuously open format to achieve consensus capable of effecting real, identifiable change in government.

It will be helpful to further expound on the role that citizen participation plays within the modern deliberative democracy framework to better understand the impact of digitally based interactions associated with E-Governance. Citizen participation in the U.S. political system that is conducted through available deliberative means can greatly contribute to reinforcing the perpetuation of important democratic principles, including accountability, flexibility and transparency. These principles become further institutionalized by creating digital means in which citizen–government interactions can accommodate accountable, flexible and transparent participative endeavors. In relation, the means in which citizens interact in dialogue events with government occurs within and contributes to the strengthening of the overall deliberative democracy framework. Therefore, a closer look at what constitutes authentic, or substantive, citizen participation is essential going forward. As such, it is important to continue to work toward cultivating an understanding of how citizen participation means help strengthen discourse with government in a deliberative democracy. This includes that citizen participation should be reflective of process diversity in which there is a structural capacity that supports both traditional and digital means. The ability of an effective deliberative democracy framework to support authentic citizen participation can directly affect government actions. This contributes to promotion of key democratic principles and further strengthens perceptions that government actions are legitimate.

Citizens can participate through a number of available means that support and encourage the intention of affecting the political system in some way. For example, citizens participate in town hall meetings with the hopes of affecting changes to, or maintaining the status quo, in the place they live. Citizens cast ballots in elections to place individuals into government office who they believe will best represent them in a manner reflecting their personal values and belief system. There is also the ability for citizens to vote on a policy referendum to enact change to the political system or to remove an elected representative from public office. Citizens can interact with the bureaucracy to provide feedback intended to influence certain activities, such as proposed agency rule changes advertised through the Federal Register or to voice displeasure with existing means in which services are provided. Regardless of the type of participation within the deliberative system, there are a number of important components associated with this process: access, intent and outcome. Substantive citizen participation (or authentic citizen participation) plays an important role in a deliberative democracy as it relates to providing greater significance to the contributions made throughout the process by empowering change. The literature provides guidance in identifying a number of expectations associated with this perspective on citizen participation, which will play a role in better understanding deliberations during the E-Governance Era. This includes expectations based on government institutionalizing access to opportunity to participate and in citizens having faith in the ability to affect outcomes if participation designs are perceived to legitimately contribute to strengthening the deliberative democracy framework.

The presence or absence of citizen trust can affect the perception of legitimacy associated with participation means provided and may ultimately influence whether government actions are considered to genuinely reflect the will of the people. In relation, the perception that citizens can affect some degree of change to the political system by participating directly with government remains a key component associated with trust in designs. Therefore, it is important to expand on how expectations associated with this dynamic may affect the perception, and use, of the means designed to facilitate citizen–government interactions such as those associated with E-Governance. Yang and Callahan (2007) indicated that a danger for citizen participation legitimacy occurs when public managers implement means that are ultimately deemed by stakeholders to be "hollow exercises," in that the participants' ability to impact government outcomes in a meaningful way is lacking, or worse, absent. Handley and Howell-Moroney (2010) echoed this idea, noting that government activities such as public hearings may focus on simply disseminating previously gathered information in an effort to convince attendees regarding the merit of already-made decisions as opposed to engaging in deliberations with citizens to determine what they think about a topic. Such activities would be relatable to rungs three (Informing), four (Consultation) and five (Placation) of Arnstein's (1969) eight-step "ladder of citizen participation" in which all three steps are classified as "Tokenism," or giving the appearance of voice to the public without including the necessary means in which to also impact changes. The concern that citizen participation mechanisms are functionally "hollow" can negatively affect perceptions of the legitimacy of the deliberative process (Arnstein, 1969; Yang & Callahan, 2007; Handley & Howell-Moroney, 2010). Turner (2014, p. 886) explained that "substantive public participation" is reflective of a process supporting "constant and equitable influence of all parties" and should be focused on "rethinking the underlying roles of, and relationships between, administrators/facilitators and citizens." Deliberative efforts that fail to consider knowledge on policy issues by those that hold interests affected by government actions may produce outcomes that are neither able to feasibly address the societal problem or could be considered by citizens to have produced potentially illegitimate outcomes that fail to reflect actual expectations (Turner, 2014). Turner (2014, p. 886) noted that citizen participation efforts may be less effective toward being capable of achieving deliberative goals when conditions exist in which there are "limited opportunities for authentic participation, predominantly one-way communication, inadequate organization and implementation, and feelings of powerlessness." King, Feltey, and O'Neill Susel (1998, p. 317) believed that authentic citizen participation associated with citizen–administrator interactions could be better facilitated by efforts to "move away from static and reactive processes toward more dynamic and deliberative processes." Significant to understanding what contributes to true citizen empowerment is recognizing the role that providing verifiable evidence of government applying components of collective intelligence derived through dialogue plays in reinforcing legitimacy (Buckwalter, 2014; Turner, 2014). Citizen participation through means such as town hall meetings or citizen advisory boards is based on assumptions that there are individuals in society that are willing to be engaged civically, have sufficient levels of free time that will allow them to pursue this interest and are generally concerned with the actions of government that may directly affect them (Heikkila & Isett, 2007). The role of two-way communication in citizen participation means is also an item of considerable importance in ensuring that true dialogue is facilitated between citizens and government (Heikkila & Isett, 2007). Buckwalter (2014, p. 574) stated that "administrators play a dual role in public empowerment, influencing both its processes and its outcomes." Buckwalter (2014, p. 583) discussed that efforts to alter perceptions associated with "empowerment in the context of government-organized citizen participation" should transition from "a control-based norm" to standards that favor "cooperation." Mutual trust between citizens and public administrators can be a key component in facilitating authentic, substantive, meaningful civic engagement (Yang, 2005). For citizens to trust that participative means are legitimate, a number of elements should exist in which an active and interested citizen base can interact in an environment supporting cooperation and in which outcomes of deliberations have the ability to affect change to the political system that are clearly identifiable.

Substantive, or authentic, citizen participation includes a number of important variables to be satisfied in order to ensure its presence and related usefulness within the deliberative system. This includes the construction of mechanisms through which citizen–government interactions can be frequently facilitated in a timely manner to determine public opinion and consistent efforts to provide verifiable evidence in which government has applied information generated through participation in the corresponding actions. In relation, there are requisites associated with ensuring that access is afforded to all parties interested in participating in deliberations. Conceptually, this is reflective of deliberative democracy principles associated with constructing cyclical participatory means allowing for open dialogue between interested parties that can result in visibly affecting government outcomes. As such, consistent access for interested parties associated with substantive citizen participation is equated to the tenets of open and cyclical interactions associated with deliberative democracy. This further integrates these concepts by highlighting the importance of expectations for deliberative participation though openly equitable means available to all interested parties. As noted, citizen participation through deliberative means is intended to some degree to be able to affect government actions. Therefore, the process of linking public sector outcomes with the information contributed to government via deliberations maintains a primary role in authentic citizen participation. The functional link between providing citizen participation means and verifiable efforts by government to apply collective intelligence derived from the process in some way contributes to the perceived guidelines for substantive citizen participation. However, the failure to allow for citizen input to consistently affect government actions can create legitimacy concerns on several fronts. This includes that failure to incorporate input derived through discursive events detracts greatly from perceptions associated with legitimacy in which open and cyclical dialogue is expected. In this sense, process legitimacy can be negatively affected by government's failure to highlight the role that consensus derived from dialogue with citizens played in influencing changes. It can also create a crisis of outcome legitimacy if government consistently fails to utilize consensus-driven change in that official actions may not represent the will of the people and that developed means are ultimately ineffective to address real problems within the political system.

Legitimacy associated with civic engagement is partly focused on determining if the collective intelligence gathered through deliberation is representative of those directly affected by resulting government actions and whether those government outcomes are linked to ideas derived from dialogue during civic engagement. It is important to recognize the adverse consequences that may result from unfavorable public perception of citizen participation opportunities. These adverse consequences have the capacity to diminish belief in civic engagement processes and political system outcomes. The continued pursuit to help ensure that civic engagement is more substantive in nature is critical in strengthening legitimacy of governance and toward ensuring that government actions provide results capable of serving the public. This relates to the importance of ensuring that the opportunity for citizens to participate is intended to facilitate genuine dialogue toward the purpose of gathering collective intelligence and ensuring that end results of participation are visibly apparent. The construction of dialogue processes is itself continual in nature without a finite point of conclusion, and the constantly developing field of study will perpetually create a non-exhaustive understanding of citizen participation though discursive means in the E-Governance Era. The scope and range of deliberative means have changed significantly over time as technology has gone through various transformations. This transformation of types of means ranges from citizen–government dialogue solely through on-site, traditional debates to the use of the telephone to contact government representatives directly, and has now significantly expanded with the creation of the Internet, which has further increased means of participation to previously unimaginable heights. The role that technology may play in authentic citizen participation has expanded over time and will likely to continue to do so, limited only by human kind's ability to make their imagination reality.

E-Governance means can contribute to the development of requisite trust levels needed to sustain authentic citizen participation, which further promotes legitimacy in this process. Empowerment has become linked conceptually with citizen participation to some degree, and empowerment requires verifiable evidence associated with government actions being representative of the end results of civic engagement processes. Therefore, it is important to determine how developing deliberative means that are perceived to be trustworthy can contribute to the legitimacy associated with authentic participation. E-Governance provides the opportunity for the development of any number of such means capable of sustaining authentic citizen participation opportunities associated with input–output dynamics. In order for citizens to trust in the legitimacy of participation, there are a number of functional criteria that should be satisfied. Here, trust is a function of opportunity of quality means available and perceptions of legitimacy of the processes. Quality means can be related to various dimensions that include provision of opportunities to participate on a consistent basis at a point in decision-making that is influential on outcomes. In this sense, interactive means are viewed as less legitimate if relegated to an advertising or educational capacity in which government utilizes the participatory event to convince parties of the merits of previously made decisions. Quality means are viewed as providing consistently meaningful opportunities for citizens to contribute during decision-making processes that ultimately guide government actions. In relation, it is important that citizen inputs derived from deliberations in participatory events manifest in public sector outcomes. In the respect, trust in the process is subject to evidence that participation will help to guide government actions. Legitimacy in civic engagement is partly rooted in the ability of citizens to trust that deliberations will result in some degree of identifiable government actions. The verifiable outcomes provide an added dimension of meaningfulness to deliberations facilitated through quality means in that citizens may trust that participation efforts are not in vain. Therefore, trust that citizen participation means are authentic is partly dependent on the provision of consistent processes for input and identifiable evidence that deliberative outcomes are capable of affecting government actions.

There is something to be said for making efforts to develop a deeper understanding associated with the relationship dynamics regarding citizens and government. In many respects, and on several levels, the constructed dialogue means can affect the relationship between government and citizens. This includes that the construction of discursive means can affect the processes in which citizen–government communication occurs and that providing deliberative means can play a role in fostering expectations associated with the ability to impact the political system. For example, the construction of participatory means by government is able to influence how and when dialogue is facilitated to a certain degree. A deliberative democracy framework that provides access to citizens by constructing infrequent means that are only reflective of traditional on-site methods is limited compared to a more diverse deliberative framework that incorporates both traditional and digital means. The structure of the deliberative framework provides the means in which various citizen–government interaction occurs and ultimately helps to shape the relationship that develops between them. The relationship can be argued to be reflective of inequitable power dynamics that place citizens at a disadvantage to some degree because how and when official dialogue events are facilitated is largely dependent on government constructs. It is important to recognize this dynamic as it relates to official discursive events as opposed to organic actions by citizens (i.e. traditional protests, signing petitions that are tangible or digital, email campaigns, etc.) to engage with government outside of formal constructions within the deliberative democracy framework. While still recognizing the potential inequitable power effects on relationship dynamics, the positive impact of official government designs for purposeful constructs to facilitate active participation toward the purposes of yielding substantive changes cannot be undersold. Without providing any such means or limiting the strength of means to significantly impact the system, the dialectic influence of citizens on government actions is reduced considerably. A deliberative framework that is reflective of limited means, or, in a most extreme scenario, an absence of dialogue means, can affect expectations regarding the ability to impact the political system and may negatively influence how citizens perceive the actions of government. This continues to highlight how a deliberative framework that applies limited means for citizens to directly engage with government in dialogue contributes to negative perceptions that government is disinterested in facilitating discourse to affect political system actions. This could result in dissatisfaction with government actions when public sector efforts to address issues of importance within the political system are perceived to ignore collective intelligence derived from dialogue with the citizen base. It also can contribute to diminished levels of citizen trust in government and the perceptions that official actions are illegitimate. Again, maintaining a deliberative framework that facilitates interactions such as those associated with authentic citizen participation is not solely the responsibility of government. There may be any number of means available to the public capable of promoting civic engagement, but without sufficient numbers of citizens willing to actively engage in consistent deliberations with government, these means lack the power to fully achieve authentic citizen participation. Here, the existence of citizens who are willing and able to engage in deliberations with government continues to be an important component. Sufficient levels of citizens willing to participate through well-publicized means serves as a foundational component providing further context to deliberative democracy. Providing means without sustaining the requisite levels of citizens willing to engage government through those means is insufficient. It is important that authentic citizen participation means are made available and efforts are made to ensure that these means are utilized. This includes conducting political marketing efforts to ensure that available means are made known to the public. However, the onus for utilizing the available participation means within the deliberative system largely falls to the citizen base.

Sometimes the will to participate is hindered by various types of limitations that may affect citizen involvement in discursive events. In relation, there may be a number of barriers that may prevent participation in deliberative means that should be recognized and addressed. Turner (2014, p. 889) referred to a type of real-world barrier to citizen participation that results from "the practical realities of life in contemporary society." Turner (2014) added that barriers to substantive citizen participation also include those related to the structural components in which the deliberation occurs and the situational processes that guide participation. Barriers may include particulars associated with a wide range of items, such as the inconvenience of traveling to the physical location in which participation occurs, the perception that opportunities to participate are too far along in the policy-making process, reflecting a selling process over true dialogue and the nature of the available means used to facilitate participation (Turner, 2014). As noted, the structural means in which citizen–government participation may occur are able to affect the nature of interactions to some degree. Lindblom (1990, p. 256) observed that the process of mutual adjustments between partisan participants is subject to a number of structural constraints that affect how the process unfolds and with whom. Fountain (2001, p. 53) similarly discussed how the structural designs of public sector entities can limit aspects of deliberative participation by noting that "partisan mutual adjustment, far from a bargaining free-for-all, is always embedded in systems of rules, including rules regarding jurisdiction and authority." Fountain (2001, p. 53) added that "when bureaucratic policymakers negotiate the best, appropriate, feasible, or acceptable uses of the Internet in their agencies, their mutual adjustment takes place within nested system of rules that constrain[s] both the innovations considered and the interests agency actors negotiate for." Here, the deliberations within government entities can affect the decisions associated with the application of technology and, in turn, this influences the nature of interactions that occur between network participants. Similarly, the participatory structural means made available can either constrain or expand citizen–government deliberative opportunities. Dahl (2006, p. 118) noted that many barriers to participation exist, but "among these, two were particularly relevant: the costs in time required for participation and the limits on the feasible size of systems that would permit them to be directly governed by assemblies of all the members." It is definitely important to recognize the possibility that participation can be costly in different ways for citizens. A wide variety of fiscally or non-fiscally oriented costs may serve as a barrier to participation in that citizens may not be able to dedicate the time to engage with government due to conflicts with real-world responsibilities such as those attributed to work and family. Here, the desire to be civically engaged may take a proverbial backseat to the avalanche of pressing responsibilities facing everyday citizens. The pursuit of the opportunity to engage with government during customary hours of operation for many citizens, whose responsibilities of the day start before the sun comes up and may conclude in the early or late evening, is oftentimes not feasible. Work and family responsibilities are very realistic barriers to civic engagement for everyday citizens. Having to balance a full-time job (or two!) while maintaining some semblance of family atmosphere may provide temporal barriers to citizens preventing them from being able to participate while government is traditionally in operation. It is also important to consider that traveling to participate at a physical location may be costly to the citizen as it relates to resources such as time and money. This may be less applicable at the local level of government, like attending a traditional town hall meeting down the street in a neighborhood, but traveling to participate in person at the state or federal level can be unrealistically costly.

The construction of digital civic engagement means that are synchronous or asynchronous can help citizens to overcome any number of real-world barriers to participation. For example, fiscal costs incurred by citizens related to traveling or having to take time off of work to participate in interactive events may be offset to some degree, and in many cases diffused entirely, by government constructing digital civic engagement tools. In addition, digital participation can reduce issues associated with travel time for citizens working to diffuse temporal-based barriers associated with process. This would be applicable for either synchronous or asynchronous digital participatory efforts. Both synchronous and asynchronous digital means can be especially relevant in diffusing barriers to citizen participation regarding costs of traveling to a locale in which engagement can be accomplished more conveniently from home. In the modern era, the scope of digital participation has also been expanded to the multitude of handheld devices, such as smartphones or tablets. Basically, any device that has access to the Internet can conceivably provide a mobile venue in which digital civic engagement can be facilitated. It is important to recognize that there are IT security concerns associated with all means in which to facilitate digital citizen participation. This will likely continue to be of paramount concern to those interested in utilizing their home computers and handheld devices. However, technical issues such as those associated with IT security for E-Governance endeavors generally remain outside of the scope of this discussion other than to acknowledge its importance. Instead, the focus will remain on E-Governance's role in facilitating participation in the modern deliberative democracy.

The proliferation of technology has continued to permeate society at a rapid rate and responsible government should seek to supplement traditional participation means with those that reflect available technological innovation. Doing so may prove beneficial for those citizens that are motivated to participate in government, but would otherwise be unable to do so as they are unable to endure the financial and temporal costs associated with civic engagement during customary hours of operation for government. This includes asynchronous digital participation, which can allow for an individual to engage with government from a computer with Internet access from any location, at any time convenient to the individual. Here, we see the power of asynchronous digital means in expanding the timeframe in which collective intelligence is gathered which can include a previously underrepresented segment of society that would have otherwise be unable to participate. This is not to say that the expansion of technologically innovative means geared toward participation will guarantee that all citizens will be engaged with every civically minded digital enterprise. Digital civic engagement is no different than the traditional in-person participative means in that the goals aren't necessarily to ensure 100-percent attendance for each online event. For example, traditional town hall meetings rarely (if ever) maintain a 100-percent attendance rate from residents in a given locality. Just because a town hall meeting may be virtual doesn't mean that everyone within a locality with Internet access will be logged in to participate. Citizen participation that is digital in nature will be subject to the same interest-based fluctuations that traditional town hall meetings are subject to. Generally, digital civic engagement tools should be viewed as being able to serve as one of many means available. Again, there is no magic formula for government in which all of societal problems will be immediately solved. Having said that, construction of digital participation tools can provide additional structural capacity to existing deliberation networks in which input from civically minded individuals can be heard. The deliberative democracy framework within the E-Governance Era should support digital and traditional means in which to conduct interactions designed for the purpose of facilitating authentic citizen participation.

As noted above, the democratic principles of accountability, flexibility and transparency are important elements associated with the participatory means available within a deliberative democracy framework. The presence of these principles can contribute to strengthening the functionality of a wide array of deliberative means associated with substantive citizen participation. For example, a system review by political actors that yields the perception that accountability is not adequately represented within the political system can lead to the refinement of existing means and/or the construction of new means to allow for goal achievement in this regard. Those means can now contribute to a broader deliberative democracy framework to facilitate interactions better suited to promote public sector accountability by providing further opportunity for citizens to voice their opinions in an effort to impact the change to the political system. The means used to conduct citizen–government dialogue can strengthen the deliberative democracy framework's ability to further promote accountable government and those means can allow citizens to maintain a dialogue with government, which serves as a measure of accountability. In turn, the whole of the deliberative framework contributes to holding government more accountable as citizens are provided more substantial means in which they engage in activities, such as expressing dissatisfaction in public sector actions and contributing to problem-solving initiatives. The cyclical process regarding political actors' assessment of accountability means available within the political system in represented in Figure 6.1.

The effort to provide a more flexible deliberative democracy framework is also of importance. The democratic principle of flexibility continues to be significant to the discussion on effectiveness for the framework of deliberative democracy. A diverse and flexible set of means in which citizen–government interactions can be facilitated generates ideas from members of society that

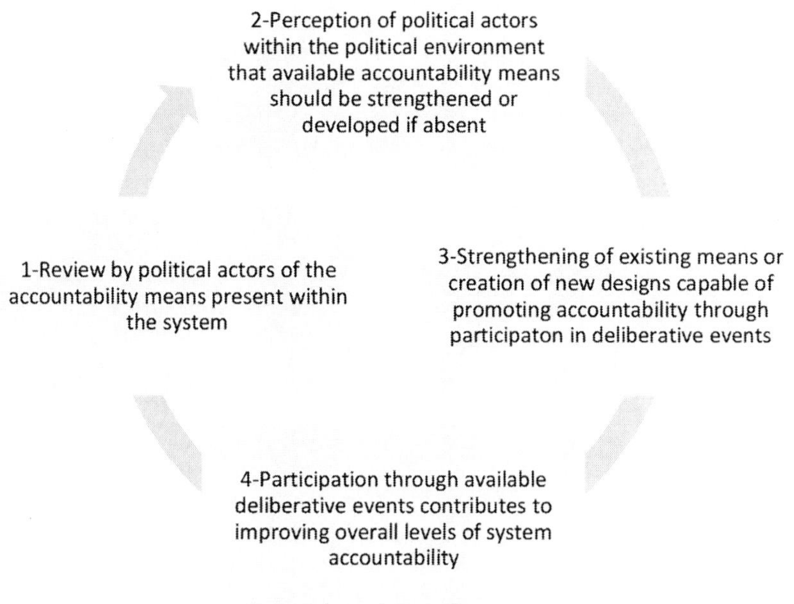

Figure 6.1 Accountability Cycle: Review, Perception, Creation and Participation

might otherwise go unheard. This yields a wider value network for the purpose of synthesizing collective intelligence with potentially higher levels of representativeness, which can further promote accountability. Here, diverse means can potentially expand the scope of those participating in citizen–government dialogue. For example, the timeframe for participation in public meetings in a traditional on-site fashion can be extended through any number of supplemental means. This could include allowing for earlier and later public meetings to be held to better accommodate the schedules of citizens who have multiple real-world responsibilities. By expanding the hours in which dialogue events could occur, government can better include those that would otherwise be prevented from participating during regular 9-to-5 hours of operation. It may also be beneficial to create a public meetings schedule in which consideration for holding meetings are extended to include a Saturday or Sunday. Utilizing digital means to facilitate deliberative events can also contribute to increased levels of citizen participation and provide additional avenues in which government can keep abreast of citizen concerns present within the political system. By expanding the timeframe and available means in which citizens may participate in deliberative events, it is possible to increase levels of feedback provided to government from citizens, which may play a role in affecting meaningful change within the system. As a reminder, providing an opportunity to participate that is either traditional or digital in nature is not a guarantee that those means will be used. However, failure to expand the means in which participation occurs increases the likelihood that this potential rich source of additional information will remain unheard.

Another point to address here is the importance of government recognizing and utilizing citizen input generated through dialogue events. As discussed previously, the most obvious efforts by government to recognize input by citizens is to ensure that consensus derived from dialogue is capable of affecting change and that examples of this dynamic in action are verifiable. However, there are other techniques in which interaction between government and citizens can be recognized. This includes any number of basic communication techniques by government to acknowledge that citizens have participated in a deliberative event. Not many individuals in any societal setting are overly keen to make an effort to participate in deliberations of any kind if they feel that their insight is being minimized or, even worse, being ignored entirely. This is true of deliberations ranging from those involving discussions between parties regarding where they will be going out to dinner to those public sector deliberative processes associated with citizen participation regarding government actions. People taking the time to participate want to be heard and it can be quite constructive to simply acknowledge those efforts. This can have an immediate positive effect, which provides evidence that the process of communication wasn't a one-way, futile exercise and that the process actually reflects genuine dialogue. A response to an e-mail or a phone call goes a long way in the private sector or public sector, even if the response is automated so that the sender can verify receipt of the original communication by the receiver. Although, for any number of reasons, there is no guarantee that action will be taken (i.e., lack of political consensus, not feasible economically, etc.), a response of acknowledgement still indicates that a traditionally communicated or digital message was heard, and can go a very long way in strengthening faith in deliberative processes. It may have a positive effect on future participation efforts in a couple ways: (a) faith in the process can be strengthened by evidence of identifiable outcomes if solutions are viable politically and (b) confirmation responses from recipients to sender can further engender trust in the process. In this sense, there are short-term and long-term implications associated with participation through deliberative means that are perceived to be both accountable and substantive.

It is important to note that although technological innovation associated with E-Governance is capable of strengthening the deliberative democracy framework, it is presently insufficient as the sole means to facilitate democratic participation. This relates in part to the understanding that the United States is a representative democracy in which deliberations on *all* government actions are not generally expected or even feasible. Dahl (1998, pp. 106–108) offered an insightful discussion regarding functionality of a small assembly democracy in the modern era by providing an analysis of issues associated with "the high price of participatory democracy," observing that "opportunities for participation rapidly diminish with the size of the citizen body." Dahl (1998, p. 109) succinctly explained this dynamic by explaining the "the law of time and numbers: the more citizens a democratic unit contains, the less that citizens can participate directly in government decisions and the more that they must delegate authority to others." Kakabadse, Kakabadse, and Kouzmin (2003, p. 55) warned against "replacing representative democracy with a new form of cyberdemocracy or virtual polis," but acknowledged that "there is room for redesigning the project of representative democracy and governance." Wholly replacing representative democracy with direct democracy—digital or otherwise—lacks feasibility associated with having deliberations that would involve all eligible citizens willing to discuss all possible interests at all levels of government. The time it would take for each eligible and willing citizen in the United States to register an opinion on every issue at every level of government would effectively immobilize the political system under the weight of unwieldy and unrealistic deliberative minutia. The total time that would be required for full participation increases to unmanageable numbers as the pool of participants progressively increases in size from a locality to a state to the nation. According to the Population Clock for U.S. Census Bureau (2016), the population of the United States is estimated to be 325 million people. Imagine the length of time that would be required for full participation from eligible citizens from a pool of that size. Therefore, the U.S. political system is reflective of a balance between decisions facilitated by government officials as a function of representative democracy while also providing opportunities for citizens to participate in meaningful dialogue as a function of direct democracy. There is plethora of possible impetus motivating government action ranging from change derived from consensus amongst elected representatives and from citizen centric change derived through participation in diverse discursive means associated with the U.S. deliberative democracy framework.

The discussion of how digital means facilitates deliberations in the U.S. representative democracy is of great relevance in the modern E-Governance Era. It is important for digital means to allow interested parties to contribute within the deliberative democracy framework in a consistently meaningful way. As such, digital participatory means applying technological innovation will have to reflect key attributes of deliberative democracy that are focused on creating opportunities for interested parties to engage with government in a cyclical nature on a longitudinal basis. Therefore, digital means used to promote deliberative democracy should be provided so that interested parties can directly engage with government through multiple points of access on a consistent basis over time. However, digital means capable of providing what is referred to as *universal citizen access* (Kakabadse, Kakabadse, & Kouzmin, 2003) is presently unfeasible in modern governance. This can be due to any number of logistical issues, including those associated with the expansive cost to government for developing a nationwide infrastructure capable of sustaining this goal. There are also possible barriers associated with the digital divide in which costs may be prohibitive for ownership by every citizen of Internet-connected devices through which to participate. The digital divide may also perpetuate the continued need for increased government efforts to facilitate deeper educational endeavors to promote a more universal understanding of complex digital deliberative democracy. Digital deliberative democracy is not capable of solving all of the inequities that may be present within the political system as it relates to participation. This includes inequities associated with variances in wealth, which may create greater access to the political system and enhanced coordination levels of interest groups that may be more successful in affecting change. Digital deliberative democracy may be able to contribute to the reduction of negative aspects associated with possible barriers to participation as it relates to expanding plausible means for citizens to participate in dialogue. In this sense, digital means can strengthen the deliberative democracy framework by increasing points of contact within the political system. This can help to encourage the application of principles of democracy centered on participation through deliberation and transparency to enhance accountability. In relation, participation though digital deliberative means can contribute to ensuring that government actions are more representative of consensus-based change derived from more inclusive citizen discourse.

It is important to reinforce that modern governance can benefit from including both traditional and digital means to construct an overarching deliberative framework which simultaneously supports elements of both representative democracy and direct democracy. A deliberative framework can support components associated with direct democracy with the understanding that it will not wholly replace the existing avenues guiding actions related to representative democracy. Enhancing the digital means capable of promoting dialogue between citizens and government strengthens components of direct democracy facilitated through deliberation, but it is still important to maintain elements associated with the integrity of the overarching representative political system. E-Governance application of technological innovation may serve to support representative democracy and direct democracy through a diverse deliberative framework capable of facilitating authentic citizen participation. The digital deliberative democracy framework should be diverse in nature regarding available means in which interested parties can engage in communications. A system that solely promotes either representative democracy or direct democracy may be insufficient to fully provide the benefits associated with democratic diversity. The same can be said for a system that solely utilizes either traditional means or modern digital means. Again, diversity in the deliberative democracy framework across a broad spectrum of criteria remains of vital importance to its effectiveness and legitimacy.

Deliberative democracy involves any number of means intended to facilitate citizen–government interactions capable of providing access to information that may be used to drive government actions. The more static features of participation in a deliberative democracy involve means in which citizens can affect the political system through events such as casting votes and completing traditional surveys. Casting a vote and interacting in town hall meetings would be reflective of actions associated with a deliberative democracy, but clearly reflect different types of activities designed to affect change in the political system. Here, where a participatory activity falls on the spectrum of interaction helps to determine its categorization for deliberative democracy. On one end of the spectrum of deliberative participation would be activities that support limited one-way communication, such as voting or contributing thoughts through a suggestion box. On the other end of the spectrum would be activities that support two-way communication, including citizen advisory panels and crowdsourcing. However, there may also be a number of deliberation means that are capable of being constructed in a manner that could support one-way and two-way communication. In relation, a citizen survey could be constructed with limited one-way communication based on closed questions, or open-ended questions allowing for some degree of discourse through two-way communication. Similarly, a public meeting may be facilitated in a manner that only allows for one-way information dissemination or a public meeting can be held in a town hall format encouraging two-way citizen–government discourse. The spectrum of deliberative participation is intended to represent a range of communication means supporting citizen–government interactions and is illustrated in Figure 6.2.

A deliberative democracy framework is intended to reflect system openness, allowing for interested parties to utilize a full range of activities, such as directly participating in dialogue with government in a cyclical fashion over an indefinite period of time. Therefore, opportunities are provided that are able to sustain dialogue through a broad range of diverse means to

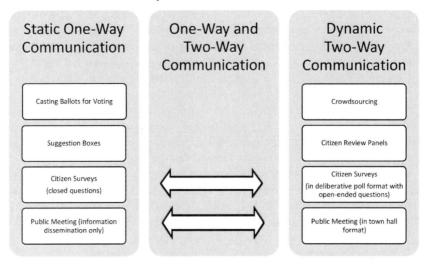

Figure 6.2 Basic Spectrum of Deliberative Democracy Activities and Communication

increase points of access linking citizens and government. Dialogue opportunities are generally not limited to single one-time events, but are continual to allow for constant feedback to help guide government actions. At any point in time in a deliberative democracy a citizen can engage in dialogue through any number of means from among a diverse range of participatory options. It is also important for there to be efforts to ensure legitimacy associated with the citizen dialogue within an effective deliberative framework. This is maintained in part by ensuring that government actions are driven to some degree by consensus derived from discursive efforts between citizens and the public sector. Consensus-driven government action derived from authentic citizen participation and verifiable evidence of this dynamic in action greatly helps to legitimize the deliberative democracy framework. A number of traditional methods of citizen participation have become especially applicable in the modern E-Governance Era, which calls for adaption to digital means to facilitate interaction with the public. This could include electronic means used to facilitate communication through social media networks, a suggestion box, crowdsourcing, citizen review panels, deliberative polls, town hall meetings and voting. The advancements in technology have opened up deliberative democracy to the possibility of a dual approach capable of simultaneously utilizing traditional and digital means to facilitate civic engagement.

References

Arnstein, S. R. (1969) A ladder of citizen participation. *American Institution of Planners Journal*, 35(7): 216–224.

Buckwalter, N. D. (2014) The potential for public empowerment through government-organized participation. *Public Administration Review*, 74(5): 573–584. doi: 10.1111/puar.12217.

Cohen, J. (1997) Deliberation and democratic legitimacy. In J. Bohman & W. Rehg (eds), *Deliberative democracy: Essays of reason and politics* (pp. 67–91). Cambridge, MA: MIT Press.

Dahl, R. A. (1998) *On democracy.* New Haven, CT and London: Yale University Press.

Dahl, R. A. (2006) *On political equality [electronic resource].* New Haven, CT: Yale University Press.

Estlund, D. (1997) Beyond fairness and deliberation: The epistemic dimension of democratic authority. In J. Bohman & W. Rehg (eds), *Deliberative democracy: Essays on reason and politics* (pp. 173–201). Cambridge, MA: MIT Press.

Fountain, J. A. (2001) *Building the virtual state: Information technology and institutional change.* Washington, DC: Brookings Institute Press.

Handley, D. M., & Howell-Moroney, M. (2010) Ordering stakeholder relationships and citizen participation: Evidence from the community development block grant program. *Public Administration Review*, 70(4): 601–609. Retrieved from http://sea rch.proquest.com/docview/853147548?accountid=32521.

Heikkila, T., & Isett, K. R. (2007) Citizen involvement and performance management in special-purpose governments. *Public Administration Review*, 67(2): 238–248. Retrieved from http://search.proquest.com/docview/197177012?accountid=32521.

Kakabadse, A., Kakabadse, N. K., & Kouzmin, A. (2003) Reinventing the democratic governance project through information technology? A growing agenda for debate. *Public Administration Review*, 63(1): 44–60.

King, C. S., Feltey, K. M., & O'Neill Susel, B. (1998) The question of participation: Toward authentic public participation in public administration. *Public Administration Review*, 58(4): 317–326.

Lindblom, C. E. (1990) *Inquiry and change: The troubled attempt to understand and shape society.* New York: Russell Sage.

Macedo, S. (1999) *Deliberative politics: Essays on democracy and disagreement.* New York: Oxford University Press.

Nabatchi, T. (2010) Addressing the citizenship and democratic deficits: The potential of deliberative democracy for public administration. *American Review of Public Administration*, 40(4): 376–399. doi: 10.1177/0275074009356467.

Roberts, N. (1997) Public deliberation: An alternative approach to crafting policy and setting direction. *Public Administration Review*, 57(2): 124–132.

Raisio, H., & Carson, L. (2014) Deliberation within sectors. Making the case for sector mini-publics. *International Review of Social Research*, 4(1): 75–92. doi: 10.1515/irsr-2014–0006.

Trotta, A. (2006) *Budget arguments and military spending in the immediate post-World War Two era.* Ann Arbor, MI: UMI Dissertation Services.

Turner, A. H. (2014) Substantive participation: A model of public participation that works for citizens and administrators. *International Journal of Public Administration*, 37(12): 885–894, 10.1080/01900692.2014.928314.

United States Census Bureau. (2016) U.S. and world population clock. Retrieved from www.census.gov/popclock/.

Yang, K. (2005) Public administrators' trust in citizens: A missing link in citizen involvement efforts. *Public Administration Review*, 65(3): 273–285. Retrieved from http://search.proquest.com/docview/197174670?accountid=32521.

Yang, K., & Callahan, K. (2007) Citizen involvement efforts and bureaucratic responsiveness: Participatory values, stakeholder pressures, and administrative practicality. *Public Administration Review*, 67(2): 249–264.

7 Modern Deliberative Democracy Means and Web 2.0 Technology

Social Media and Crowdsourcing

The advancements in innovations since the start of the E-Governance Era in the early 1990s has continued to grow in scope so that a vast array of technologies have been introduced within society. The modern era has seen a rapid growth in communication technologies, such as those associated with modernizations classified as "initial wave" and the newer Web 2.0 variety. The initial wave and Web 2.0 reflect continued advancements in innovation with a different interpretive understanding of facilitating interactions while maintaining societal relevance for E-Governance. The continued relevance for initial-stage and Web 2.0 technology is representative of an interpretive assessment determining whether respective means would qualify as a *doubling-time effect* (whose relevance is magnified with continued use) or a *half-life effect* (whose potency potentially rapidly degrades in significance over time). The first wave of development included innovations such as the Internet and e-mail, whose proliferation since being conceived is more indicative of a doubling-time effect associated with the technology. The Internet and e-mails were technological innovations at the outset of the E-Governance Era in the 1990s in which the wide-scale proliferation of these innovations was far from immediate. The use of the Internet and e-mail innovations gradually proliferated the private and public sector, eventually reaching a critical mass threshold in which these technologies were deemed stable, acceptable and ready for wider scale applications. In relation, the relevance of the Internet and e-mails in government expanded significantly since these innovations were originally introduced in the early 1990s. Today, the role of initial-stage ICT innovations within the deliberative democracy framework is widely accepted and has proliferated all levels of government to facilitate any number of citizen–government activities. This also provides a significant boon to potential analysis associated with the E-Governance movement, as there is a vast array of observable material that has accumulated in the past 25-plus years associated with the application of first-wave technological innovations.

The development of Web 2.0 technologies broadened the scope of innovations applicable in the E-Governance Era. It is then vital to further define and discuss issues of importance associated with the applicability of newer

Web 2.0 technologies within the deliberative democracy framework at all levels of government. Web 2.0 technologies include a wide range of developments that may be applicable to E-Government and E-Governance, including RSS feeds, crowdsourcing, blogs, wikis, virtual worlds and social networks, which can be utilized in activities that actively promote communication, encourage innovation, support collaboration and facilitate knowledge management within organizations (Nelson, Christopher, & Mims, 2009; Andriole, 2010; Sadaf, Newby, & Ertmer, 2012; Taylor, 2012; Bolivar, 2015). Although these examples would qualify as relatively new innovations in recent years, Web 2.0 technologies are becoming increasingly more relevant in many areas associated with modern governance. There are a number of "political variables" that may affect decisions to pursue usage of Web 2.0 technologies, including political ideology, form of government, expectations of citizens and efficiency in service delivery (Bolivar, 2015). The application of Web 2.0 technologies will be dependent on the public sector reacting to a number of cues stemming from the political system and may be utilized to facilitate a wide range of citizen–government interactions. Bolivar (2015, p. 199) observed that the expectations that innovations become utilized toward the completion of bureaucratic duties has led "service delivery towards a more personalized, outcome-driven, participative, efficient and collaborative model." Bolivar (2015, p. 199) added that the role of Web 2.0 technology is potentially significant toward "supporting public engagement" to be utilized "to improve public services" and to facilitate "information sharing and dialogue" for the purpose of establishing "relationships between government and citizens." The capacity for Web 2.0 technology to facilitate citizen–government dialogue potentially pertains to all levels of government within the U.S. federal system. However, it is argued that local governance may be particularly suited to the application of Web 2.0 technologies to cultivate citizen–government dialogue based on system norms focused on "citizen participation at the local level" in which there is a greater expectation to "use more mechanisms that permit direct citizen involvement" (Bolivar, 2015, p. 205). This may be especially true in the U.S. federal system in which adoption of this form of government was based partly on the assumption that local problems could be more accurately identified, better understood and more readily solved by participants more familiar with a policy issue at the local level because they have directly experienced its effects.

Taylor (2012) recognized that recent advancements in technology, such as those associated with Web 2.0 social networking, have affected information organization and dissemination processes for government, the business sector and citizen-consumers. Here, the potential for the application of Web 2.0 technologies may be influential in any number of activities that involve citizen–government deliberations, information dissemination, transactions and service provision (Taylor, 2012). Schlozman, Verba and Brady (2010) advocated caution regarding overselling the potential of Web 2.0 technologies to overcome all structural communication barriers and to improve levels of citizen participation based on age and socioeconomic status demographics. As such, it is important to remain mindful of the effect of applying technological innovation as it relates to digital divide participation. This includes understanding the potential inequity of participation derived from the decision to utilize exclusivity of Web 2.0 supportive means to facilitate public sector interactions with citizens. Schlozman, Verba, and Brady (2010, p. 501) noted that citizens' comments posted through social media websites like Facebook or through blogs are "less likely to be viewed by public officials or their staff than are ordinary communications" through more traditional communication means. The high-turnover rate due to rapid technological advancements in social media tools creates instability in communication means and the somewhat low threshold for qualifying as an expert blogger in comparison to other forms of political discourse further diminishes the potential for these "modes of involvement" to facilitate constructive citizen participation (Schlozman, Verba, & Brady, 2010). There are concerns that participation through some Web 2.0 technologies may not be able to significantly impact the system in select instances. One has to consider also the effect of the mercurial nature of shifting preferences for innovations. Web 2.0 technologies also have the potential to affect perceptions of modern public sphere participation in which the focus is shifted from being exclusively on the domain of the purely physical to extend to include digital considerations. For example, in the past, government could gauge the displeasure of the public by viewing obvious events that transpired in physical space like a protest. Now, citizens may voice displeasure through means such as staging a traditional protest at a physical location, but the public sphere has been expanded to include digital elements of participation. Here, government can monitor citizens voicing their displeasure via any number virtual venues supporting participation through Web 2.0 technology; these innovations provide legitimate means in which to facilitate citizen–government interactions within the context of deliberative democracy.

In the E-Governance Era, emerging technologies continue to broaden the scope of participative means. This alters the communication dynamics associated with civic engagement to some extent. Traditional means are now increasingly complemented with modern designs that seek to take full advantage of emerging technologies. In relation, harnessing the ideas shared through emerging mediums such as social networking websites presents new challenges to government (Mergel, 2011). The overabundance of comments that a government agency may receive from citizens via social networking websites like Facebook and Twitter may ultimately create difficulties associated with transcription, assessment and application of information (Mergel, 2011). Medici (2013) raised a unique E-Governance Era question: "should tweets directed at proposed federal agency regulations be included in the record?" In addition, determining which comments are subject to official consideration may require some further qualifications. The qualifying distinctions can be limited by incorporating remarks through officially sanctioned channels, such as comments on recommended agency rule changes though corresponding official means affiliated with the online Federal Register. Fortier (2000, p. 459) commented, "through computer networking, the mass of information, rather than its scarcity, often becomes problematic." Organizations need to be prepared to manage flows of information. Today, virtually anyone may share comments regarding topics of interest from anywhere in the world as long as they are within reach of the technological means to do. Computers and handheld mobile devices have become an increasingly popular way in which individuals communicate via any number of Internet platforms. In relation, comments regarding a wide range of societal topics can be expressed directly via e-mail, message boards, blogs and social media networks. This seemingly endless stream of comments regarding any number of private sector and public sector topics through multiple modern communications means may result in an information overload to some extent. Social media networks and crowdsourcing are two examples of Web 2.0 technologies that will be expanded on further as they relate to the potential impact to contribute to citizen participation.

A vast array of innovations has been generated since the advent of the Internet. Many of the recent generation of innovation attributed to Web 2.0 technologies, such as social media networks, have been less applicable in directing activities related to service delivery to citizens and are presently better constituted to facilitate information dissemination. Citizens can utilize social media networks to register opinions directly with government regarding any number of issues. The communication flow from government to citizens via social media networks can facilitate the dissemination of information in all manner of areas, including being used for emergency management alerts, upcoming scheduled public meetings or even informing citizens of scheduled public auctions (https://twitter.com/usagov). The usage of social media networks in the case of emergency management alerts provides a digital means in which management can be coordinated by public sector entities at all levels of government to provide an aggregate source of helpful information. For example, during Hurricane Sandy in 2012, social media networks served as one of many digital methods that were utilized by federal, state and local government entities to disseminate important updated emergency management information to citizens in affected areas. This includes coordinating information flows from federal agencies such as FEMA with state/local government in New Jersey, New York and Connecticut (https://twitter.com/fema and www.fema.gov/news-release/2012/11/29/follow-fema-twitter). Again, it continues to be important to recognize that due to the existence of the digital divide, a more universally tenable diverse communication system is more advantageous to better ensure a wider target audience will receive information. However important it is to maintain diversity in means that allows for system cohabitation of traditional and digital deliberative tools, the potential for the usage of Web 2.0 technologies such as social media networks for information dissemination should not be ignored.

It is important to recognize that social media networking is far from limited to citizen–government two-way dialogue. There are multiple relationships that can be facilitated through this version of Web 2.0 technology. This includes that social media networks are able to involve citizen-to-citizen and citizen-to-businesses dialogue that may be capable of affecting long-term change to the government system based on resulting actions. In relation, Web 2.0 technology supporting this type of social media network dialogue may be used in a more organic way in which citizens communicate with one another to offer support to those in need or to express dismay with government. In this sense, citizens can use social media networks to provide a digital forum for like-minded voices on a global level and to attract media attention to a cause. Social media network communication can also allow citizens to organize a political rally at a predetermined location, as has been the case with a number of recent movements organized by the public through electronic means. This includes any number of citizen efforts electronically supported through social media networks in the United States, like Twitter's role in the Occupy Wall Street movement in 2011 (https://twitter.com/OccupyWallSt). Social media network tools, whether applied in a private or public sector setting, are also capable of creating a virtual community that can cultivate a sense of belonging and encourage future interactions between system actors. This is evidenced by any number of social media network coordinated events, such as those associated with live interactions between communities of people during televised events ranging from presidential debates to season finales of a popular television show. The capacity for Web 2.0 technologies to create a virtual community whose collective participation may be organized in the hopes of affecting change cannot be overstated. Social media network's role in modern society has continued to expand since its inception in the mid-2000s; it has experienced a rapid proliferation on a societal level in a private–public sector capacity. The development and nurturing of virtual communities through Web 2.0 technology means such as social media networks is a modern element associated with the E-Governance Era that deserves recognition and continued consideration regarding the potential impact in strengthening the deliberative democracy framework.

The application of such Web 2.0 technologies may raise a number of concerns regarding the potential to directly impact the political system in a meaningful way. This includes the dangers associated with hollow participation through social media network tools in which meaningful citizen–government discourse is supplanted by vapid commentary or uninspiring feedback strictly limited to "liking" or "disliking" a government service or entity. Providing digital access to government without citizens' having any intentions to utilize these means to engage in meaningful dialogue for purposes such as addressing real concerns within the political arena will be insufficient unto itself to strengthen the deliberative framework. To enact changes consistent with the expectations associated with this framework, there must be a willing citizenry to engage in meaningful dialogue with government though technologically innovation means. In addition, there may be government-centered social media network limitations for collaboration if the provision of a virtual forum to facilitate citizen–government dialogue is done so without the intention to utilize that feedback. In this scenario, the usage of social media networks may create a proverbial digital soap box in which citizens provide input regarding government activities that go largely, or completely, unused. Whether this is intentional is largely inconsequential. This can degrade, instead of strengthening and nurturing, trust in citizen–government relationships while also diminishing perceptions of government legitimacy. It is important that there is some link between citizen efforts to provide deliberative input through social media networks intended to affect changes to the system and a corresponding pursuit by government toward the purpose of engaging in effective two-way interactions that could culminate in some form of change. Authentic citizen participation through a social media network requires the provision of interactive means to be coupled with the intention that feedback derived from dialogue will potentially be able to affect the political system in the future in some way. This is not to say that all feedback derived from citizen–government dialogue is able to affect the political system, as this would be both an unrealistic and unwieldy proposition. The expectation that collaborative discourse is capable of driving changes to government serves as standard guiding the usage of technological innovation in the public sector during the E-Governance Era. The usage of applicable technological innovation such as social media networks could be utilized to further cultivate meaningful relationships between citizens and government by increasing access and mutual interaction. This reality associated with this aspect of social media networks has yet to be fully explored, but the interactivity resulting from increased accessibility has potential within the context of deliberative democracy.

The levels of accessibility to government created through the applications of first-wave and Web 2.0 technological innovations are unprecedented in the E-Governance Era. In relation, open innovation is a private sector technique that seems to have great relevance in public sector deliberative endeavors related to E-Governance. Although the full impact of Web 2.0 technologies on citizen participation has yet to be fully determined, there are some forms of this generation of technology that have proven quite compelling thus far. This is especially true as it relates to the usage of technological innovation associated with crowdsourcing, which can be designed to support authentic citizen participation in which outcomes derived from interactions are intended to affect real changes within the political system. The open innovation technique referred to as *crowdsourcing* is another modern electronic phenomenon. Crowdsourcing has more recently been growing in relevancy as a means in which to facilitate citizen–government interactions and its potential role within the digital deliberative democracy framework deserves some additional attention. It is important to identify crowdsourcing's conceptual motivation for digitally expanding networks to collectively construct solutions and to determine basic guidelines for how crowdsourcing can be utilized to contribute to authentic citizen participation. Like many emerging Web 2.0 innovations, the full potential for crowdsourcing is largely undetermined in the E-Governance Era. However, the potential of crowdsourcing to contribute to authentic citizen participation by allowing for government to electronically engage the public in collective problem-solving efforts is deserved of great consideration moving forward. Doing so can strengthen the overall deliberative democracy framework by further encouraging meaningful digital participative means capable of affecting change.

The concept of crowdsourcing is relatively new to the political system, even within the 25 years or so since the advent of the E-Governance Era. This newly emerging technological endeavor reflects how innovations are utilized by government to consistently work toward achieving important expectations within the framework for deliberative democracy. Crowdsourcing is one of many means available within the E-Governance Era capable of supporting meaningful citizen–government dialogue events. Technological advancements have allowed for the development of open innovation means such as digital crowdsourcing to be incorporated into the deliberative democracy framework. Highlighting how *crowdsourcing* is defined and noting the conceptual methodology utilized to achieve deliberative goals through the modern era innovation of crowdsourcing merits further discussion here. The crowdsourcing literature provides a conceptual link for using technological innovation to broaden network participation in the hopes of generating unique perspectives that can contribute to societal problem solving.

The term *crowdsourcing* can be originally traced back to Howe (2006), who is oft credited with coining the phrase. He expands on the role of using technological innovation within networks for collective problem solving. Howe (2006, sec. 3, para. 6) explained that "the most efficient networks are those that link to the broadest range of information, knowledge, and experience." Howe (2006) noted that the continued advancements in communication technology has reduced the costs of participating in some instances, creating a more inclusive participative environment with a more level playing field between amateurs and professionals. Howe (2008, p. 14) added that "crowdsourcing capitalizes on the deeply social nature of the human species" in which technological innovation is utilized for cooperative endeavors to generate insight derived from "online communities" to help solve problems. Lebraty and Lobre-Lebraty (2013, p. 17) built on this ideal by stating, "crowdsourcing is the externalization by an organization, via an application using the Internet protocol, of an activity to a large number of individuals whose identities are most often anonymous." Brabham (2012, p. 307) explained, "crowdsourcing is an emerging problem-solving model that leverages the collective intelligence of online communities for specific purposes." Isaacson (2014, p. 261) noted that the Internet can be utilized to encourage participation through "a networked commons, a place where innovations could be crowdsourced and open-source" while simultaneously recognizing the potential impact of the digital divide in limiting online participation only to those individuals with access to and understanding of technology. Murphy (2015) added that although online crowdsourcing is useful in generating ideas derived from two-way communication processes it is "not a stand-alone tool." Brabham (2012, p. 308) explained, "new online participatory arrangements, such as crowdsourcing, hold the potential to improve government process by complementing traditional, face-to-face public participation methods." Mergel (2011, p. 6) noted that for crowdsourcing endeavors, "the focus is on innovation, creativity and the generation of new ideas from stakeholders and/or subject matter experts." The practical applications for E-Governance usage of crowdsourcing could be to generate ideas from citizens, which government can then apply to influence the shaping of public policy development and the rule-making process for agencies (Medici, 2013). Overall, it is helpful to consider that crowdsourcing for E-Governance applies technological innovation intended to facilitate digital network participation between citizens and government toward the purpose of generating non-anonymous collective solutions capable of solving pre-identified problems. The usage of technology in crowdsourcing endeavors is capable of expanding communication networks by providing means allowing for the inclusion of digital participants that can contribute to the problem-solving process. However, the digital divide can limit crowdsourcing's ability to achieve collective intelligence-based solutions derived from full participation. Crowdsourcing efforts represent an application of technology to expand network participation by supplementing sources of input derived via modern era electronic innovations to determine solutions based on collective intelligence. As such, it will be helpful to further expand on what constitutes collective intelligence as it relates to crowdsourcing efforts.

E-Governance crowdsourcing is a form of open innovation in which modern digital means are used to facilitate citizen participation intended to generate collective intelligence, which contributes to government problem solving. There are a number of conceptualizations that are applicable to the type of group-based knowledge collected through crowdsourcing that includes terms such as *collective intelligence* (Levy, 1997; Luft, 2010; Howe, 2006; Howe, 2008; Tamosiunaite & Balezentis, 2013). Surowiecki (2004) referred to this type of knowledge as *collective wisdom*, which is derived from actively mining group intelligence. Tamosiunaite and Balezentis (2013, p. 419), in discussing the role of technology in collective intelligence (CI), observed, "CI does not form itself: a certain technology is necessary to form the CI." Tamosiunaite and Balezentis (2013, p. 427) noted that "collective intelligence is an artificial form of intelligence, which exists only organized purposefully." There may be diverse technologies that are more applicable toward different collective intelligence–gathering processes representing different goals and problem sources (Tamosiunaite & Balezentis, 2013). Nguyen and Wagner (2014) recognized that collective intelligence can be a derivative of cooperation and competition in which either focus can be utilized to motivate group participation. Surowiecki (2004, p. 29) noted that the logic of this type of participation is based on the belief that "generating a diverse set of possible solutions isn't enough. The crowd also has to be able to distinguish the good solutions from the bad." Levy (1997, p. 13) explained that cyberspace cooperation can yield collective intelligence, which can be defined as "a form of universally distributed intelligence, constantly enhanced, coordinated in real time, and resulting in the effective mobilization of skills." Luft (2010, p. 1570) stated that collective intelligence is based on "knowledge gained from observing the behavior of many independent actors adapting to changing situations." Here, crowdsourcing group dynamics for E-Governance involve digital civic engagement between multiple parties focused on collectively developing solutions to problems. Adaptability is important because the environment in which governing occurs is constantly changing and responsible government must be able to adapt in kind by developing equally responsive solutions capable of addressing an identified problem. As applied to crowdsourcing, collective intelligence is derived from a process with cooperative and competitive components, which can also include a level of universal responsibility of all participants to assess solution feasibility from among the pool of choices. Generating solutions to policy problems through crowdsourcing links the benefits of collectivized citizen participation with modern technological means utilized to create a broader network. The broader digital network is capable of providing more diverse levels of insight by expanding the scope of participants toward generating collective intelligence used in problem-solving endeavors. Open innovation efforts by government such as crowdsourcing is rooted in the belief that increased access to multiple sources of ideas can considerably expand the knowledge base during the process of formulating solutions to identified problems. Crowdsourcing can be a useful tool in the E-Governance Era in which online citizen participation can be a contributing factor in solution generating public sector efforts to address important problems.

The purpose of crowdsourcing in the context of E-Governance is to provide digital means allowing for citizens to participate in problem-solving endeavors put forth by government. There is some importance in further determining what constitutes the crowd participating in this digital deliberative means, the logic associated with utilizing groups to generate solutions to government problems and how crowdsourcing endeavors are constructed to best achieve collective intelligence. The literature provides additional insight of the expectations associated with these elements of crowdsourcing participation that are applicable to E-Governance. This includes further highlighting the logic behind incorporating collective intelligence derived from digital participation to solve problems, the importance of public sector efforts to communicate with citizens to collect knowledge that originates from a different origin point and issues that may diminish the integrity of solutions generated through crowdsourcing. Juni and Eckstein (2015, p. 1) reflected that collective wisdom is sought by problem solvers because it is believed that "group decisions typically outperform individual decisions." Piezunka and Dahlander (2015, p. 56) observed that "soliciting suggestions is a form of distant search, since it allows organizations to tap into knowledge that may not reside within their organizational boundaries." In addition, it is important that crowdsourcing processes should be reflective of efforts to ensure crowd diversity to generate heterogeneous solutions and ideas which may not otherwise be obtained from the homogenous entity of origin (Stieger et al., 2012). The freedom for participant groups to be able to creatively generate possible solutions without restrictive oversight from crowdsourcers is also important to ensure the legitimacy of the problem solving process (Stieger et al., 2012). Stieger et al. (2012, p. 47) noted, "crowdsourcing requires the collaboration of larger numbers of people." Stieger et al. (2012, p. 65) added that success in crowdsourcing is achieved in part by creating "a suitable process to encourage and guide employees in their participation." Murphy (2015, pp. 49–50) discussed that online crowdsourcing is beneficial in that it provides "direct and efficient two-way communication" and that "to make a better decision, you follow a process of collecting ideas and suggestions from a large group of people." Mergel (2011, p. 6) provided helpful insight regarding the importance that the crowd-sourcing process should have an identifiable structure guiding expectations for participation, which are summarized in Table 7.1.

Providing an identifiable process for crowdsourcing can help to diffuse confusion regarding participation criteria and allows for evidence of

Table 7.1 Crowdsourcing: Procedural Guidelines

Procedural Guidelines
State the problem that is being crowdsourced without the usage of unnecessarily complex technical or industry jargon.
Ensure that time limits are established, creating a window for participation.
Develop incentives to encourage participation (e.g., monetary prize, publication of winners in an online forum/traditional newsletter, etc.).
Articulate clearly the crowdsourcing processes associated with evaluating "winning" solutions.
Publically announce the source responsible for generating the winning solution and why this solution was selected.
Show evidence of the winning solution being implemented and positive effects resulting from its usage.

Source: Mergel, 2011.

outcomes derived from crowdsourcing to be highlighted publically. However, the provision of an identifiable process does not mean that there may not be issues of concern associated with crowdsourcing. In relation, the sizeable influx of new suggestions derived from crowdsourcing to generate solutions from outside of the organization may create a number of processing concerns including those associated with the paradoxical nature of "crowding" (Piezunka & Dahlander, 2015). Piezunka and Dahlander (2015) discussed that the substantial influx of suggestions from crowdsourcing may create logistical limitations, which actually cause the organization to process familiar knowledge from common sources before considerations of unfamiliar distant knowledge. Piezunka and Dahlander (2015) posited that reliance on input from a small external group, establishing set ratio goals for usage of a combination of distant and close knowledge and developing means that allow for distant knowledge to be prioritized during the review process may help to diffuse negative effects of crowding on crowdsourcing processes. The spirit of crowdsourcing can be upheld through utilizing such solutions to better facilitate the assessment and incorporation of distant knowledge generated by this digital design. Mergel (2011, p. 6) noted that crowdsourcing dialogue could be expanded to include the opportunity for those submitting solutions "to provide additional information on how their idea can be executed, and every participant can comment on all other submitted ideas."

For E-Governance, crowdsourcing utilizes the Internet to create digital bridges in order to expand the participation network in which interested parties can contribute electronically in public sector problem-solving events. Crowdsourcing is founded on the belief that groups are better equipped in some cases than individuals to determine solutions to societal challenges because of their ability to generate collective intelligence from participants contributing to cooperative problem solving. Here, collective intelligence can be considered preferable to individual knowledge in its ability to better address complex societal problems. The use of digital bridges to include outside sources of knowledge that would not otherwise have been integrated into the problem-solving process can contribute to better ensuring diversity in the constitution of the group participating when gathering collective intelligence during crowdsourcing. Crowdsourcing should be open to all interested parties that seek to contribute to helping solve problem(s). In addition, participation should be cyclical in nature in which success/failure in submitting the winning solution is not prohibitive to contributing in future crowdsourcing events. In fact, the continued participation may breed familiarity with the process itself and develop a comfort level in tailoring winning solutions to better address identified problems. In this sense, crowdsourcing may benefit from the adoption of deliberative democracy expectations calling for the process to be open and cyclical in nature. The construction of a deliberative digital forum without restrictive oversight by the crowdsourcing host can contribute to the goal of ensuring that more genuine, unfettered collective intelligence is gathered. It is important to acknowledge that group solutions based on collective intelligence are not infallible and should not wholly replace decisions made by individuals within the political system. For example, an individual may be more qualified in some circumstances than a group (and visa versa) dependent upon the parties involved and the policy issue to be addressed. However, collective intelligence derived from crowd-sourcing endeavors can prove to be a very instrumental tool within the context of digital deliberative democracy. Efforts to develop crowdsourcing opportunities can add another layer to the modern deliberative framework and provide access to increased sources of knowledge that can contribute to informed decision making.

It is also important to recognize that the digital divide relegates crowd-sourcing to one of many supplemental discursive means and that traditional means should not be wholly supplanted by this digital measure. Digital and traditional means both still maintain a place in their ability to contribute to meaningful citizen participation within the deliberative democracy frame-work. Crowdsourcing is focused on end-stage problem solving in which government provides an issue and groups generate the best possible solutions reflecting the end results of collective intelligence. This is not to say that crowdsourcing is required to be a standalone means because it may be well suited to coupling with other preliminary-stage digital and traditional participatory means. For example, it may be beneficial for government to interact with citizens to assist in identifying societal problems through other online means, such as deliberative polls, electronic surveys, digital sugges-tion boxes or digital town hall meetings. It is also possible to utilize more technically sophisticated electronic means to identify societal problems that are of concern to citizens, such as tracking issues of importance posted though social media networks and determining what topics are important by calculating website hits by visitors. Traditional means that are beneficial in problem identification include on-site town hall meetings and traditional surveys sent though the postal system. Therefore, multiple digital and tra-ditional deliberative tools may be used in conjuncture to create a broader architecture capable of facilitating deliberative participation that is more inclusive during the problem-identification stage. Once problems have been identified through initial stage digital and traditional deliberative means, crowdsourcing can then conceivably serve as the next step in the progression in which interested parties contribute to solving the identified problem. As a note, the process of crowdsourcing should endeavor to assuage the negative impact of groupthink, which would diminish overall creativity in developing solutions and devalue the practical usefulness of solutions resulting from collective intelligence derived under groupthink conditions.

In sum, the overall framework of deliberative democracy in the E-Governance Era can be strengthened by the continued application of both traditional and digital means to identify, and ultimately solve, problems. In relation, crowdsourcing seeks to leverage digital means to expand the scope of parti-cipants to include a wider range of perspectives in which collective intelligence can be used to generate solutions to previously identified governmental problems. Processes like crowdsourcing use technological innovation to expand the scope of participants to include those outside of the organization and can create an influx of insightful new perspectives that can be used for problem solving. Crowdsourcing is an attempt to cast a wider conceptual net in which to access a more diverse perspective of interests that extends outside of the original organization or group. The motivations in which crowdsourcing was founded are based on collectively determining solutions to identified problems and serves to provide context for its continued use in citizen–government interactions. Specifically, this form of open innovation can contribute to the deliberative framework by providing digital authentic citizen participation means in which collective intelligence can be generated to help guide government problem solving efforts. Crowdsourcing can allow government to actively generate adaptable solutions through a more inclusive process by utilizing citizen driven collective intelligence directed toward open innovation problem-solving endeavors. Crowdsourcing serves as just one of many digital means capable of facilitating authentic citizen participation in the E-Governance Era. Crowdsourcing is one such digital participatory means that has great potential for contributing to the deliberative democracy framework in the E-Governance Era.

Although crowdsourcing is still relatively new within the context of the E-Governance Era, there have been a number of encouraging examples in recent years that have shown great potential in meeting the deliberative expectations that government provide means in which to facilitate authentic citizen participation. Crowdsourcing has merit for various components of government and when problem-solving events are applicable for multiple topics of interest affecting the political system. Crowdsourcing has begun to emerge as a means within the E-Governance Era to collectively develop solutions to problems associated with a wide range of policy issues identified by government and this dynamic is well represented through the public sector website Challenge.gov (www.challenge.gov/list/). Challenge.gov is a government website in which public sector entities advertise crowdsourcing contests and interested parties can participate electronically by providing solutions to problems identified by government. The concept of collective intelligence in this government-crowdsourcing endeavor contributes to providing the groundwork guiding this process and leads to what is ultimately the selection of the winning solution(s) identified through digital participation. The Memorandum on Transparency and Open Government (President Barack Obama, 2009) was an early stage initiative developed at the outset of President Obama's administration which begun to pave the way for what would become Challenge.gov (https://obamawhitehouse.archives.gov/the-press-office/2015/11/16/memorandum-transparency-and-open-government). The president's memo called for "executive departments and agencies" to work toward creating an open government that was more "transparent, participatory and collaborative." On December 8, 2009, the director of the Office of Management and Budget (OMB), Peter R. Orszag, issued a corresponding memo calling for governmental executive departments and agencies to set forth specifications for an "Open Government Initiative" consistent with President Obama's directive to promote greater levels of "transparency, participation and collaboration" (Orszag, 2009). Section 3, subsection *d* of the memo, which is entitled "Create and Institutionalize a Culture of Open Government," set the foundation for what would later become the Challenge.gov initiative by requiring action based on the following statement as highlighted in Box 7.1.

Box 7.1. OMB: Open Government Directive memo

Within 90 days, the Deputy Director for Management at OMB will issue, through separate guidance or as part of any planned comprehensive management guidance, a framework for how agencies can use challenges, prizes, and other incentive-backed strategies to find innovative or cost-effective solutions to improving open government.

https://www.treasury.gov/open/Documents/m10-06.pdf

This subsection within the OMB memo set forth the conceptual foundation in which Challenge.gov was based on. Here, the memo's language allowed for the conceptualization of crowdsourcing problems collectively through electronic means in order obtain access to innovative solutions to problems identified by government to become reality. The Challenge.gov website was established in 2010 and has since greatly contributed to providing solutions derived from collective intelligence for a plethora of digital government problem-solving endeavors through crowdsourcing contests. During the initial years of operation, Challenge.gov contributed various essentials associated with the crowdsourcing process as highlighted in Box 7.2.

Box 7.2 Challenge.gov Essentials

1   640+ competitions launched
2   More than $200 million awarded in prizes
3   250,000+ solvers participated
4   More than 4.5 million site visits
5   Visitors from every country around the globe
6   Participants from every state in the USA

https://www.challenge.gov/about/

In relation, the following information highlights key outcomes and processes associated with crowdsourcing participation through Challenge.gov between 2010 and 2015:

> Between September 2010 and December 2015, more than 80 federal agencies ran 640+ challenge and prize competitions. The use of this tool to drive innovation and collaboration with citizens continues to expand.
>
> The platform is available at no cost to all federal agencies to help them list their challenge and prize competitions and learn how to engage the public through this innovative approach.
>
> (Challenge.gov, 2016c)

A significant volume of crowdsourced contests have been facilitated through Challenge.gov since its inception in 2010 and these digitally facilitated events provided solutions to address policy topics for agencies such as the National Aeronautics and Space Administration, Department of Health and Human Services, Department of Agriculture, Department of Energy, National Park Service, Department of Education, Internal Revenue Service, Department of Defense, Department of State, Environmental Protection Agency and the Social Security Administration. There are also examples initiated by other government entities such as the Congressional App Challenge (Challenge. gov, 2016b), which was "a congressional coding challenge for U.S. High School Students." An interesting component associated with the contests issued by the government at Challenge.gov is the vast array of policy topics derived from different government entities and the inclusive nature in which contests are provided for multiple ages, interests and skill sets. For example, there are a number of crowdsourcing contests that are intended for high-school-age students such as the aforementioned "Congressional App Challenge" offered by the U.S. House of Representatives. There is a wide array of contests reflecting diversity in requirements for participation (i.e., age, membership in organization/entity, citizenship, etc.) in which solutions are sought for complex technical, political and social problems provided by government.

According to Challenge.gov, interested parties can register via the crowdsourcing website at no cost while the only requirement guiding registration is the creation of a username and the provision on an e-mail account. There are a number of ways in which interested parties can search available crowdsourcing contests via the Challenge.gov website, such as typing in information via the search menu and by utilizing the interactive "Sort" option in which searches can be narrowed through any number of the following criteria: "Agency Search," "Prize Amount Range: Prize Start From to Prize End To," "Challenge Type: Software/Apps, Ideas, Designs, Scientific/ Engineering, Multimedia (photo, video, poster), Other." Within this Sort option is a "Sort By" tab in which searches can be further filtered based on: "Newest Challenge, Submission Date-Latest, Submission Date-Oldest, Open-Ending Soonest, Open-Ending Latest, Prize–High to Low, Prize–Low to High." The Challenge.gov website also provides a user-friendly, visually pleasing homepage in which interested parties may click on "Menu Options" to learn more details about a wide variety crowdsourcing competitions. The selection from the available competitions listed within the Menu Options leads an interested party to a supplemental webpage with additional information related to participation in this crowdsourcing contest. This includes the crowdsourcing event entitled "2016 CDFI Fund Prize Competition" in which the identifying information guiding participation is summarized in Table 7.2.

There are also a number of interactive tools available to participants such as a discussion threads to facilitate questions pertaining to the contest, tabs linking to social media networks (e.g., Facebook, Twitter, etc.), means to receive information by subscribing to RSS feeds and an e-mail option. The Challenge.gov website represents the application of democratic principles of

Table 7.2 Participation Details and Information 2016 CDFI Fund Prize Competition

Participation Details	Information
The problem to be solved	New ways to increase CDFI Investments in Underserved Rural Communities
What agency posted the event	The U.S. Department of the Treasury
Evaluation grids with criteria that will be used by the judges to select winners	Evaluation criteria for idea that has been implemented within two years (Location, certified CDFI or partnership with a CDFI, Implementation, Depth of Need, Design, Scalability or Replicability, Outcomes, Innovativeness, Community Involvement and Persistent Poverty)
	Evaluation criteria for idea that has not been implemented (Location, Certified CDFI or Partnership with a CDFI, Depth of Need, Design, Scalability or Replicability, Expected Outcomes, Innovativeness, Expertise, Community Involvement and Persistent Poverty)
Submission dates outlining the window of participation	June 16th, 2016 1:30 pm EST to July 29th, 2016 5 pm EST
Judging dates	August 3rd, 2016 through August 31st, 2016
Expected prize money	Up to $1,000,000 that will be allocated to the number of winners (approximately 4)
Date in which the winners will be announced	September 30th, 2016

Source: Challenge.gov (2016a) 2016 CDFI Fund Prize Competition located at https://www.challenge.gov/challenge/2016-cdfi-fund-prize-competition/.

transparency and openness which serves as further motivation for crowd-sourcing solutions to government problems through digital participation. The Challenge.gov website will likely continue to be very relevant in the future because of its ability to contribute to strengthening the deliberative democracy framework by providing digital means to facilitate authentic participation between citizens and government.

The trend of growth in innovations has continued in recent years in which the list of available digital tools that may be applicable to E-Governance has expanded from initial stage developments to include considerations of Web 2.0 technologies. As is the case with all new emerging innovations that require further exploration, usage and refinement, the full significance of Web 2.0 technologies in modern governance is still yet to be determined. Assessing the viability of emerging 2.0 technologies in governance, such as social media networks, can be especially challenging given the continued advancements in which electronic innovations are seemingly being replaced by newer versions at a rapid rate in some cases. For example, the rapid turnover rate for what constitutes a popular social media app may cause difficulty when determining if such means would serve as viable options for E-Governance. Sometimes the potentially high replacement tendency for innovation is a variable rendering the study of rapidly emerging technologies very mercurial in which the window of opportunity is relatively small. This may ultimately render the relevance of emerging technologies that are subject to potentially high turnover rates to be interpreted as having an innovative half-life whose wide-scale usage in society may likely quickly dissipate. It is sometimes difficult to immediately determine the effectiveness of emerging technologies when applied to E-Governance especially if the usage of said technology has a finite timeframe in which its application is replaced by newer, seemingly more attractive innovations. In cases such as this, the application of an emerging innovation in E-Governance may not provide sufficient time to determine its effectiveness, strengths, weaknesses, and wide-scale societal impacts before the expectations for a newer technology to be applied occurs. The longer a technology is utilized in society and continues to gain relevance as it proliferates the private and public sector, the stronger the consideration for its application in E-Governance seems plausible. This in part is derived from a number of considerations for use validity associated with identifying a broadly proven societal track record of successful application, determining the fiscal viability of an established technology to assuage budget stress and gauging the growing demands stemming from the political environment for government to incorporate its function on a wider scale. Therefore, it is important to take a somewhat measured and patient approach to the application of emerging technological innovation, especially when it applies to the whole-of-government approach. It is not implied that government should not endeavor to be on the cutting edge of innovation—both in its development and application. However, a tempered approach to the application of popular technologies like social media apps may be most prudent to avoid having to constantly adjust and readjust government applications to meet the quickly shifting nature of such innovations on the vast societal scale. Acquiescing to rapidly shifting public demands for use of trendy and popular social media tools for E-Governance should be resisted if possible in order for that tool to be properly vetted before considering its application on a broad scale. If the growing demand is too significant to stall its immediate application in governance for any number of reasons, political or otherwise, then it is possible to consider applying the technology on a trial basis. This could seemingly allow for the public desire for this emerging technology to be utilized by government to be sated while simultaneously creating a small trial session that can help to better determine if its applicability on a broader scale may warranted at a later time. The logistical, societal and fiscal successes associated with established innovations lends further credence to a measured overall E-Governance schema that seeks to apply more proven means while being cautious of utilizing the technological "flavor of the month." This can be especially important on the federal scale in which the whole of government is not likely able to constantly readjust to apply each new innovation to fulfill a wide range of responsibilities. However, it would be irresponsible to simply ignore the continued rapid advancements in innovations that may potentially play a meaningful role in E-Governance that are associated with newly developing Web 2.0 technologies. The applicability of Web 2.0 technologies supporting communication, such as social media and crowdsourcing, in E-Governance has undeniably become ever more relevant in recent years. Despite the somewhat volatile nature of shifting preferences of Web 2.0 technologies associated with social media, which can often reflect a rapid turnover rate more representative of a technology-based half-life, these conceptualizations deserve consideration for the role in contributing to the deliberative democracy framework. The potential of two Web 2.0 manifestations, social media networks and crowdsourcing, to contribute to citizen–government deliberative expectations are deserved of continued exploration in the future.

It is important to reiterate the role that political context plays as it relates to the decision to utilize technological innovation associated with E-Governance. There often needs to be a convergence of a number of contributing factors, including a large enough demand for innovative change in government stemming from a technologically savvy citizen base, the existence of proven applicable technologies that would enhance public sector goal achievement and the will of government to pursue the adoption of said innovations. There are also contextual considerations associated with the budgeting environment that will play a role in determining whether the usage of technological innovation associated with E-Governance will be fiscally sustainable. The political contexts that affect the expectations for the application of innovative technologies have a broad scope of focus in the E-Governance Era. This includes maintaining relevance for each of the branches of government at all levels of the federal system and across a considerable spectrum of government activities. The usage of technological innovation in public administration can be applied toward collaborative endeavors facilitating participation between citizens and government, which are more reflective of the expectations associated with a deliberative democracy framework. The potential applicability of Web 2.0 technologies is related to previous discussions associated with the deliberative democracy framework that utilizes innovation to facilitate a number of citizen–government interactions for the purposes of civic engagement.

The digital tools associated with Web 2.0 technologies, such as social media networks and crowdsourcing, add to the plethora of preexisting established first-wave technologies associated with ICTs that can contribute to a higher number of overall means available within the overarching deliberative democracy framework. Thus far, social media network technology is still somewhat limited in scope within the deliberative framework and is not without some potential pitfalls in its application in governance. Social media networks allow for two-way citizen–government communication flows generally more suited for information dissemination while presently providing less capacity to realistically facilitate meaningful service delivery associated with E-Government or to support authentic citizen participation associated with E-Governance. An area of interest in the future is whether Web 2.0 technologies related to social media networks will be more instrumental in a wider range of citizen–government activities associated with E-Government-based service delivery or with E-Governance-related deliberative events. This includes the possibility of utilizing social media networks to facilitate the delivery of online service to the public like renewing a driver's license, filing taxes or voting in elections. Government crowdsourcing efforts such as Challenge.gov are designed to generate solutions based on collective intelligence derived from digital deliberation. In this sense, collective intelligence derived from participation via digital bridges contributes a unique source of insight used for solving predetermined government problems. Although relatively new to the digital deliberative democracy framework, crowdsourcing measures have shown great promise to promote cooperative problem solving through electronic interactive events. It is also important to continue to recognize the role that the digital divide may have in limiting universal access to participation through Web 2.0 technologies. Here, participation through Web 2.0 technologies occurs if parties have interest in using the electronic means, knowledge of how to utilize innovations and access to the technology required to facilitate digital participation. As such, traditional means and digital means should continue to coexist within the deliberative democracy framework in the E-Governance Era in order to provide diversity in means supporting authentic citizen participation.

References

Andriole, S. J. (2010) Business impact of Web 2.0 technologies. *Communications of the ACM*, 53(12): 67–79. doi: 10.1145/1859204.1859225.

Bolivar, M. P. R. (2015) The influence of political factors in policymakers' perceptions on the implementation of Web 2.0 technologies for citizen participation and knowledge sharing in public sector delivery. *Information Polity*, 20(2/3): 199–220.

Brabham, D. C. (2012) Motivations for participation in a crowdsourcing application to improve public engagement in transit planning. *Journal of Applied Communication Research*, 40(3): 307–328. doi: 10.1080/00909882.2012.693940.

Challenge.gov. (2016a). 2016 CDFI fund prize competition posted by Department of the Treasury. Retrieved from www.challenge.gov/challenge/2016-cdfi-fund-prize-competition/.

Challenge.gov. (2016b). Congressional app challenge-MA-07-Rep. Capuano. Retrieved from www.challenge.gov/challenge/congressional-app-challenge-ma-07-rep-capuano/.

Challenge.gov. (2016c). About Challenge.gov. Retrieved from www.challenge.gov/about/.

Fortier, F. (2000) Virtual communities, real struggles: Seeking alternatives for democratic networking. In M. Gurstein (ed.), *Community informatics: Enabling communities with information and communications technologies* (pp. 446–469). Hershey, PA: IGI Global.

Howe, J. (2006) The rise of crowdsourcing. *Wired Magazine*. Retrieved from www.wired.com/2006/06/crowds/.

Howe, J. (2008) *Crowdsourcing: Why the power of the crowd is driving the future of business*. New York: Crown Business.

Isaacson, W. (2014) *The innovators: How a group of hackers, geniuses and geeks created the digital revolution*. New York: Simon & Schuster.

Juni, M. Z., & Eckstein, M. P. (2015) Flexible human collective wisdom. *Journal of Experimental Psychology: Human Perception and Performance*, 41(6): 1588–1611. doi: 10.1037/xhp0000101.

Lebraty, J., & Lobre-Lebraty, K. (2013) *FOCUS series: Crowdsourcing: One step beyond*. Somerset, NJ: John Wiley & Sons. Retrieved from www.ebrary.com.

Levy, P. (1997) *Collective intelligence: Mankind's emerging world in cyberspace*. Cambridge, MA: Perseus Books.

Luft, H. S. (2010) Data and methods to facilitate delivery system reform: Harnessing collective intelligence to learn from positive deviance. *Health Services Research*, 45(5), 1570–1580. doi: 10.1111/j.1475-6773.2010.01148.x.

Medici, A. (2013) Policy-making may be next level of crowdsourcing. *Federal Times*, 49(10): 8.

Mergel, I. (2011) Crowdsourced ideas make participating in government cool again. *PA Times*, 34(4): 4–6.

Murphy, P. K. (2015) Communications gridlock? Try crowdsourcing. *Educational Leadership*, 72(9): 48–52.

Nelson, J., Christopher, A., & Mims, C. (2009) TPACK and Web 2.0: Transformation of teaching and learning. *TechTrends*, 53(5): 80–85.

Nguyen, T. B., & Wagner, F. (2014) Collective intelligent toolbox based on linked model framework. *Journal of Intelligent & Fuzzy Systems*, 27(2): 601–609. doi: 10.3233/IFS-131084.

Orszag, P. R. (2009) Director of the Office of Budget and Management. *Memorandum for the Heads of Executive Departments and Agencies*. Retrieved from www.whitehouse.gov/open/documents/open-government-directive.

Piezunka, H., & Dahlander, L. (2015) Distant search, narrow attention: How crowding alters organizations' filtering of suggestions in crowdsourcing. *Academy of Management Journal*, 58(3): 856–880. doi: 10.5465/amj.2012.0458.

President Barack Obama. (2009) Transparency and open government: Memorandum for the heads of executive departments and agencies. *Presidential Documents: United States Federal Register*, 74(15). Retrieved from www.gpo.gov/fdsys/pkg/FR-2009-01-26/pdf/E9-1777.pdf.

Sadaf, A., Newby, T. J., & Ertmer, P. A. (2012) Exploring factors that predict pre-service teachers' intentions to use Web 2.0 technologies using decomposed theory of planned behavior. *Journal of Research on Technology in Education (International Society for Technology in Education)*, 45(2): 171–196.

Schlozman, K. L., Verba, S., & Brady, H. E. (2010) Weapon of the strong? Participatory inequality and the internet. *Perspectives on Politics*, 8(2): 487–509. http://dx.doi.org/10.1017/S1537592710001210.

Stieger, D., Matzler, K., Chatterjee, S., & Ladstaetter-Fussenegger, F. (2012) Democratizing strategy: How crowdsourcing can be used for strategy dialogues. *California Management Review*, 54(4): 44–68. doi: 10.1525/cmr.2012.54.4.44.

Surowiecki, J. (2004) *The wisdom of crowds*. New York: Anchor Books.

Tamosiunaite, R., & Balezentis, A. (2013) How useful and possible collective intelligence technologies are in programming of public sector's decisions? *Socialines Technologijos*, 3(2): 415–431. Retrieved from http://search.proquest.com/docview/1509822013?accountid=32521.

Taylor, J. A. (2012) The information polity: Towards a two-speed future? *Information Polity: The International Journal of Government & Democracy in the Information Age*, 17(3/4): 227–237.

8 Modern Deliberative Democracy Means and Web 2.0 Technology

Suggestion Boxes, Deliberative Mini-Publics, Citizen Review Panels, Deliberative Polls and Public Meetings

The scope of means available within a deliberative democracy could include those that are supportive of more static, one-directional citizen input, such as suggestion boxes. In relation, the traditional suggestion box is a citizen participation means that may benefit from technology updates associated with modernization efforts prevalent in the E-Governance Era. It is important to develop an understanding of the expectations associated with who participates, possible motivations for participation and by which measures that participation is facilitated as it relates to suggestion box use in the E-Governance Era. A suggestion box can provide important insight from a range of different sources in the hopes of utilizing that feedback to improve the organization in some way. Opt (1998, p. 77) explained that "on an individual level, the box can provide a voice for subordinates or customers, and, on a collective level, it can provide feedback important for organizational survival." Suggestion boxes serve as a communication device that can be used to generate information associated with consumer preferences and employee satisfaction (Guiniven, 2000). For Lloyd (1999), participation means such as suggestion boxes are representative of "upward problem-solving" mechanisms. Lloyd (1999, p. 873) suggested that the three most important reasons motivating participation through suggestion boxes are that individuals are "frustrated with work process and wanted to change it," are seeking to "improve the success of the organization" and want to "save the organization some money." Suggestion boxes also have the capacity to motivate participation due to the prospect that prizes can be provided to the individual whose suggestion is applied within the organization ("The Old Suggestion Box," 2014). An individual's decision to participate through suggestion boxes could be based on the desire to effect positive change to the organization for altruistic purposes or participation could be rooted in more self-serving reasons reflecting an agenda focused on personal gain. Regardless of the motivational force behind suggestion box participation, the main goal of this effort is focused on generating bottom-up feedback that is capable of identifying changes that may contribute to improving the organization. The suggestion box as a participatory tool within a deliberative framework is applicable to situations in which government seeks input through applying technological innovation to facilitate citizen-consumer feedback with the hopes of yielding organizational and system improvements.

The suggestion box can be a means to facilitate bottom-up feedback to ascertain internal insight from within an organization that is representative of a traditional hierarchical structural dynamic. It is also a means by which to determine the opinions from sources of interest outside the organization such as the consumer. Therefore, a suggestion box is a participatory means in which organizational decision makers can generate individualized feedback from inside and outside an organization. Although suggestion boxes are generally used to determine bottom-up feedback from within or from outside an organization, these do not necessarily qualify as an "exclusionary device" preventing other points of interests from participating. Viewpoints can encompass a wide range of topics, including individual perceptions associated with the effectiveness of organizational standard operating procedures, fiscal components regarding spending decisions and the scope of responsibilities performed by the organization. Participatory means such as suggestion boxes can provide an opportunity for individuals to offer insight while allowing for decision makers to have access to alternate viewpoints on organizational activities. The ability of a governmental organization to obtain external feedback from citizen-consumers serves as the foundation in which the suggestion box technique is applicable within the deliberative democracy framework for the purposes of this discussion. A government entity can construct a suggestion box that utilizes traditional and electronic means to determine citizen-consumer feedback geared toward improving the organization. A traditional suggestion box allows for an individual to physically write down their opinions on tangible mediums such as paper and then submit those thoughts on topics geared toward improving the organization. The electronic version of the suggestion box is clearly missing the tangible submission of ideas written on paper and is instead facilitated through virtual interactions reflecting the same idea submittal concept. In this case, the medium used is less important than the intent behind the dialogue event in which government has the opportunity to obtain citizen feedback that may be used to guide organizational change.

When constructing suggestion boxes it may be helpful to consider that there may be some variance in regard to the level of anonymity employed through this participation means. As such, the duality of anonymity is an interesting component associated with suggestion box participation. The opinions can be submitted to a suggestion box, tangibly or digitally, in an anonymous fashion by individuals or publically in which participating individuals attach their personal information with the proposed recommendations. The choice associated with anonymity can better promote engagement with interested parties through suggestions boxes by attracting a wider array of potential participants. Individuals may prefer to make suggestions to an organization in an anonymous fashion for any number of reasons. In a traditional organizational setting that utilizes suggestion boxes to determine internal feedback, anonymity could be preferred for the discretion that is provided if an individual feels their potentially unfavorable input may result in backlash from bosses or coworkers. In relation, participation could be limited in some cases if external participants are also apprehensive of being subjected to backlash if they make an unfavorable suggestion or critique. On the other hand, individuals that participate with the hopes of receiving recognition like a plaque and/or fiscal reward may also be attracted to providing feedback via a suggestion box. For example, opinions can be submitted with identifying information to allow for the prospect of the receipt of rewards associated with what constitutes a "winning" suggestion that is to be implemented within the organization. The duality of anonymity is also relevant in online suggestion boxes in which IT departments may create a digital message board that allows for choice associated with disclosing whom submits suggestions ("The old suggestion box," 2014). The context of anonymity for suggestion boxes is subject to user preferences, which can either display or conceal a participant's identity.

The suggestion box can contribute to the strength and usefulness of a deliberative framework in a number of ways. For example, a key benefit associated with online suggestion boxes can be to expand the time frame of participation significantly. Traditional suggestion boxes within an organizational setting may be limited to on-site participation during regular hours of operation. However, online suggestion boxes can allow for this type of participation to occur asynchronously at any time during the day from virtually anywhere that has an Internet connection. This increases the participatory timeframe for individuals who may have previously been prevented from being able to contribute due to any number of real-world responsibilities that served as a barrier during regular hours of organizational operation. Suggestion boxes can ultimately contribute to enhancing the overall levels of means used to promote authentic citizen participation in modern government as well. This includes the important expectation for authentic citizen participation in which the inputs derived from participation are linked with verifiable outputs in governance to assist in further cementing legitimacy associated with civic engagement processes. Opt (1998) provided some interesting insight associated with competing myths surrounding suggestion boxes involving establishing the belief that input derived from participation is capable of positively affecting the organization vs. the perceptions that suggestion boxes are simply for show without providing meaningful opportunity to affect organizational change. Porter (1986, p. 76) observed that for organizational "visible dialogue" means such as suggestion boxes, "the critical factors in the success of the program appear to be the promptness of the responses, the patience displayed in the responses as comments and complaints repeat themselves, and the serious consideration of suggestions as demonstrated by visible changes." Here, the process of making visible the changes resulting from suggestion box input reinforces the importance of providing evidence that authentic citizen participation can affect changes to government within a deliberative democracy. The link between providing a consistent opportunity to contribute judgments and the importance of highlighting identifiable manifestations of the suggestions that affected change continues to maintain an integral role in authentic citizen participation means, including digital suggestion boxes.

In a large representative democracy such as the United States, it is not feasible to engage directly with all citizens to determine opinions regarding undertakings at all levels of governance. Therefore, it is important for government to continue to employ logistically manageable means in which citizens can participate in meaningful dialogue. Here, the concept of mini-publics contributes to the foundation for constructing deliberative means through which small groups of citizens can communicate in meaningful dialogue with government for a vast array of purposes. The focus of mini-publics is somewhat different than other forms of citizen–government dialogue tools in that the intent is to communicate with a small, predetermined target audience. Raisio and Carson (2014, p. 76) defined a *sector mini-public* as "a mini public assembled to represent a particular section of the population." Raisio and Carson (2014, p. 89) added that these designs are markedly qualified to "have the potential to bring forth the voice of marginalized sections of the population." Here, the mini-public is representative of an even smaller subsection of the overall population that may be more directly affected by policy efforts. Chambers (2009) noted that "abandoning the mass public in favor of mini-publics risks sending deliberative democracy on a path toward participatory elitism where citizens who participate in face-to-face deliberative initiatives (and only a small fraction do) have more democratic legitimacy than the mass electorate." Olsen and Trenz (2014, p. 117) explained that the concept of deliberative mini-public is generally untenable as an instrument capable of replacing "established forms of representative democracy," but has merit in completing complementary activities geared to "inform government about the distribution of votes and the direction of public policies." Olsen and Trenz (2014, p. 119) noted the importance of maintaining the view that "deliberative mini-publics are *part* of the democratic process." In the context of E-Governance-based deliberations, the mini-public itself is a small, subset of individuals selected by government from among the larger population to provide voice to those that are more directly affected by a specific government action or may not have otherwise participated in discursive events. This conceptualization can be especially informative when seeking to determine feedback from a specific group of citizens that may be affected by recommended policy changes. For example, a national deliberative open-ended survey may be used to question a group of citizens that is representative of the whole of society regarding proposed changes to the Affordable Care Act that was signed into law by President Obama in 2010. However, polling a mini-public composed of citizens that have signed up for this program through open enrollment can be utilized to determine feedback from those that will be most directly affected in the immediate future by recommended policy changes to the Affordable Care Act.

A mini-public may also be engaged to determine feedback from marginalized groups of citizens that may not have initially had the interest to participate of their own volition or may not have otherwise been afforded the opportunity to participate for any number of reasons. In marketing terms, the mini-public could be likened to some degree to a specialized focus group in that the deliberations are conducted with a predetermined group of individuals to generate feedback that can contribute to later actions. A mini-public can be engaged through any number of participatory means available within the deliberative framework. For example, a mini-public could be engaged through citizen review panels, surveys, deliberative polls or town hall meetings facilitated through digital means and traditional on-site means. An important observation here is to remember feedback mined from mini-public deliberations is not wholly representative of the public at large and that similarly feedback mined from deliberations with the public at large may not be wholly representative of the mini-public. This speaks to the importance of utilizing mini-public based deliberations as one means, among many, to engage in meaningful participation to provide a more accurate assessment of the pulse of citizens regarding governance. Instead of singling out one means in which mini-publics are engaged to obtain input in the deliberative process, it may be helpful to consider the larger role of all deliberative endeavors in contributing to the creation of an aggregate understanding on a much broader scale. This allows both macro and micro discursive events representing a diverse scale of participants to contribute toward meaningful citizen participation and to have great merit within the deliberative framework. The deliberation may occur through traditional means including face-to-face interactions or through the application of persistent traditional technologies that have maintained system relevance for an extended period of time prior to the E-Governance Era (e.g., telephones, written letters, etc.). Also, including technologically innovative modern means that facilitate digital civic engagement may contribute to strengthening the overall deliberative nature of the U.S. political system. In this sense, the deliberation democracy framework is an aggregate of traditional means and technologically innovative means supporting mini-publics and macro-publics engagement in dialogue that contributes insight intended to be more representative of the whole of the U.S. political system.

There are additional discursive means that can be facilitated digitally or traditionally that can contribute to further strengthening the deliberative democracy framework including deliberative polls (DPs) and citizen review panels (CRPs). These deliberative conceptualizations are introduced here and then related to the expectations associated with citizen–government participation in the E-Governance Era. A *deliberative poll* is a variation of the conceptualization of the traditional poll in which an individual responds to a specific set of predesigned questions. Fishkin et al. (2004, p. 56) explained that "deliberative polling is an attempt to harness social science to better consult the public" and that this interactive means is focused on issues of democratic importance related to "representativeness and deliberation." Fishkin et al. (2004, p. 57) added that a deliberative poll, when "compared to the snapshots of an inattentive public typically offered by conventional polls, it assesses informed public opinion produced through a balanced process of informative discussion that we call deliberation." Olsen and Trenz (2014, p. 210) noted that to promote legitimacy for democratic governance it is important to "represent the informed opinions of the general public (*representation* of public judgement)" while providing opportunity to determine input from "citizens to whom collective decisions apply (creating *publicity* and public accountability)." A deliberative poll not only provides individuals from within society with a predetermined set of questions but also allows for them to expand on their perspectives by affording the opportunity for further dialogue. In this sense, the opportunity for dialogue supplements the information gathered through polling questions that can provide the government with access to richer, more complex levels of information that can be used in decision-making.

Falling under the umbrella of the wide scope of available participatory means is also citizen review panels (CRPs), which play a role in facilitating deliberation between citizens and government (Jones, 2004; Jones & Royse, 2008; Buckwalter, 2014; Jones, 2014). Citizen review panels offer a unique opportunity for the public to interact with government and to provide recommendations based on the results of deliberations between participants. The composition of a citizen review panel includes a combination of citizen volunteers, government officials and private sector experts in a given field. Buckwalter (2014) observed that there are some instances in which government-organized participation means, such as citizen review panels (CRPs), have been formed as the result of legislative mandates in which public sector administrators initiate dialogue with the public in order to receive access to designated funds. Here, citizen participation can be organized on behalf of government, which initiates the deliberative endeavor in compliance with a mandate linked to corresponding funding stipulations. A prevalent example of mandated CRPs are those associated with budgeting stipulations set forth in various incarnations of the Childhood Abuse and Prevention and Treatment Act (CAPTA). CAPTA mandates the usage of child abuse citizen review panels in circumstances in which "each State to which a grant is made under this section shall establish not less than 3 citizen review panels" (Children's Bureau, 2003, p. 34). CAPTA requires that annual recommendations be submitted by a minimum of three citizen review panels in circumstances for which federal funds are distributed to the states that are over the established minimum allotment of $175,000 articulated within the legislation.

There are a number of concerns with participation dynamics and logistics to be aware of when considering the usage of citizen review panels. Buckwalter (2014, p. 583) noted that "having a venue in which to participate does not guarantee that the participant will have a voice in shaping administrative decisions." The provision of participative means like citizen review panels does not guarantee usage by the public, and usage does not necessarily guarantee that changes will automatically be made to the political system based on citizen–government deliberations. This is where dual citizen–government responsibility becoming ingrained in expectations associated with deliberative democracy maintains significance if real changes within the political system are to occur based on authentic citizen participation. Jones and Royse (2008, p. 159) noted that a consideration associated with traditional citizen review panels is that "the logistics of implementing CRPs in such geographically vast states as Alaska or Wyoming also needs to be considered when discussing barriers to participation." Here, logistical barriers are very real considerations associated with traditional on-site citizen review panels and may negatively affect levels of participation among the intended audience. The development of logistical awareness with traditional participation endeavors can involve recognizing potential travel difficulties affecting those citizens who are geographically dispersed and acknowledging the realities that people experience regarding transportation concerns. E-Governance techniques can play a role in diffusing some of the travel-related logistical issues associated with traditional in-person civic engagement means like citizen review panels. This includes that conducting digital citizen review panels may significantly reduce having to travel long distances by personal automobiles or through public transportation to participate in such forms of deliberations. This ideal is applicable across many deliberative means that can be facilitated in a digital capacity to assist in overcoming travel-based logistical barriers to citizen participation. Diffusing the travel-oriented logistical limitations associated with traditional on-site participation can be achieved in part by developing supplemental digital participatory means providing access to knowledge based on interactions from an expanded pool of participants. The citizen preferences identified through participation in citizen review panels and deliberative polls is clearly not representative of the thoughts of everyone on every topic associated with governance at a given point in time. However, preferences identified through deliberative participation are representative of some semblance of the larger whole and can contribute to understanding the influence of multiple means in which preferences can be gathered over an extended period of time. This can also help to provide a longitudinal dynamic associated with understanding deliberative techniques utilized to ascertain citizen preferences on a continuous basis through digital and traditional means.

There are numerous means in which citizens may directly participate with government within a deliberative democracy framework that can utilize digital applications, including public meetings, citizen review panels, deliberative polls and crowdsourcing. These means are similar to casting a vote electronically or to online suggestions boxes in that they fall within the broad framework of deliberative democracy, but differ in that there is an ability to provide consistent direct dialogue opportunities between citizens and government. Such dialogue techniques create the opportunity for citizens to participate directly with government to receive information and to provide feedback on preferred changes to the system across a multitude of societal topics. This includes citizens providing feedback to government identifying concerns within the community, expressing preferences for changes to existing policy, making suggestions for policy solutions to iden- tified problems or constructing arguments intended to affect government budgeting expenditures. Here, open dialogue between citizens and govern- ment can ultimately yield consensus-based changes to the political system as expected with authentic citizen participation within a deliberative democ- racy. In this sense, deliberative means allow government to consistently engage with citizens to determine the proverbial pulse of the public regard- ing issues of concern within the political arena and to take actions accord- ingly when applicable. One such means available within the deliberative democracy framework capable of facilitating citizen–government dialogue is a town hall meeting, which serves as a type of public meeting. For the pur- poses of this discussion, these related terms refer to an event in a public set- ting that facilitates the exchange of some level of information between citizens and government. A public meeting may only allow for the basic transfer of information while a town hall meeting also provides the opportunity for par- ticipants to engage in deliberative exchanges. As a note, government often uses the terms interchangeably when posting an announcement for an upcoming town hall meeting or public meeting when deliberation is expected.

There is a broad spectrum of public meetings forms within a deliberative democracy framework that supports different levels of participation. This relates to the possibility that one type of public meeting may be designed to facilitate one-way communication in which government disseminate infor- mation to the citizen base. Another type of public meeting is one that facil- itates two-way citizen–government communication, like a town hall meeting, in which dialogue is more closely attributed to the expectations associated with authentic citizen participation. Lastly, it is plausible that a public meeting may be constructed in a way that facilitates both one-way and two-way communication as represented in Figure 8.1.

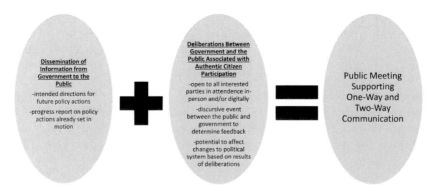

Figure 8.1 Public Meetings and Communication

Here, there may be an allowance for government to disseminate information followed by traditional town hall interactions based on citizen–government deliberations. Many items of concern associated with traditional citizen participation are applicable to digital participation endeavors; this is relevant when it comes to means designed to facilitate dialogue. These compatible concerns for traditional or digital public meetings may be focused on some combination of perceived inadequacies that are procedural and outcome-based in nature. An introduction to public meetings that are structured to facilitate one-way communication, two-way communication and directionally blended communication is provided below. The elements associated with how public meetings serve to promote citizen–government dialogue events in the E-Governance Era are highlighted. In relation, it is also important to discuss how dialogue events are capable of playing a role in deliberative democracy as it relates to authentic citizen participation.

A functionally diverse deliberative democracy framework is expected to include means that support various types of citizen–government communication. The communication means are expected to support activities such as allowing for the dissemination of information from government to the public. These means can also create dialogue events intended to contribute to consensus-based changes to the political system, changes that are to be made visible at a later date. Participation expectations can play a role in guiding the structuring of town hall meetings and denotes the importance of ensuring that such efforts are reflective of important deliberative democracy principles. This includes ensuring that town hall meetings are supportive of meaningful citizen–government communication and that there is an effort to fulfill the expectation that participation can affect changes to the political system in the future. As noted, a chief concern associated with deliberative democracy frameworks is that dialogue events are capable of supporting authentic citizen participation, which can guide future government changes. It is beneficial to expand further on this dialogue expectation associated with a deliberative democracy framework as it relates to town hall meetings. Guiniven (2000, p. 22) expanded on the negative notion of non-substantive town hall meetings applied in an organizational setting by noting that "too frequently, town hall meetings renege on their implied promise of dialogue." There have also been discussions of the potential weaknesses associated with civic engagement means, such as traditional town hall meetings, as it relates to failing to affect real change in a timely manner (Lukensmeyer, 2010). The public meeting as a participatory event, traditional or digital, is served well by visibly connecting government actions with the means utilized to guide consensus-based change to ensure that outcomes are legitimized within the deliberative framework. In relation, the importance that government outcomes reflect "policy choices based on authentic, collective voice of citizens" (Lukensmeyer, 2010, p. 278) is a key consideration for deliberations conducted through town hall meetings. Adams (2004, p. 43) stated, "public meetings are frequently attacked as useless democratic rituals that lack deliberative qualities and fail to give citizens a voice in the policy process." Determining the effectiveness of means to successfully provide a platform for citizen voice is determined in part by the ability to both be heard and to be able to have dialogue directly affect the system at some point. This includes the ability to effectively shape public policy development efforts by government based on results of deliberations in town hall meetings. It has been argued that public meetings may play a less impactful role in the deliberative framework than other forms of participation available to citizens, as they may lack the necessary power to directly affect public policy making in a timely fashion (Adams, 2004). For Adams (2004), the deliberative power associated with public meetings may be diminished somewhat in relation to the ability to directly impact the public policy cycle. This is not to say that the present state of public meetings is completely devoid of deliberative capacity or is irreparably diminished in the ability contribute to strengthening expectations of dialogue events in a deliberative democracy. Adams (2004, p. 44) posited that alternatives to participation designs can be used to further involve citizens in policy making including noting that an "alternative has been to modify the format of public meetings, discarding the structured and non-deliberative hearing forms in favor of a roundtable or small group setting." Therefore, there are a number of structural factors that are applicable when considering the role of public meetings within a deliberative framework. The structure of a public meeting dictates citizen–government communication flows, which are then expected to influence processes and outcomes associated with a dialogue event. Dialogue events may also reflect various levels of usefulness in their ability to directly affect the political system in a timely and consistent fashion. A town hall meeting's place in the broad deliberative framework is to provide dialogue tools allowing for the dissemination of information and that are capable of yielding consensus derived from discursive events to yield real changes to the political system. Dialogue events such as town hall meetings may not immediately impact the system in the same fashion as voting, but there is great merit in a public meeting's ability to contribute to strengthening the overall deliberative democracy framework.

A public meeting can be constructed to facilitate one-way communication in which interaction is limited to government dissemination of information to citizens. A public meeting reflecting one-way communication could be used for a number of activities serving an educational capacity, such as to inform the public of upcoming policy plans or to share pertinent data associated with the fulfillment of government responsibilities. For example, a public meeting in a specific locality could announce upcoming plans for the construction of a new traffic light or plans to expand the local community ballpark system. The same locality could also use public meetings to share information with the community associated with budget expenditures. This includes informing the public of possible fiscal shortfalls caused by emergency circumstances resulting from higher-than-expected costs for snow removal due to a series of blizzards. In this sense, the one-way nature of communication is based on procedural limitations in which a public meeting simply serves to disseminate information from government to citizens in attendance. The outcome for this type of public meeting is also limited to citizens being the recipient of one-way dissemination of information and is devoid of the ability of citizens to utilize discourse to yield consensus to directly affect changes to the system at that time. This could be further illustrated by the aforementioned example pertaining to the local government's use of public meetings to announce intended government actions such as expanding the local ballpark system by adding more athletic fields and constructing a new indoor gym facility for winter sports. In this case, the public meeting uses one-way communication only to inform citizens of upcoming plans that will affect the community. For this type of public meeting, the opportunity to engage in citizen–government dialogue is reserved for a later date if at all.

There are some critiques attributed to public meetings that are one-sided in nature. Handley and Howell-Moroney (2010) explained that mandated government-sponsored participatory events such as public hearings may lack effectiveness as a means of deliberation if held too infrequently to consistently determine citizen preferences or are designed simply as an opportunity for government to share information in an educational capacity instead of being exploratory in nature. McComas, Besley, and Black (2010, p. 122) noted, "public meetings are often referred to as 'rituals' to denote a largely symbolic activity with little concrete meanings." They added that "with regard to public meetings, people may lose faith in the process and cease to participate if they believe participation is limited through the strategic manipulation of rituals" (McComas, Besley, & Black, 2010, p. 127). A deliberative democracy framework that only supports public meetings used to disseminate government information to citizens would ultimately prove ineffective toward achieving authentic citizen participation. Relatedly, the sole usage of one-way communication may result in public meetings being relegated to a largely symbolic function if more substantive measures are not available. This could ultimately reduce levels of trust in government if citizens perceive that deliberative democracy principles associated with having the ability to consistently engage in meaningful dialogue capable of affecting the political system are not being consistently upheld. However, there is room within the deliberative framework supporting public meeting designed for information sharing if there is some level of a diversity in use of such means. It may serve as a complementary measure in which information disseminated through a public meeting format serves as the precursor to later dialogue events in which deeper citizen–government discourse is then facilitated. A public meeting that facilitates one-way communication has merit in the ability to contribute within a deliberative democracy framework by expanding the list of available civic engagement means. Dissemination of information in this type of public meeting can serve a purpose in the deliberative framework because it may allow for citizens to obtain information that could be utilized to help guide more informed citizen participation in future substantive deliberative events. There is room within the deliberative framework for interactive events such as public meetings that are partly symbolic and through which information is communicated from government to the public in a one-sided in nature. This type of public meeting can serve as one important means that ultimately contribute to the creation of a diverse deliberative democracy framework that supports authentic citizen participation.

A deliberative framework can include public meetings that function in an educational capacity through one-way communication; however, this is with the understanding that the facilitation of one-way communication creates *a* type (not *the* type) of public meeting available. Again, the whole of an effective deliberative framework is representative of the sum of multiple means that contribute to facilitating citizen–government interaction. Therefore, it is important to consider the usage of other types of public meetings that can contribute to a more comprehensive deliberative democracy framework. This includes the possibility of constructing a public meeting in a fashion in which citizen–government dialogue is based on two-way communication flows or a combination of directional flows of communication. A public meeting as a dialogue event that supports citizen–government two-way communication is more closely aligned with the expectation of authentic citizen participation. Here, whether the government holding a public meeting is mandated or voluntary is less important than the expectations associated with deliberative events being viewed as legitimate in their ability to eventually impact the political system. In this sense, substantive two-way citizen participation may be unintentionally hindered by the possibility that the dialogue event may have fallen short of deliberative democracy expectations in some way. This may be due to a public meeting being unsuccessful in upholding deliberative democracy principles associated with the expectation that meaningful dialogue was facilitated and was eventually capable of yielding actual change to the system. Like town hall meetings within a traditional brick-and-mortar setting, virtual town hall meetings can provide quality means in which the opportunity to consistently participate is facilitated to determine citizen insight across a wide array of government responsibilities. The provision of virtual town hall meetings on a consistent basis can be utilized to promote deliberation with citizens to identify issues of importance that may eventually require government actions. This could include digital deliberations with citizens capable of identifying newly emerging problems that have yet to register on the proverbial radar of government decision makers. Consistent digital deliberations can also allow government to assess citizen opinions to determine if current efforts by government to address previously identified problems are considered to be inadequate in some (or all) ways. Therefore, a public meeting can be designed in a way that supports deliberative democracy expectations for two-way citizen–government dialogue. In relation, the two-way communication between citizens and government is expected to be able to be used to affect change to the political system at some point.

Unlike the results of voting for public officials or on policy referendums in which verifiable changes to the system are more immediate, the ability to directly affect the political system through participation in public meetings are generally subject to a time delay. As such, identifiable changes to the political system resulting from input derived from citizen–government dialogue is expected to occur sometime in the immediate future. For example, a town hall meeting may be called by government to assess the public's view on issues of concern within a given locality. This includes allowing for citizens to express opinions on the intended direction of government actions previously announced in public meetings conducted through one-way communication. Here, the expectation is that citizen–government dialogue is capable of contributing to consensus-based changes, which at some time in the near future manifest as verifiable government actions. This can relate to the example above in which a public meeting utilized one-way communication to inform citizens of an upcoming plan to expand the ballpark system in the locality. A public meeting facilitating two-way communication may provide the opportunity for both opposition groups and support groups to construct policy arguments designed to affect changes to the political system on the topic of expanding the ballpark system. This includes providing the opportunity for citizens to comment on fiscal implications associated with the costs of expanding the ballpark system in terms of tax dollars being spent versus the potential long-term positive financial effect on the community. It also includes allowing for a discussion of issues such as those associated with whether an expansion will yield significant environmental concerns and possible traffic implications caused by increased motorists traveling to and from the expanded ballpark system. A public meeting that allows for citizens to engage directly with government with the expectation that dialogue events will contribute to consensus-based change to the political system is more reflective of authentic citizen participation in a deliberative democracy framework.

One-way communication, which is devoid of the opportunity for citizens to contribute input capable of directly impacting the political system, may be reflective of too narrow of an interpretation of deliberative expectations. In relation, two-way communication may be hindered somewhat by citizen–government discursive interactions that occur without the benefit of prior opportunities for information dissemination, leading to dialogue events in which participants are impassioned but not completely informed on the topic at hand. There may be a relatively simplistic solution to this dilemma that involves constructing a tiered public meeting structure that involves both types of communication. Conceptually, there is room within the deliberative framework for a public meeting format that accommodates both one-way and two-way communication. This includes the possibility that public meetings are structured in a way that allows for some combination of both types of communication. For example, a public meeting may begin with an opening session in which one-way communication allows for government to disseminate information to the public to be discussed at a later time. The next stage of the public meeting could facilitate open dialogue between citizens and government concerning a variety of issues of societal important. The usage of one- and two-way communication may create a public meeting structure that is more able to address deliberative democracy expectations reflected in the ability to disseminate information while still accounting for authentic citizen participation through dialogue events. In relation, technological innovation available in the E-Governance Era could add another dimension to the interaction process associated with public meetings. Technology could be used to create supplemental means to facilitate multiple communication types for different stages of public meetings. For example, an initial public meeting could be held online in which information is disseminated to citizens in a one-way capacity. At a later date, a town hall meeting that is facilitated online or on site can be conducted through two-way dialogue between citizens and government on the previously announced topical information. The public meeting tool can be utilized in a flexible and diverse fashion that takes advantage of available technological innovation while facilitating multi-directional citizen–government dialogue flow. This also reinforces the importance of ensuring that democratic government remains flexible in its ability to react to cues from within the political environment. In this case, flexibility is reflected in part by the ability of government to utilize advancements in technology to fulfill government responsibilities associated with public-meeting deliberations. As such, it will be helpful to further expand on the role of digital technology in facilitating public meetings in the E-Governance Era.

In the E-Governance Era, it is important that citizen participation methods are capable of integrating modernized elements of communication to provide a broader deliberative platform. This speaks to the importance of developing diversity in means for activities within a deliberative democracy framework that can better facilitate increased levels of participation. Here, it is possible that the use of technological innovation to facilitate deliberations through an online town hall meeting finds some relevance in this regard. Online town hall meetings can expand the scope of those participating in deliberations on topics of societal importance with the understanding that such dialogue efforts should avoid being solely symbolic in nature. Public meetings within the deliberative democracy framework can be structured to sustain traditional in-person discourse and digital discourse promoting participation through a more diverse structure. Therefore, it is important to continue to recognize the role that combining technologically advanced means with traditional low-tech means can have in creating a more comprehensive deliberative framework in the E-Governance Era. The modern deliberative framework that includes traditional and digital communication means may be capable of providing access to citizen input derived from a wider array of societal demographics. Digital dialogue means may allow for individuals to participate in town hall meetings who had previously been unable to attend on site due to time constraints or geographical impediments or who are simply more comfortable participating online. It is also possible that facilitating town hall meetings supporting digital dialogue may encourage the aforementioned tech-savvy demographic into being more engaged by providing opportunity for citizen–government participation through their preferred means.

It is also helpful to acknowledge an issue of importance associated with town hall meetings as it relates to the possibility of deliberative events potentially reflecting questionable levels of representativeness of participants. If a deliberative democracy is intended to provide dialogue means to contribute to achieving consensus-based changes to the system, then the levels of representativeness is important in determining if these outcomes truly reflect the will of the public. It is possible to incorporate techniques to ensure that public meetings are reflective of the expectations associated with authentic citizen participation as it relates to contributing to a more inclusive and representative processes. This includes the application of technological innovation to simultaneously support citizen–government dialogue through traditional and digital means to create a more open deliberative framework. Here, incorporating modern technical aspects associated with E-Governance can expand the deliberative capacity of traditional town hall meetings to include a diverse range of perspectives. The degree of openness is enhanced by a deliberative framework that is reflective of diversity in available means. Creating diversity in available deliberative means and incorporating town hall meeting designs capable of sustaining a combination of such means can help to create a more responsive framework. The dialogue processes associated with deliberative democracy are expected to be open to all interested parties and increasing the means available to include a more diverse participant base contributes to enhancing the overall levels of representativeness participating in dialogue events. This can be especially true regarding the usage of digital deliberative means to ensure that the aforementioned tech-savvy demographic of digital participants is more adequately represented. As a reminder, issues associated with representativeness related to the digital divide require that E-Governance Era participation remains focused on providing structural means that are diverse in nature to ensure inclusion of a vast array of societal perspectives. It also includes a shared responsibility on behalf of government and citizens who are required to provide diverse deliberative means and to actively participate on a consistent basis.

The frequency and timing of public meetings can also play an important role in determining their overall usefulness within the deliberative democracy framework. In this respect, determining the usefulness of public meetings in regard to the ability to affect the political system is more representative of a dynamic sliding scale than a static concern. Public meetings that are held too infrequently may not allow for citizen–government deliberations to identify issues and to work toward collectively developing solutions to those issues in a consistent and timely manner. However, it is also unfeasible to hold public meetings too frequently. Given the size and scope of modern society, holding public meetings for the purposes of addressing all possible societal issues or to discuss all possible public policy alternatives is unrealistic. Doing so would inundate the system through endless debates on political minutia at each level of government, overloading the deliberative framework. Too many public meetings may slow down the system and too few public meetings may yield a system that isn't able to consistently address actual concerns stemming from the polis in a timely fashion. Therefore, finding the right balance is critical. This is equally true regardless of the format, whether digital or traditional. At present, there is no formula that provides an identifiable threshold for the number of town hall meetings that will be able to adequately facilitate authentic citizen participation within a deliberative democracy framework. The usefulness of town hall meetings to contribute to the deliberative expectations will likely require some form of trial and error on a case-by-case basis at each respective level of government.

It is helpful to acknowledge that technology can be applied in a political marketing capacity to highlight how citizen participation in dialogue events was able to affect real government changes. This could include any number of digital means utilized to publish outcomes derived from traditional and electronic town hall meeting. Perceptions associated with the legitimacy of authentic citizen participation is partly dependent on the ability to directly affect change though deliberation, and online publication of subsequent changes that may have occurred during civic engagement helps to provide verifiable evidence of successful efforts in this regard. Advertising the subsequent modifications to the political system that resulted from citizen–government dialogue helps to promote the deliberative expectation that through participation government, change is feasible and constant. In this sense, publication of successful efforts to influence the system provides evidence of authentic citizen participation in which deliberations directly effected change in government. This component is reflective of a certain degree of political marketing in which making visible the deliberative successes contributes to actualizing the authenticity of citizen participation and in enhancing the legitimacy of available deliberative means. E-Governance-related efforts are able to reinforce expectations for authentic citizen participation by providing digital means to supplement existing traditional means for participation and for the purposes of advertising the outcomes that resulted. It is possible that deliberations with citizens may result in visible outcomes within the community, such as the creation of a much-needed traffic light or the construction of a monument honoring an issue of federal/state/local significance. The deliberations with citizens through various manifestations of public meetings can result in visible government outcomes in the community; these real-world results of deliberation can be further promoted through supplemental online means. As such, a website at any level of government may highlight actions that were derived from ideas generated through available deliberative means, including town hall meetings. Publishing information online provides verifiable evidence that input from citizens during deliberative participatory processes resulted in actual outcomes within the political system. This provides input–output linkages between deliberations and corresponding government actions affected directly by this process. This can also help foster the required levels of trust in substantive citizen participation to further legitimize the usage of the process in a deliberative democracy based on a combination of both traditional and digital means. E-Governance can utilize technology toward accomplishing ends, such as conducting citizen–government participation through digital town hall meetings, and technology can also be used in a political marketing fashion to advertise to the public that participation in dialogue events successfully impacted the system. In this sense, technological innovation available in the E-Governance Era can be used as a means to facilitate citizen–government discourse and can also serve as the means through which changes to the system resulting from authentic citizen participation are digitally advertised. Town hall meetings are one such dialogue event available within a deliberative democracy framework that adheres to the expectations for modern authentic citizen participation while applying technological innovation available in the E-Governance Era to facilitate digital discourse and related processes associated with advertising outcomes.

References

Adams, B. (2004) Public meetings and the democratic process. *Public Administration Review*, 64(1): 43–54. Retrieved from http://search.proquest.com/docview/197171507?accountid=32521.

Buckwalter, N. D. (2014) The potential for public empowerment through government-organized participation. *Public Administration Review*, 74(5): 573–584. doi: 10.1111/puar.12217.

Chambers, S. (2009) Rhetoric and the public sphere: Has deliberative democracy abandoned mass democracy? *Political Theory, 37*(3): 323–350. Retrieved from www.jstor.org/stable/25655484.

Children's Bureau: An Office of the Administration for Children and Families. (2003) The Childhood Abuse and Prevention and Treatment Act of 2003. Retrieved from www.acf.hhs.gov/programs/cb/resource/capta2003.

Fishkin, J. S., Rosell, S. A., Shepherd, D., & Amsler, T. (2004) ChoiceDialogues and deliberative polls: Two approaches to deliberative democracy. *National Civic Review*, 93(4): 55–63.

Guiniven, J. (2000) Suggestion boxes and town hall meetings: Fix 'em or forget 'em. *Public Relations Tactics*, 7(2): 22.

Handley, D. M., & Howell-Moroney, M. (2010) Ordering stakeholder relationships and citizen participation: Evidence from the community development block grant program. *Public Administration Review*, 70(4), 601–609. Retrieved from http://search.proquest.com/docview/853147548?accountid=32521.

Jones, B. (2014) Citizen review panels. *Policy & Practice, 72*(2): 26–27.

Jones, B. (2004) Effectiveness of citizen review panels. *Children and Youth Services Review*, 26(12): 1117–1127.

Jones, B., & Royse, D. (2008) Citizen review panels for child protective services: A national profile. *Child Welfare*, 87(3): 143–162.

Lloyd, G. C. (1999) 'Stuff the suggestions box.' *Total Quality Management*, 10(6): 869–875.

Lukensmeyer, C. J. (2010) Learning from the past, committing to the future: A practitioner's view of our democracy. *Public Administration Review*, 70(S1): S273–S283. Retrieved from http://search.proquest.com/docview/853425360?accoun tid=32521.

McComas, K., Besley, J. C., & Black, L. W. (2010) The rituals of public meetings. *Public Administration Review*, 70(1): 122–130. Retrieved from http://search.pro quest.com/docview/853757624?accountid=32521.

Olsen, E. H., & Trenz, H. (2014) From citizens' deliberation to popular will forma-tion? Generating democratic legitimacy in transnational deliberative polling. *Political Studies*, 62(S1): 117–133. doi: 10.1111/1467–9248.12021.

Opt, S. K. (1998) Confirming and disconfirming American myth: Stories within the suggestion box. *Communication Quarterly*, 46(1): 75–87.

Porter, P. (1986) The suggestion box: New light on an old technique. *Journal of Academic Librarianship*, 12(2): 75–78.

Raisio, H., & Carson, L. (2014) Deliberation within sectors: Making the case for sector mini-publics. *International Review of Social Research*, 4(1): 75–92. doi: 10.1515/irsr-2014-0006.

HR Specialist: Compensation & Benefits (2014). 'The old suggestion box: How to make it work.' 9(10): 6.

9 E-Governance, Deliberative Democracy and Voting Processes
Part One

Voting processes are multidimensional, as there are static and dynamic deliberative components associated with this type of E-Governance interaction. The casting of votes electronically, on site or online, serves as an example of a more static-oriented deliberative democracy function in which citizens can participate in the electoral process. Voting provides citizens with a consistently cyclical opportunity to participate in government interactions in which outcomes are intended to be capable of affecting real changes to the political system. Participation through voting provides citizens a voice, which may contribute to yield verifiable changes to government including affecting who is elected to, or in some cases recalled from, public office. Voting may also result in directly observable changes, such as determining policy initiatives resulting from a public referendum process. The act of casting a vote does not generally involve citizen-government direct dialogue, but it does fit along the spectrum of deliberative democracy interactive means in that it allows for open and cyclical input from citizens that is capable of directly affecting the political system. In addition, there are components associated with the overall voting process prior to casting a vote that can involve more dynamic citizen–government interactions involving information dissemination that are more deliberative in nature. This includes citizen–government interactions that may affect the voting process, such as those associated with active information dissemination (i.e., town hall meeting, Internet campaigning, etc.). As such, the whole of electronic voting processes contributes to an overarching digital deliberative democracy framework as it relates to E-Governance.

Electronic voting, on site or online, is a means that is full of possibility in modern era democracy. Electronic voting on site through e-machines is presently a critical component associated with the electoral system in the United States. Electronic voting that occurs online from virtually anywhere an Internet connection is present may potentially create a level of convenience when participating in elections or on policy referendums in the future. The ease of voting from devices that have Internet access, such as home computers or smartphones, may promote higher levels of citizen participation simply based on the convenience of use. If voting online can be facilitated with the same level of convenience as banking electronically or posting messages to social media, then this may help to increase levels of participation associated with voting. Online voting presents a number of challenges, however, associated with maintaining a secure electoral process and in ensuring representativeness of voters. Electronic means can contribute to increasing levels of participation for citizens that may have otherwise abstained due to being unable to make it to the voting booths because of conflicting real-world responsibilities. A citizen that is balancing working multiple jobs while attending to numerous family responsibilities while also pursuing a higher education may be unable to make it to the voting booths during regular hours of operation. Voting online may circumvent such logistical barriers that would have otherwise prevented an individual from participating. Electronic voting can benefit these citizens by providing a timely and accessible means in which to participate in the voting process.

Recognizing that real-world responsibilities may create a legitimate barrier to participating in events such as voting is not a blanket societal "hall pass" justifying low levels of voter turnout in U.S. elections. Voting is a critical foundational element associated with U.S. democracy and is of great importance to the legitimacy of the political system itself. Citizens elect candidates to office who are expected to represent the will of polis, and those elected officials develop government actions based in part on consensus attained from cues within the political system. Those individuals in society classified as the voter-eligible population or "VEP" (McDonald, 2002; File, 2015) are citizens who qualify to vote in an election, and who may benefit from electronic methods that either strengthen the voting process or create increased access points for voting. If for some reason voter turnout in elections for government representatives or on policy referendums is low in relation to the VEP, then it is possible that the resulting government actions by elected officials may not be fully representative the whole of society. This is a risk in a representative democracy in which a potential consequence of having low voter turnout is a domino effect that ultimately may yield government action within the political system that isn't truly reflective of the populace's preferences. There is a citizen responsibility to consistently participate in deliberative events such as voting, as failure to engage may have a negative effect on the representativeness of system outcomes. By association, this may create discord between citizens and government if policy-oriented actions are viewed as far removed from actual concerns affecting the whole of society. The disjoint between actual citizen preferences and government actions initiated by elected officials representing a disproportionately small percentage of participating eligible voters may negatively affect perceptions of legitimacy. Here, the future usage of online means may contribute to creating government actions that more accurately reflect a wider variety of citizen preferences. The e-voting option may help to increase levels of voter turnout in the future simply by increasing the means in which citizens may cast their vote. The future of electronic voting, or e-voting, in which innovations are utilized to facilitate on-site or online elections, is filled with great promise and also potential pitfalls that should be acknowledged.

A government focused on developing an e-voting strategy that reflects an electoral structure with on-site and online components is not without some plausible issues. One particularly important issue is that of security. Breaches of security in any online interaction, private or public, could potentially lead to identity theft and related consequences, such as an individual incurring a financial loss or damaged credit. This includes having personal bank accounts emptied and loans taken out in the name of the victim of the identity theft. In the modern era, many citizens have either been the victim of identity theft or have known others that have experienced it. With the proliferation of digital activities in society used toward completing many public or private tasks, the dangers associated with identity theft have correspondingly been expanded. Citizens may be subject to identity theft related to any number of online activities, such as making electronic purchases through a company's website or when registering personal information online with their health-care provider. This concern has been quite relevant in the modern era in which there have been a number of recent public examples of customer information being leaked due to breaches of security involving corporate entities. Any online transaction, public or private, should be able to be facilitated through a secure website that is capable of protecting personal information. However, there is a larger issue of significance associated with the requirement that online e-voting processes are secure as it relates to perceptions of democratic legitimacy. Online e-voting in elections and on policy referendums cannot afford to have breaches in security that may create the perception, or in the worst case scenario, reflecting a current reality, that voting outcomes were altered by outside parties in some capacity. A breach of security during online voting processes may directly erode the integrity of this type of participation, and by default, the whole of the deliberative democracy framework. Voting is a cornerstone of democracy itself—the outcomes of participating in e-voting, on site or online, need to be beyond reproach to maintain democratic integrity.

The voting system in the United States has had to continuously evolve to meet the changing expectations from within the political arena as it relates to the development of measures designed to promote equality and to combat threats associated with voter fraud. This includes U.S. government efforts to mandate voting equality through legislation such as the 19th amendment in 1920 (which prevented gender-based discrimination granting suffrage rights to women voters) and the 1965 Voting Rights Act (which sought to remove all state/local racial discriminatory barriers preventing the practice of universal suffrage for all citizens of legal voting age). The subject of voter fraud and its negative impact on degrading the integrity of the electoral process is also not a new issue facing U.S. democracy. There have been numerous examples of voter fraud in U.S. history ranging from the activities associated with William "Boss" Tweed in the Tammany Hall Era of the 1800s in New

York City (i.e., an individual voting multiple times, the sale of votes, votes being cast for the deceased, etc.) to modern examples from Clay County, Kentucky in which elected officials and residents were convicted of multiple instances of voter fraud in 2010 (https://archives.fbi.gov/archives/louisville/press-releases/2010/lo032510.htm). The prevention of voter fraud and the maintenance of equality of access are important components in preserving the integrity of the electoral system and in strengthening democratic legitimacy. In the E-Governance Era, the nature of voter fraud may change due to innovations used to facilitate elections so that the application of technology requires government to alter the focus of security concerns in some instances. In addition, the governmental focus on developing means capable of ensuring voting equality has shifted somewhat to include considerations associated with diffusing, or preferably eliminating, the negative effects derived from the digital divide as it relates to the electoral process. Although the nature of these electoral issues has evolved with time, the importance of maintaining a secure and equitable voting process still remains of utmost importance to the integrity of the U.S. democracy. Citizen participation in elections is an integral part of the U.S. deliberative system. As such, the means utilized to facilitate voting should be capable of promoting a secure, trustworthy and equitable process.

Recounting each pivotal moment associated with the vast history of governmental voting reforms will not be the focus of the following discussion. Instead, a seminal electoral event in recent U.S. history, the 2000 presidential election, will be highlighted, serving as the vehicle through which to analyze a number of contemporary issues of importance related to e-voting in the E-Governance Era. A brief summation of voting irregularities that transpired in the state of Florida during the 2000 presidential elections and a number of resulting short-term/long-term implications on U.S. voting processes are introduced for illustrative purpose. At that time, there were a number of voting irregularities that made it unclear in determining if George W. Bush or Al Gore was the winner in the immediate aftermath of the election. Due to voting irregularities related to the confusion with how to tally the punch-card ballots that resulted in "hanging chads," the Florida Supreme Court ordered a recount of votes for a wide array of disputed ballots in the state. The U.S. Supreme Court eventually ruled on this matter in *Bush v. Gore*, in which it was determined in a 5–4 vote that "standardless manual recounts" were unconstitutional, effectively halting the recount process in Florida (U.S. Supreme Court, 2000). George W. Bush had won the state of Florida by a narrow margin, receiving the requisite number of overall electoral votes that would ultimately allow him to become the 43rd president of the United States despite losing the overall popular vote. The 2000 presidential election illuminated a number of issues associated with the voting process that resulted in a U.S. governmental legislative response designed to address these concerns.

   The 2000 presidential election brought a number of potential weaknesses associated with the voting process into the light of a national debate. At the forefront of this debate was the belief that voting technologies being used during elections were in some cases antiquated and should be updated to take advantage of innovations available in the modern era. Doing so could help ensure that future citizens are not disenfranchised, as some had been in the 2000 presidential election because an unclear vote was not counted due to the existence of the now infamous "hanging chads." In response, Congress passed the Help America Vote Act (HAVA) of 2002, which sought to rectify a number of possible weaknesses within the voting system by attempting to modernize both the processes and the equipment. HAVA was designed to address voting system weaknesses identified during the 2000 presidential election, and throughout this legislation, there are components that worked toward developing standards intended to strengthen the electoral process. In accordance with U.S. federalism, HAVA includes numerous elements focused on creating national standards for all voting systems used in federal elections. Section 202 of the original HAVA called for the Election Assistance Commission (EAC) to develop "Voluntary Voting System Guidelines," and by 2015, the EAC had developed the third version of this initiative. According to the EAC (2016), "Voluntary Voting System Guidelines (VVSG) are a set of specifications and requirements against which voting systems can be tested to determine if the systems meet required standards. Some factors examined under these tests include basic functionality, accessibility, and security capabilities. HAVA mandates that EAC develop and maintain these requirements." However, "these guidelines are voluntary" and "states may decide to adopt them entirely or in part prior to the effective date" (EAC, 2016, para. 3). The VVSG are intended to ensure that machines used during the electoral process have been certified in accordance with an identifiable set of standards prior to their use in elections, but the voluntary nature creates parameters lacking in a certain degree of enforcement power to ensure compliance throughout the federal system. HAVA Sec. 301, entitled "Voting System Standards," established a number of requirements to be adopted by the states that would be applicable during all federal elections. Components of Sec. 301 required that voting systems (i.e., lever, optical scanning, DREs, etc.) provide voters with the means in which to "verify (in a private and independent manner) the votes selected by the voter on the ballot before the ballot is cast and counted." Sec. 301 components also indicate that voting systems should alert the voter if overvotes occurred and should allow the voter to change or correct errors prior to casting their ballots. Sec. 301 components require that voting systems include an "audit capacity" in which a record is created of ballots cast and "accessibility for individuals with disabilities," allowing for participation "in a manner that provides the same opportunity for access and participation (including privacy and independence) as for other voters." In relation, components of HAVA Sec. 301 mandate "the use of at least one direct recording electronic voting system or other voting system equipped for individuals with dis-abilities at each polling place." The specifics set forth in Sec. 301 of HAVA created standards for state voting systems without providing a blueprint to the states for how exactly to go about implementing such changes to ensure com-pliance. In relation, this left a great deal of discretion to the states regarding the methods in which localized voting systems would be constructed in order to be compliant with HAVA standards. This legislation was also reflective of incremental policy that sought to progressively affect changes at the state and local levels for the federal election process. It is important to note that implementing incremental policy is a process in which changes occur slowly over time and where new, and often unintended, problems may emerge. This dynamic is also applicable to electoral system changes associated with HAVA; these issues are discussed at greater length further in the chapter.

The initial changes to the voting system associated with HAVA were intended to improve and modernize the process in many respects. These changes sought to modernize the electoral process by introducing means for citizens to register to vote online and by promoting the usage of voting machines that applied modernized innovations. HAVA was designed to modernize the electoral process at the state/local level in a number of respects while also supporting the federal components that have tradition-ally served as part of the fabric of American government. In relation, there were a number of elements of federalism associated with the voting pro-cesses targeted for changes in accordance with HAVA. This includes the development of fiscal guidelines illustrating how the federal government would allocate funds to the states for the purposes of affecting changes to voting equipment and voter registration processes. This includes Sec. 102(a), subsection 2, which was intended to encourage voting machine updates by allowing for federal funds to be allocated to the states "to replace punch card voting systems or lever voting systems." It also encompasses Sec. 252(b), which established a formula to calculate the "state allocation percentage" based on population numbers of voting age citizens which would be utilized to determine the amount of funds allocated to the states by the federal government, and Sec. 257(b), which established additional minimum funding levels for states from 2003 through 2005. The funding was established in accordance with federal principles and allowed for money from the federal government to be distributed to states implementing changes to their respective electoral systems in accordance with HAVA. The allocation of federal money to the states would be dependent on compliance with state efforts to actively apply HAVA guidelines to correct voting flaws that became apparent during the 2000 presidential election. In this sense, federal money is distributed to the state level to fund efforts intended to overcome perceived weakness of voting equipment and voting processes associated with participating in federal elections. The allocation of federal funds was intended to assist the states in developing means to make improvements to equipment and processes by incorporating available technological innovation as expected of the public sector in the E-Governance Era. Initially, the motivation for implementing HAVA was to make changes to compensate for perceived shortcomings of federal elections to preserve the integrity of the process. The successful application of technological innovation during federal elections can contribute to enhancing levels of citizen trust in government by maintaining the legitimacy of voting processes and outcomes.

Another component of federalism that was reflected in HAVA was the degree of discretion left to the states regarding how to implement changes to the voting system and the allowance for states to exceed minimum standards if they wish to. This is indicated in a number of excerpts from HAVA that reinforce the federalist approach by the national government, allowing for state discretion in the implementation process. This includes Sec. 304 and Sec. 305, which read as follows in Figure 9.1.

The discretion afforded to the states to exceed minimum federal standards for activities such as developing a single entity to maintain voter registration information and to address technological components associated with utilizing a secure database of registered voters may ultimately yield a lack of congruence in the electoral system on the national level. This is also true regarding the fact that discretion afforded to the states may create a lack of national congruency associated with voting machine usage from state to state, and perhaps from locality to locality within each state. Allowing for state discretion in lieu of creating specific guidelines to achieve legislative stipulations in HAVA and the lack of enforcement power granted to the federal Election Assistance Commission (EAC) to ensure compliance both serve to diminish the effectiveness of the legislation to some degree. The dynamics

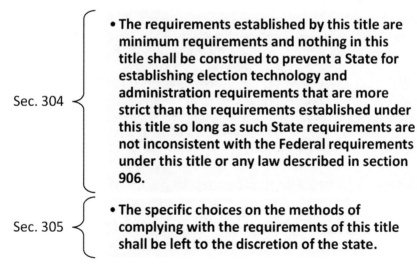

Sec. 304
- **The requirements established by this title are minimum requirements and nothing in this title shall be construed to prevent a State for establishing election technology and administration requirements that are more strict than the requirements established under this title so long as such State requirements are not inconsistent with the Federal requirements under this title or any law described in section 906.**

Sec. 305
- **The specific choices on the methods of complying with the requirements of this title shall be left to the discretion of the state.**

Figure 9.1 HAVA: Sections Sec. 304 and Sec. 305
Source: Help America Vote Act of 2002: http://www.eac.gov/assets/1/workflow_sta ging/Page/41.PDF.

associated with how states implement specific changes to the electoral system based on HAVA regarding the online registration process and in updating voting machine technology are discussed at greater length below.

It is important to recognize the existence of a number of components inherent within HAVA that highlight the efforts to apply E-Governance Era technological innovation to modernize the voting processes. This includes Sec. 303, which called for the creation of "computerized statewide voter registration list requirements and requirements for voters who register by mail" (United States Congress, 2002). HAVA sought to modernize voter registration processes at the state level by advocating for a single state-level entity to coordinate personal information of eligible voters and called for technological advancements to be used to facilitate this process. HAVA standards sought to contribute to the state's ability to strengthen the voter registration process by creating a digital database of eligible voters, developing means for potential voters to register online and allocating federal funds to be used for the development of modern voting means. However, the technology-based components associated with the implementation of HAVA are capable of creating a number of newly emerging unintended concerns—for example, security concerns in the efforts to maintain a single database of voter registration information. This includes requiring the secure maintenance of the computerized registered voter list and highlights the important role that Internet security plays in protecting voter information maintained electronically at the state government level. The security concerns for registration processes involve protecting multiple points of contact, including voters' use of a computer or smartphone device to submit personal information through a government website and the location in which that voter registration information is stored electronically by government. The usage of technological innovation in E-Governance may create new and unexpected problems such as those associated with the security of electronic information during the voter registration process. As such, government must remain aware of this possibility and proactively develop means capable of addressing any negative effects that may develop during the implementation of innovation being used toward the fulfillment of public sector responsibilities. This is a common theme when considering the application of E-Governance Era technology in which the usage of innovations may create many unintended problems that are technologically oriented in nature.

The 2000 presidential election also highlighted a number of flaws with the U.S. voting system related to the existence of confusing and/or antiquated voting means. During the 2000 presidential election, equipment flaws were speculated to have caused votes to not be counted within the state of Florida due to a number of butterfly ballot overvotes (in which an individual casts a vote for too many candidates during the elections) or punch-card ballot undervotes (reflecting insufficient votes for all for the offices on the ballot). The voting methods utilized at that time resulted in a number of examples in Florida in which "hanging chads" caused votes to not be counted, creating a scenario reflecting disenfranchisement by default for those citizens whose votes were not registered in such circumstances. This election also highlighted that there was great deal of inconsistency related to the types of technology used in voting booths. Underhill (2012) noted that "in 2000, it wasn't just Florida's equipment that posed risks. All across the nation, voting machines varied in terms of type, age and function." This resulted in meaningful efforts by Congress to create a more consistently effective voting system in the United States.

According to the United States Election Assistance Commission (2015), the Help America Vote Act (HAVA) of 2002 "creates new mandatory minimum standards for states to follow in several key areas of election administration. The law provides funding to help states meet these new standards, replace voting systems and improve election administration." HAVA provided financial assistance to local jurisdictions for purposes such as updating from traditional mechanical voting machines to more modern direct recording electronic (DRE) voting machines (Claassen et al., 2013). For example, Section 102 required that states make specific alterations to voting processes within a set timeframe for all federal elections and would allow for the states to receive federal money for overseeing related activities, such as the "replacement of punch card or lever voting machines" (United States Congress, 2002). The states were required to make efforts to modernize the voting machines that would be used in upcoming federal elections and were tasked with creating higher levels of consistency in the voting machines utilized throughout the country. Upgrading and modernizing voting machines used by the states to facilitate federal elections is not without concerns. For example, there may be issues associated with the design of upgraded modern voting machines that make participating in the electoral process confusing and intimidating to non-tech-savvy participants. There is also a concern associated with the integrity of DRE technology categorized as "unintentional machine flaws" or intentional attempts to perpetrate machined-based voter fraud. Such machine-based concerns manifesting in reality could alter electoral outcomes and negatively affect citizen trust in government's ability to fulfill expectations associated with facilitating its democratic responsibilities during the voting process. An assessment of key unintentional machine flaws and intentional voter fraud efforts are highlighted. Then, a discussion of plausible methods designed to preserve voter machine integrity is provided.

Several voting machine improvements associated with HAVA were reflective of government applying innovations representative of E-Governance Era expectations for the application of technology in the performance of duties. The belief is that updating to DREs will yield more precise electronic vote counting because of the elimination of mechanistic mishaps (i.e., hanging chads) and that these machines can be programmed to alert voters if an overvote occurs (Claassen et al., 2013). In relation, a reduction, or preferably elimination, of mistakes attributed to the voting process by utilizing technological advancements such as DREs can contribute to enhancing how citizens perceive the legitimacy of the electoral process. This logic contributed to efforts to replace older election technology like lever machines and punch-card machines with more modern voting equipment such as DRE machines that could apply buttons or touchscreen technology much like the interface for a bank ATM. HAVA of 2002 was designed in part to promote actions so that older voting machines are systematically replaced. As noted previously, the advancements in technology applied toward facilitating government actions are capable of raising a number of new concerns unto themselves. In relation, there are still a number of concerns that should be recognized when applying technological innovation to the voting process in association with HAVA of 2002. This includes that there may be consideration for the negative impact of unintentional machine flaws, user error because of lack of familiarity with updated technologies and unique security concerns when applying technological innovation in voting processes, which will be discussed at greater length shortly. In this sense, HAVA's implementation opened the door to a contemporary discussion of electoral machine technology functionality that is applicable to better understanding participatory means associated with E-Governance Era voting.

There have been a multitude of established voting methods utilized during past U.S. elections that includes ballots cast through punch-card machines, lever machines, optical scan machines and handwritten entries. This also includes the recent widespread proliferation of DRE machines during elections, which serves as an example of the application of technological advancement in the E-Governance Era. One of the key results of HAVA was the effort by the states to improve voting technology. This includes ensuring that older, out-dated methods such as lever machine voting and punch-card voting are eventually phased out completely. The Federal Election Commission (2016) indicated that mechanical lever machines are no longer produced and that there is a "trend is to replace them with computer based marksense or direct recording electronic systems." In relation, the 2013 survey conducted by the U.S. Election Assistance Commission (EAC, 2013) indicated that no jurisdictions in the United States used lever machines during the 2012 presidential election. Gilbert et al. (2013) observed that many voting methods, such as punch-card ballots and optical scan ballots, have design flaws that may affect election outcomes in some cases. This includes that punch-card ballots may yield selection errors that cannot be altered by the voter, which requires the ballot to be officially voided, and that optical scan machines may have issues tallying improperly marked selections of candidates, as human interpretation is non-existent in the vote-tallying process (Gilbert et al., 2013). Although the wide-scale replacement of older voting technology has been facilitated based on HAVA, this is not to indicate that all modern technology such as DRE machines is without possible issues. In relation, DRE machines are susceptible to any number of design flaws that may unintentionally influence the electoral process. DRE machines are also susceptible to intentional voter fraud efforts to alter electoral outcomes. As such, the increased usage of DREs during elections as a result of HAVA raises the importance of better understanding the functionality of such devices. The functionality of voting machine technology can be very influential in affecting citizen perceptions associated with the legitimacy of the electoral process. The perceived legitimacy of a voting system may affect the levels of participation in some respects and can affect levels of trust in the overall nature of government. A closer look at the functionality and some key issues associated with the importance of maintaining voting machine integrity, specifically DRE machine technology, is presented.

The direct recording electronic (DRE) machine technology usage in elections has increased since the inception of HAVA in 2002. For example, the Election Assistance Commission (2007) indicated that, as it relates to general elections, "there has been a dramatic rise in the number of jurisdictions using electronic systems compared to what was previously reported in the EAC's 2004 survey. In 2004, just 9.3% of the jurisdictions reported using electronic voting equipment, but this increased 53.6% two years later." The continued wide-scale proliferation of DRE usage in U.S. federal elections highlights a growing importance of developing an understanding of this innovative design. The DRE machines operate differently than other voting technologies, and it is helpful to provide some brief introductory information associated with the device's functionality. Saltman (1988, p. 1189) explained that DRE voting occurs without a ballot and in which a "voter enters choices directly into a storage unit of the machines with the use of pushbuttons, a touch screen, or similar devices." The DRE machine design supports a constituent casting a vote in which "this system stores an electronic record of the ballot in the computer's memory" (Zaino & Zaino, 2004, p. 17). Zaino and Zaino (2004, p. 17) added that DRE-machine benefits include that it "gives instantaneous results, does not rely on human interpretation and is not subject to clerical error, and is 'chad-free'." The process in which this type of vote is cast and how that vote is calculated is reflective of how government applies available technology toward the completion of duties. In this case, the vote is cast and calculated electronically on site through the DRE machine. The DRE machines are capable of contributing to strengthening electoral system processes and in further promoting legitimacy in voting outcomes in many respects. For example, positives associated with DRE voting machines include the adaptability capacity to develop means in which to accommodate disabled citizens and non-English speaking citizens (Card & Moretti, 2007). The United States Government Accountability Office (2005, p. 14) reported on electronic voting systems indicates that DRE's include a number of features that are able to accommodate citizens with disabilities including "braille keyboards and audio interfaces," "head movement switches and 'sip and puff' plug-ins" and "voice recognition capability, which allows voters to make selections orally." In addition, a DRE machine can be programmed to allow for non-English speaking citizens to participate in the voting process by selecting a language preference. The DRE machine is intended to compensate for weaknesses associated with alternate voting technologies to ensure greater ease in voting access, create more easily understood voting processes and reduce errors associated with votes being cast. However, as with any available means used to facilitate voting, there are still concerns associated with DRE machine usage in the U.S. electoral system. The application of DRE machines on a wider scale since the implementation of HAVA in 2002 does not mean that this technology is free of potential issues. Voting through DRE machines raises concerns associated with the lack of verifiability provided to the voter or poll worker to ensure that the vote for a specific candidate is actually registered as intended when the ballot is officially cast and the possible deficiencies associated with an inability to perform a machine-based recount should the need arise (Saltman, 1988; Zaino & Zaino, 2004; Card & Moretti, 2007). Saltman (1988, p. 1189) explained that because "no voter-generated records of choices exist, and no recount independent of the machine is possible," it is of importance that DRE machines are dependable "to assure complete confidence in the reported results." The use of DRE machines potentially yields benefits and detriments that should be considered in order to remain fully aware of the capacity of this innovative means to impact the processes and outcomes associated with the electoral system.

The functional integrity of the technology utilized during the electoral process in the E-Governance Era can impact whether citizens trust in the process and perceive that corresponding outcomes are legitimate. In relation, one of the key motivations guiding Congress to pass the HAVA of 2002 was to ensure that greater voter confidence was instilled in the public at large for election processes (Claassen et al., 2013). For Moynihan and Lavertu (2012), there are political ramifications associated with the adoption and rapid wide-scale proliferation of unreliable voting innovations if voting outcomes may be altered or are unreliable, which may irreparably damage the trust levels of citizens in elections. Gardner, Bishop, and Kohno (2009, p. 82) explained that "voting enables citizens to elect their public officials and voice their opinions about the laws and policies that form their society" and that potential vulnerabilities with the electronic voting system that affect electoral outcomes may greatly impact the legitimacy of democracy. There are also a number of security-related concerns and functionality issues that must be recognized when applying technological innovation in modern voting procedures related to HAVA (Kakabadse, Kakabadse, & Kouzmin, 2003; Moynihan, 2004; Moynihan & Silva, 2008; Moynihan & Lavertu, 2012). Card and Moretti (2007, p. 672) explained that touch screen voting issues associated with unreliable equipment or deliberate incidents in which votes are tampered with may lead to a "further deepening of the public distrust in the electoral and democratic system." Concerns associated with DRE machine usage include unintentional "software bugs" capable of affecting election outcomes and intentional efforts to perpetrate voter fraud in which "parties with access to voting machines might manipulate the software to favor or disadvantage particular candidates or parties" (De Jong, van Hoof, & Gosselt, 2008, p. 399). Moynihan and Lavertu (2012) observed that software complexity utilized within the DRE machine is subject to both internal tampering by hackers and expected software-related errors associated with application of this technology. In relation, it has also been noted that voting facilitated through e-machines is vulnerable to a variety of types of hacking (Barr, Bishop, & Gondree, 2007; Moynihan, 2004). Zaino and Zaino (2004, p. 19) stated that security issues could relate to instances when "DRE software could be modified by malicious computer codes," which could ultimately influence voting outcomes. The Diebold optical scan machines and Diebold DRE machines were both found to be subject to massive security weaknesses in which an intentional attack could alter vote tallying (Hursti, 2005; Hursti, 2006). Moynihan (2004) noted that securing a completely error-free e-voting system is not plausible due to the software complexity associated DRE machine usage, potential hardware malfunctions and the unfortunate fact that the United States has a history of election fraud. Software used in DRE machines is vulnerable to both intentional hacks designed to achieve voter fraud and typical everyday technical malfunctions that may cause issues with the voting process. The unfortunate reality is that software and hardware for voting machine technology such as DRE machines is not completely perfect, as perfection is not plausible in any circumstances. It is also not possible to ensure that all voting machine technology is completely safe against intentional attempts to perpetrate voter fraud. Voter fraud is, unfortunately, an established problem with historical precedence. However, proactively identifying potential security risks making voting machine technology susceptible to intentional voter fraud and reducing the frequent occurrence of machine-based software/hardware malfunctions should be a practice that is vigilantly maintained. Therefore, consistently making best efforts to ensure the functionality and security of voting machine technology is paramount to preserving the integrity of an election and upholding the overall legitimacy of a democratic government.

The DRE machine should reflect a high level of precision to ensure that votes are cast as originally intended and be as secure as possible to protect against attempts to commit voter fraud. Despite continued efforts to actively strengthen the usage of advanced voting technologies during the electoral process, it needs to be recognized that a completely flawless and entirely secure voting system is not likely—there is no guarantee against human error or intentional fraud. There are both perceptual concerns and genuine issues associated with DRE functionality and security that can be exacerbated by the existence of questionable dynamics with the machine verifiability processes. Barr, Bishop, and Gondree (2007, p. 9) explained that criticism of the process of e-voting could be related to issues associated with believability in the certification of e-voting technologies due to "the practice of having voting machine vendors pay the independent testing authorities raises questions about the impartiality and rigor of the certification process itself." There may also be issues affecting the credibility of e-voting machines based on the possibility that source code proprietary restrictions may prevent an outside review to determine the functionality and security of the source code being used (Barr, Bishop, & Gondree, 2007). The proprietary issue is one that can potentially result in failure to adequately ensure that DRE machines placed in circulation during elections are secure and function as intended. The security and functionality deficiencies resulting from this circumstance may affect actual election outcomes while potentially degrading overall perceptions for the legitimacy of the electoral process. There are also potential failings associated with the verifiability process because responsible due diligence can be supplanted by deliberate omission of intent to actively verify voting machine integrity. For example, Hursti (2005, p. 2) noted that "security by obscurity" is an ineffective technique that relies on the "secrecy of design and implementation," but largely results in creating the "illusion of security" instead of providing true system safeguards. Hursti (2005, p. 2) continued by noting that "a system relying on security through obscurity may have serious security vulnerabilities, while its owners and designers wish that simply by not informing others of the flaws, no attacker will find them." The concerns raised by the exclusivity-based dilemma can be mitigated in part by utilizing inclusive measures to expand the participant list of those conducting the review process for determining the integrity of voting machine technology. Barr, Bishop, and Gondree (2007, p. 24) focused on this possibility by noting that "computer scientists, voting officials and the body politic" can cooperatively develop "effective and meaningful standards for electronic voting machines" to "help secure these systems and, thereby, our rights as voters." The security-by-obscurity approach can result in an environment in which electoral system integrity is subject to doubt because proprietary rights associated with machine functionality are favored over full transparency. Utilizing a more inclusive effort welcoming input from a wide array of electoral system participants over the security-by-obscurity approach serves as a potentially more effective and democratically responsible means in which to ensure voting machine integrity. Here, the future of establishing more universal electronic voting machine standards may evolve through collective efforts from a wide spectrum of talent involving citizens, government, proprietary owners and technical experts. This speaks to the importance of incorporating multiple perspectives when constructing solutions to address societal issues and the importance of being vigilant to address an area of E-Governance that is still in a state of flux because of the high degree of technological innovation involved in modern voting.

If a more inclusive and democratic approach to testing voting machine integrity is favored over relying on a method supporting proprietary secrecy, then there will be specific technical areas subject to review in relation to the recommended transparent process. As such, there are various means available prior to the election that can be useful in determining if the voting machine is functioning as intended. Saltman (1988) stressed the importance of pre-election testing of software and hardware to ensure the expected functionality of e-machines, helping to preserve the integrity of election results and strengthen citizens' trust in the process of e-voting. In the event a software issue is identified, then it is important that efforts are made to correct the issue or remove the machine from circulation prior to the election. Gardner, Bishop, and Kohno (2009) analyzed security patches for Premier (formerly Diebold) touch screen DRE machines and optical scan machines and found that the intended fixes to safeguard the voting integrity for a wide range of issues (e.g., voter cards, data being transferred, software, vote counts for optical scan systems) was not absolute. Therefore, the initial concerns for security issues for DRE machines and optical scan machines should also extend to include the review of patches designed to prevent election fraud, which are themselves fallible. To better preserve the overall integrity of the electoral process, security concerns should include a continual assessment of the machines, and the security patches designed to address identified weakness associated with use that may be capable of affecting the electoral outcomes. It is also important to avoid becoming over reliant on software patches that are utilized to address DRE machine functionality and security concerns. A software patch can be a useful and important tool to preserve voting machine integrity, but it is not a foolproof, or even permanent, measure.

As noted, the continual gauging of the functionality and security of the software utilized in voting machine technology may benefit from efforts focused on inclusivity. Moynihan (2004) recommended a technique to help diffuse unforeseen issues with complex DRE voting systems that could include using the open-source method to verify operational software by a community of individuals with a vested interest in creating a reliable electoral system. The open-source method helps to "reassert the public ownership of the process" by giving greater precedence to societal verifiability over proprietary ownership for the DRE software and by allowing for a vast array of interested parties, from outside and inside government, to work toward identifying potentially catastrophic software issues (Moynihan, 2004, p. 525). However, the open-source approach is unable to provide a complete guarantee that DRE machines will be wholly and completely reliable. The open-source method is not foolproof. Software is always subject to being manipulated by those that seek to do so, and there still may be DRE machines that are put to use that have not been part of the verification process (Moynihan, 2004). Utilizing the open-source method may also prove ineffective in some cases due to "natural accident theory" associated with complex systems, which indicates that software bugs will always exist despite proactive preventive efforts (Moynihan, 2004). The natural accident theory is predicated on the belief that within a highly complex system, unpredictable issues will inevitably occur that can affect functionality despite efforts to prevent such occurrences and this dynamic is applicable to understanding the application of DRE machines during the electoral process (Moynihan, 2004). The inability to fully predict complex system failures can be applicable to e-voting designs associated with DREs partly because "testing itself is imperfect and is likely to miss bugs that inevitably occur in complex software;" this may create "an illusion of security," allowing for the appearance of accurate votes being cast (Moynihan, 2004, p. 518). It is important to recognize that it is not feasible to completely ensure DRE voting technology is devoid of all design flaws, is error-free regarding voter usage or is not susceptible to voter fraud attacks. Instead, it is necessary to remain proactive and aware of electoral system issues facing participants in the E-Governance Era. The open-source method can help to (a) improve transparency, which promotes faith in democratic processes; (b) integrate a cooperative approach to identify software issues before elections are conducted with machines that are potentially flawed to better ensure greater reliability of voting technology; and (c) work to enhance the overall legitimacy associated with the voting process by proactively verifying machine integrity.

Proactive preventative measures to assess machine integrity prior to elections is an integral step in ensuring legitimate voting outcomes. It is also important to make efforts during the electoral process to help ensure that machine integrity is preserved by taking measures to strengthen means to verify the accuracy of the votes cast. One of the solutions to assist with verifying the vote count and strengthening faith in the integrity of the electoral system is to require that a paper trail is created of the vote cast through modernized voting means such as DREs (Zaino & Zaino, 2004; Card & Moretti, 2007; Moynihan & Lavertu, 2012). Voter-verifiable paper trails (VVPTs), or paper audit trails, may promote trust in on-site e-voting results by providing visible evidence that this electronic means performs as intended during elections, by creating a paper trail that can be used for tallying votes for verification purposes and by serving as the tangible means on which recounts are based (Mercuri, 2002; Zaino & Zaino, 2004; De Jong, van Hoof, & Gosselt, 2008). De Jong, van Hoof, and Gosselt (2008) noted that DRE paper audit trails could (a) serve as the official tally of election results (rendering the calculation of digital results as preliminary), (b) represent a redundancy safeguard to ensure voting machine integrity, and (c) act as the means for which recounts are facilitated. Mercuri (2002, p. 49) observed the importance of maintaining transparency in e-voting means in order "to provide auditability" and to "enhance voter confidence" by which trust in the process can be strengthened in part through the usage of "voter-verified physical audit trail for use in recounts." Since HAVA was passed, the move toward states requiring that modernized voting technologies such as DREs issue a VVPT has gained momentum. HAVA's large-scale replacement of traditional means with more modern voting applications created newly emerging security issues associated with voting machine integrity and led 27 states to adopt DRE paper trail provisions as of 2007 (Schlozman, Verba, & Brady, 2010). The usage of VVPTs for DRE machines can contribute to the verification of e-voting outcomes, potentially reduce digital voter fraud and can serve to strengthen faith of citizens in elections that are conducted through electronic means on site at polling locations. It is important to reinforce that proactive efforts to ensure voting machine integrity such as VVPTs does not guarantee a perfect electoral system and will not ensure that voter fraud or machine malfunctions won't occur in some instances. In this case, a citizen is given a receipt that serves as physical evidence of the political transaction to verify the vote was cast correctly and a corresponding receipt can be utilized for government recount purposes if necessary in the future. However, it is plausible that a machine malfunction or an intentionally malicious alteration of a vote could be extended to the paper trail receipt process as well. If a DRE machine does malfunction or a DRE ballot is altered purposefully as part of voter fraud, then it is possible that these issues could also be extended to the process of issuing a receipt. In this case, the unintentional flaw or purposeful attempt to commit electoral fraud could result in a citizen being furnished with a false receipt of the voting transaction. This false receipt could indicate to the citizen that his or her vote was cast as intended, but the official vote cast was actually altered to reflect an unintended choice. The expectation that electoral outcomes are perfect and completely free from error, intentional or otherwise, is impractical in nature. Although targeted efforts can significantly reduce fraud and unintended errors, achieving the goal of perfection in all facets of elections is not realistic (though this should still be the goal).

The implementation of HAVA in 2002 resulted in an expanded usage of modernized voting equipment such as DRE machines. The previous section highlighted a number of efforts that can be utilized to better ensure the technical reliability associated with maintaining voting machine integrity. There are also considerations with ensuring that individuals who have direct contact with voting machines during elections have a better understanding of machine functionality. This speaks to the sometimes-overlooked human element. Considerations in this regard can focus on educating poll workers and voters, who have the most direct contact with voting machines during elections, as to expectations associated with technical functionality. A lack of training for poll workers and voters regarding how to troubleshoot and utilize e-machines respectively could ultimately lead to a loss of votes causing disenfranchisement (Zaino & Zaino, 2004). In relation, there is a need to recognize the impact that the training of election officials can have in ensuring that they may be of assistance to voters regarding how to utilize modern technology during the voting process (Johnson & Lybecker, 2011). The importance of training poll workers on changes to the electoral system resulting from HAVA can assist to familiarize participants with the new modernized equipment for their own benefit and for the benefit of those citizens that may need assistance using the new voting devices. As important as training and educating poll workers is in contributing to strengthening the understanding of voting technology functionality used in the electoral system, there are some political system–based concerns associated with how this process is facilitated throughout the United States. Here, accounting for educational efforts faces a unique challenge in the U.S. federal system in which HAVA allows for localized development of training programs of poll workers that makes development of a universal electoral system unfeasible. As such, there are considerations associated with how implementing technological innovation may affect "local elections officials" that facilitate the changes to voting procedures associated with HAVA (Moynihan & Silva, 2008). Claassen et al., (2013, p. 233) observed that "the decentralization of election administration in the United States means that electoral jurisdictions will differ with regard to voting technologies, resources for recruiting and training poll workers, and their histories of electoral administration." The original HAVA training components for election officials are not standardized between the states because the legislation does not mandate that money is spent on training (Zaino & Zaino, 2004). This can result in a disjointed usage of voting machine technologies throughout the federal system and variable levels of training initiatives for poll workers between electoral jurisdictions. Training and education become important in ensuring that election officials are proficient in the usage of voting equipment that may be continuously updated in the E-Governance Era. This can be especially challenging in the United States in which HAVA allows for jurisdictional differences in training on various voting technologies used throughout the nation during federal elections.

The educational and training efforts associated with developing a functional understanding of DRE voter technology clearly also includes citizens voting in elections. Citizens serve as the most integral part of the electoral process by casting a vote and it is important that their participation through modern electoral technology is based on a proficient understanding of machine functionality. Therefore, it may be helpful for government to develop education programs for citizens to better familiarize them with voting machine technology that has been used more frequently as a result of HAVA. These educational programs on how to use modernized voting machines could include any combination of on-site training seminars, online educational efforts that provide video walk-throughs and traditional mail campaigns in which informational pamphlets are mailed to registered voters. A multifaceted educational approach, composed of traditional and digital means, could more adequately contribute to ensuring that registered voters have a better understanding of new voting technology that will be used at their local election station before they show up to vote on election day. There is also something to be said for the impact of practical experience and the more elections that are held with the new voting technologies over an extended period of time the greater the potential for developing higher levels of citizen proficiency with how to use these devices.

Overall, it is plausible that actively cultivating an understanding of DRE functionality can serve as an additional safeguard against negative consequences associated with malfunctioning machines or intentional voter fraud. A poll worker or voter that is more familiar with how a voting machine should work can be more apt to spot an unintentional malfunction or voter fraud efforts in which an intended vote has been altered. A lack of training for election officials working the polls that would have enabled them to assist with technical issues and failure to develop educational efforts designed to familiarize citizens participating in e-voting could lead to technical-based disenfranchisement. Educational efforts to cultivate poll worker and voter familiarity with machine usage helps to ensure accuracy of voting outcomes, promoting higher levels of electoral system integrity, and is capable of strengthening democratic legitimacy within the U.S. deliberative framework. The development of proactive educational efforts on DRE machine usage prior to elections and participation yielding practical experience gained through use over an extended period of time helps to mitigate election-day issues that could potentially affect voting outcomes.

The above sections highlight the importance of ensuring voting system integrity through developing means to gauge machine-based technical effectiveness and through educational endeavors to familiarize individuals with technological functionality of modern voting means. Such purposeful designs may assist in maintaining democratic legitimacy by preserving the integrity of voting outcomes. However, there are also naturally occurring political system components that may be instrumental in preventing wide-scale, voting machine–based election fraud. There are allowances in the federal system for state variances in the usage of voting machine technology that may serve as an additional electoral safeguard against the threat of voter fraud. Mercuri (2002, p. 48) explained that "whereas earlier technologies required that election fraud be perpetrated at one polling place or machine at a time, the proliferation of similarly programmed e-voting systems invites opportunities for large-scale manipulation of elections." In the event of a congruent application of machine technology on a federal scale, this type of electoral system could be more susceptible to coordinated, wide-scale voter fraud attack. At present, the whole of the U.S. electoral system is generally disjointed in the implementation of voting machine technology, creating variances from state to state as a result of federal discretion associated with HAVA. The U.S. federal system in some ways may render "widespread fraud unlikely" because states are left to their own volition to implement a number of HAVA requirements associated with e-voting machines, resulting in diversity in both "vendors" and "software" (Zaino & Zaino, 2004, p. 19). Barr, Bishop, and Gondree (2007, p. 19) critiqued the design and testing plans for certifying voting machines because the standards of the Election Assistance Commission (EAC) are constructed without "a coherent set of requirements for electronic voting systems," which makes it difficult to some degree to determine how related digital HAVA requirements should be implemented on a national scale and in identifying what threats this system should be ready and able to combat. However, the resulting lack of consistency in the design of voting machine technologies can also serve as a natural safeguard to some degree to help prevent electoral fraud on a coordinated national scale. For example, a wide-scale attempt at voter fraud through intentional DRE machine manipulation would require seemingly unlikely electoral system conditions to be able to adequately facilitate a coordinated effort on a national scale. To some degree, election fraud could be limited in scope by the inherent nature of the federal system in which state variances for the implementation of multiple e-voting means serves as a natural safeguard. In this sense, the adoption of a multitude of HAVA-compliant electoral technologies at the state/local level reflective of variable levels of innovations helps to mitigate the threat of wide-scale machine-focused attempts at voter fraud. The EAC's Election Administration Voting Survey (EAC, 2015) of approximately 371,600 voting systems during the 2014 federal elections indicates that voting technology variances may be evidenced locally in circumstances in which "a jurisdiction may employ a scanner for absentee ballots but Direct Recording Electronic (DRE) machines for in-person voting. Polling places may have more than one type of voting technology in use on Election Day." In relation, the EAC's Election Administration Voting

DRE machines with a voter-verified paper audit trail (VVPAT)

DRE machines without a VVPAT

Optical or digital scan systems, in which voters fill out a paper ballot that is then read by a scanner

Hybrid system combining a DRE with an optical scanner

Punch card systems

Paper ballots

Other systems

Figure 9.2 EAC's Election Administration Voting Survey (2015) and Voting Technologies
Source: Help America Vote Act of 2002: www.eac.gov/assets/1/1/2014_EAC_EAVS_
Comprehensive_Report_508_Compliant.pdf.

Survey (2015) highlighted the following voting technologies that were used within voting systems as indicated in Figure 9.2.

Here, the usage of technology during an election may be diverse even at a single local polling station within a state. This diversity in means used to facilitate an election is compounded significantly when considering the multitude of jurisdictions within a given state and even more so when considering the levels of diversity in voting means representing the whole of the national voting system. This is not to say that the federal system is completely immune to voter fraud attempts simply because of variances in manufacturers' designs and software used in voting machines at the state/local level. The level of coordination required to conduct a machine-based attack during general elections on the national scale is arduously intricate when there is a vast array of machine technologies in use and consistency in that usage may vary from locality to locality within each state. This would render a national-scale, coordinated attack to conduct election fraud by targeting on-site e-voting machine technology improbable due to present logistical limitations. There are clearly still system concerns in which an accumulation of successful localized attempts at voter fraud could constitute a significant overall alteration to election outcomes. As noted, the discretion afforded through HAVA creates a national voting system that is reflective of differences between election technologies used as the state and local level. This may also make it difficult to assess the wide-scale effectiveness of voter technologies to some degree in which there will be variances in use on a state/local level, which will render a national approach to understanding more difficult. For example, the success or failure of a voting technology in one locality may not be applicable in a different locality for various demographic and logistical reasons.

There are several unique voting components that bridge traditional election concerns with technical elements prevalent in the E-Governance Era, and the state of voting machine technology utilized on site during elections serves as an illustrative example of this dynamic. This includes maintaining awareness that the voting system in the United States (a) may be lacking in universal implementation standards throughout the nation, (b) may be subject to questionable certification processes of voting machines due to an inherent partiality in the vender-tester fiscal dynamics, (c) may suffer from limitations in analysis of source code utilized for proprietary reasons, and (d) may include the application of innovations that are not completely secure. Since the passing of HAVA in 2002, there are a number of methods available to better ensure voting machine integrity and to strengthen voter faith in the electoral process, including a wide range of technical-based efforts by government to preserve the functionality and security of voting machines in use. These technical-based preventive means can occur prior to the election to ensure that voting machines are functioning properly and are adequately secure against intentional voter fraud attacks. In relation, utilizing the more democratically conscious, transparent open-source method could be useful in reviewing software utilized in voting machines. Conducting tests prior to the election regarding voting machine functionality can be an important component associated with government efforts to ensure the integrity of the electoral system. There are also technical-based preventative measures that could be utilized during the election to ensure voting machine reliability, such as furnishing a voter-verified paper trail (VVPT). In addition, there are educational-based methods designed so that voting machine usage can be better understood and facilitated by individuals who have the most frequent direct contact with those machines during an election. Educating poll workers and voters regarding how to utilize voting machine technology can contribute to a reduction in voting errors. This includes ensuring that poll workers are sufficiently trained regarding machine functionality and that voters are comfortable with how to cast votes when utilizing voting machine technologies such as DREs. Doing so may help to provide an additional safeguard in which malfunctions or intentional voter fraud efforts can be more readily identified by participants who are more familiar with how voting machines are intended to function. The experience gained over time by individuals participating in elections through advanced voting technology can also contribute to cultivating a higher comfort level derived from a practical understanding of machine functionality. There may also be natural system protections inherent within the federal electoral structure because HAVA guidelines creates a wide disparity in which voting machine technology is being utilized on a national level. The lack of continuity regarding software and hardware utilized by different manufacturers of voting machine technologies can make wide-spread voter fraud attacks less logistically feasible on a national scale. The variances in the application of voting machine technologies utilized at the state/local level can serve as a natural system protection against wide-scale voter fraud. For example, wide-scale technology variances in the types of voting machines utilized on site at polling stations could make it more difficult to perpetuate intentional voter fraud to alter the outcomes of general elections in the U.S. federal system. Ultimately, the success or failure associated with creating an effective E-Governance Era voting system can have significant social and political consequences. An electoral system that utilizes voting machines with questionable, or in the worst case scenario, a verified security or functionality issue can affect electoral outcomes, which calls into question the legitimacy of government. Therefore, ensuring voting machine integrity and developing an understanding for participants with how to use such technology contributes to establishing a more democratically sustainable and trustworthy modern electoral system.

The decision to utilize a specific modern voting technology like DRE machines may be based on any number of political factors. This includes the role that budgeting may play when considering which modern voting technologies can be implemented at a given time. Card and Moretti (2007) discussed a number of influential factors that may determine whether DRE technology is adopted within a locality in which the decision to obtain such machines may be cost prohibitive due to a relatively high initial purchase price and the cost of maintaining the machines over time. Card and Moretti (2007, p. 663) also highlighted that there may be considerations associated with "the adjustment costs of switching to a new technology." In addition, there may be customization variances regarding how state and local governments utilize the same exact DRE machines, variances that can dictate technology adoption decisions (Card & Moretti, 2007). As noted above, not all U.S. states require a paper trial to be included with DRE voting; the discretion left up to localities in these instances will affect levels of adaptability. Here, there are a number of realistic fiscal concerns that may contribute to decision makers' pursuit to further expand DRE technology use in the voting process. This includes the cost of purchasing, customizing, maintaining and operating DREs. Government is responsible for gauging the levels of demand from the political environment indicating whether there is a need to enact changes to the voting technology presently in use. There may also be cost considerations associated with replacing existing voting technology that still has a longer operational life expectancy before it is warranted simply because there may be a perceived need to utilize emerging technologies.

The decision to implement a state-of-the-art voting technology may have significant implications associated with the perception of the public regarding the legitimacy of government. It is important to remain aware that decisions to apply modernized voting technologies should avoid being unintentionally or intentionally designed to affect voting outcomes by exploiting demographic preferences. Card and Moretti (2007) explored the possibility that the application of specific voting technology like DRE machines may have the capacity to influence election outcomes if specific demographics are generally less apt to utilize these innovations during elections. There are a number of related factors regarding how the choice of voter technology may affect election outcomes, including demographic-based distrust of or discomfort with utilizing the innovation (Card & Moretti, 2007). Card and Moretti (2007) also noted the unfamiliarity of citizens with the usage of voting technology such as DREs could have a logistical effect, unintentionally creating longer lines and increasing the length of time it takes to vote. In such instances, choices to utilize a specific voting technology may unintentionally disenfranchise citizens that opt to leave before voting when presented with massive lines at polling stations because they may not have the desire to wait or the additional available time to do so. The decision to apply voter technology that may unknowingly, or the worst case scenario, knowingly, adversely affect the participation levels of a demographic, whatever that demographic may be, could ultimately affect election outcomes by dissuading a significant percentage of a given demographic from becoming involved in the election. This can degrade levels of citizens' trust in the outcomes of an election and may strike at the very fabric of faith in democracy, which denigrates a key activity—voting—within the deliberative framework. If citizens within demographic "A" (e.g., age, ethnicity, gender, political party, race, residency location, etc.) are distrustful of, disinterested in or intimidated by a specific voting technology, then the utilization of that means may affect elections on the micro level (i.e., voting participation within that demographic) and macro level (i.e., influencing the overall outcome of elected officials). The decision to apply voting technologies may be based on any number of political factors in which fiscal considerations or public demand dictates action. However, a diverse approach to utilizing voting technologies in elections to provide means to accommodate preferences of voters should be considered. Government must ensure that choice is provided to citizens in which participation at the voting polls may be facilitated by different types of HAVA-compliant voting machines to assist in avoiding technical-based disenfranchisement.

References

Barr, E., Bishop, M., & Gondree, M. (2007) Fixing federal e-voting standards. *Communications of the ACM*, 50(3): 19–24. doi: 10.1145/1226736.1226754.

Card, D., & Moretti, E. (2007) Does voting technology affect election outcomes? Touch-screen voting and the 2004 presidential election. *Review of Economics and Statistics*, 89(4): 660–673.

Claassen, R., Magleby, D., Monson, J., & Patterson, K. (2013) Voter confidence and the election-day voting experience. *Political Behavior*, 35(2): 215–235. doi: 10.1007/s11109-012-9202-4.

De Jong, M., van Hoof, J., & Gosselt, J. (2008) Voters' perceptions of voting technology: Paper ballots versus voting machine with and without paper audit trail. *Social Science Computer Review*, 26(4): 399–410. doi: 10.1177/0894439307312482.

File, T. (2015) Who votes? Congressional elections and the American electorate, 1978–2014: Population characteristics. Retrieved from www.census.gov/content/dam/Census/library/publications/2015/demo/p20-577.pdf.

Gardner, R. W., Bishop, M., & Kohno, T. (2009) Are patched machines really fixed? *IEEE Security & Privacy Magazine*, 7(5): 82–85.

Gilbert, J. E., Dunbar, J., Ottley, A., & Smotherman, J. M. (2013) Anomaly detection in electronic voting systems. *Information Design Journal*, 20(3): 194–206. doi: 10.1075/idj.20.3.01gil.

Hursti, H. (2005) The black box report: July 4, 2005 critical security issues with Diebold optical scan design. Retrieved from www.blackboxvoting.org/BBVreport.pdf.

Hursti, H. (2006) Diebold TSx evaluation security alert: May 11, 2006 critical security issues with Diebold TSx a black box voting project. Retrieved from www.blackboxvoting.org/BBVtsxstudy.pdf.

Johnson, D. N., & Lybecker, K. M. (2011) Does HAVA (Help America Vote Act) help the have-nots? U.S. adoption of new election equipment, 1980–2008. *Growth and Change*, 42(4): 601–627.

Kakabadse, A., Kakabadse, N. K., & Kouzmin, A. (2003) Reinventing the democratic governance project through information technology? A growing agenda for debate. *Public Administration Review*, 63(1): 44–60.

McDonald, M. P. (2002) The turnout rate among eligible voters in the States, 1980–2000. *State Politics & Policy Quarterly*, 2(2): 199.

Mercuri, R. (2002) A better ballot box? New electronic voting systems pose risks as well as solutions. *IEEE Spectrum*, 39(10): 46–50.

Moynihan, D. P. (2004) Building secure elections: E-voting, security, and systems theory. *Public Administration Review*, 64(5): 515–528.

Moynihan, D. P., & Lavertu, S. (2012) Cognitive biases in governing: Technology preferences in election administration. *Public Administration Review*, 72(1): 68–77.

Moynihan, D. P., & Silva, C. L. (2008) The administrators of democracy: A research note on local election officials. *Public Administration Review*, 68(5): 816–827.

Saltman, R. G. (1988) Accuracy, integrity and security in computerized vote-tallying. *Communications of the ACM*, 31(10): 1184–1191.

Schlozman, K. L., Verba, S., & Brady, H. E. (2010) Weapon of the strong? Participatory inequality and the Internet. *Perspectives on Politics*, 8(2): 487–509. doi: 10.1017/S1537592710001210.

Underhill, W. (2012) Election 2000: Before and after. *State Legislatures Magazine*, September. Retrieved from www.ncsl.org/research/elections-and-campaigns/election-2000-before-and-after.aspx.

United States Congress. (2002) Help America Vote Act (HAVA) of 2002. Retrieved from www.eac.gov/assets/1/workflow_staging/Page/41.PDF.

United States Election Assistance Commission (EAC). (2007) 2006 election administration and voting survey and data sets (executive summary). Retrieved from www.eac.gov/assets/1/AssetManager/2006%20EAVS%20Executive_Summary.pdf.

United States Election Assistance Commission (EAC). (2013) 2012 election administration and voting survey: A summary of key findings, September. Retrieved from www.eac.gov/assets/1/Page/990-050%20EAC%20VoterSurvey_508Compliant.pdf.

United States Election Assistance Commission (EAC). (2015) The 2014 EAC election administration and voting survey comprehensive report: A report to the 114th congress. Retrieved from www.eac.gov/assets/1/Page/2014_EAC_EAVS_Comprehensive_Report_508_Compliant.pdf.

United States Election Assistance Commission (EAC). (2016) Voluntary voting system guidelines. Retrieved from www.eac.gov/testing_and_certification/voluntary_voting_system_guidelines.aspx.

United States Federal Election Commission. (2016) Mechanical lever machines. Retrieved from www.fec.gov/pages/lever.htm.

United States Government Accountability Office. (2005) Report to congressional requesters: Elections federal efforts to improve security and reliability of electronic voting systems are under way, but key activities need to be completed. Retrieved from www.gao.gov/assets/250/247851.pdf.

United States Supreme Court. (2000) *Bush v. Gore*. Retrieved from www.oyez.org/cases/2000/00-949.

Zaino, J. S., & Zaino, J. T. (2004) A new era in voting technology: The changing landscape of election disputes. *Dispute Resolution Journal*, 59(3): 11–21.

10 E-Governance, Deliberative Democracy and Voting Processes

Part Two

The E-Governance Era includes a wide range of activities of democratic importance, including the potential role that Internet-based voting processes may play in modern governance. The present state of Internet-based e-voting is that it is generally underutilized consistently on a wide scale and its potential has yet to be even remotely fully realized. The process of Internet-based e-voting has generated much interest in the modern era as it relates to the ability to contribute to electoral participation. The possibility of Internet-based e-voting being conducted on the international scale and domestic scale has continued to generate great interest in recent years. This includes considerations associated with the potential role that Internet-based e-voting may play in enhancing levels of citizen participation in a deliberative democracy in South Korea (Jin-Wook, 2006). There has also been significant research associated with the application of Internet-based e-voting on the global level, including in Argentina and Columbia (Alvarez, Katz, & Pomares, 2011), Brazil (Avgerou et al., 2009), Estonia (Lust, 2015) and India (Krishnan, 2014). Estonia is somewhat unique in the context of the larger considerations with the E-Governance Era due to the unusually high levels of government-related activities that are facilitated online. The government of Estonia has a rich tradition of utilizing innovations to facilitate delivering services to the public online and in the development of a nationwide initiative to incorporate Internet and computers in schools (Lust, 2015). The Estonian government created an online opportunity for public sector officials to dialogue with each other during each stage of the legislation process and for citizens to participate via the Internet by making suggestions to proposed legislation (Lust, 2015). Lust (2015) noted that Estonia is the only nation in which voters can participate in national online elections and that 31 percent voted online in the 2015 elections. The Estonia case study is one that provides a rich area of future study as it relates to determining how security issues may affect the process, understanding the influence of online-voting levels of citizen participation and considering the potential role of the digital divide in affecting electronic elections (Lust, 2015).

There are some examples from within the international community in which online voting has been used during elections, and this continues to serve as justification for further consideration of its potential future use. Bannister and Connolly (2012) observed that, generally, online voting is reserved for application in "limited contexts" in which its proliferation has been somewhat restricted to an almost trial-balloon capacity for "small, closed electorates" to determine future effectiveness. In relation, the application of Internet voting has been somewhat limited in practice, and this political context is applicable to online voting in the United States in the present E-Governance climate. In addition, there are some limited examples in the United States in which elections have been facilitated online. This includes two examples in the United States from Michigan and Arizona in which online voting was used to cast official ballots in a binding election for presidential primaries (Solop, 2001; Kenski, 2005; Prevost & Schaffner, 2008). These limited examples of online voting in U.S. elections provide information that may prove vital as the field of Internet-based voting expands. Solop (2001) studied demographic and attitudinal differences of citizens participating in the first binding online election that occurred in the 2000 presidential Democratic primary in Arizona. Solop (2001) observed that Internet voting was most popular among demographics that were white males, well-educated, middle-age (36–65), liberal Democrats with higher incomes when compared to non-Internet voter demographics. Factors such as availability of online voting, citizen efficacy associated with perceived impact of political participation and raised awareness of online voting due to media attention were contributing factors that led to increased levels of participation in the online election of the 2000 Arizona Democratic primary (Solop, 2001). These findings highlight the importance of recognizing multidimensional factors that led to increased voter turnout during the binding online election. This layered perspective contributes to a better understanding of how the future of online voting may affect this type of political participation in a deliberative democracy.

There are contemporary considerations for the role that modern innovation could play in influencing the voting process and the applicability of Internet-based e-voting for citizens that reside overseas has received some attention in the E-Governance Era. According to the U.S. Department of Justice (2010), "the 1986 Uniformed and Overseas Citizens Absentee Voting Act (UOCAVA) protects the right of service members to vote in federal elections regardless of where they are stationed. This law requires that states and territories allow members of the U.S. Uniformed Services and merchant marine, their family members and U.S. citizens residing outside the United States to register and vote absentee in elections for federal offices." The advancements in technology that could be applied to facilitate participation in elections for overseas voters have changed dramatically since the UOCAVA was implemented. As such, the potential for the usage of the Internet to facilitate a range of e-voting activities for overseas voters generated greater focus on behalf of the federal government. The Government Accountability Office (2007, p. 10) reported that upon receiving a

Congressional mandate as part of the National Defense Authorization Act (NDAA) of 2002, the Department of Defense (DoD) began to move forward with "the Secure Electronic Registration and Voting Experiment (SERVE) for Internet-based absentee registration and voting" which was to be facilitated by the Federal Voting Assistance Program (FVAP). However, SERVE was temporarily delayed before it could be implemented by FVAP prior to the 2004 general elections. The Government Accountability Office (2007, p. 10) highlighted the fact that a delay was issued "because DoD did not want to call into question the integrity of votes that would have been cast via SERVE, the Deputy Director of Defense terminated the project in early 2004, and DoD did not use it in the November 2004 election." The seed of doubt associated with the usage of the Internet for overseas voting was planted by the unfavorable results stemming from a review of SERVE conducted by members of the Security Peer Review Group (SPRG), which dealt a major blow to the confidence in the ability of the government to fulfill wide-scale online overseas voting in a secure environment. Jefferson et al. (2004) of the SPRG were tasked with the responsibility of determining whether the SERVE system would have been secure against any number of cyber-attacks if allowed to facilitate online voting for a projected 100,000 overseas voters in the 2004 primaries and general elections. Jefferson et al. (2004) concluded that "because the danger of successful, large-scale attacks is so great, we reluctantly recommend shutting down the development of SERVE immediately and not attempting anything like it in the future until both the Internet and the world's home computer infrastructure have been fundamentally redesigned, or some other unforeseen security breakthroughs appear." The mandated requirements for the development of SERVE was suspended by Section 567 of the Ronald W. Reagan National Defense Authorization Act (United States Congress, 2004, pp. 1919–1920), which called for a "repeal of requirement to conduct electronic voting demonstration project for the Federal election to be held in November 2004" until which time "the first regularly scheduled general election for Federal office which occurs after the Election Assistance Commission notifies the Secretary that the Commission has established electronic absentee voting guidelines and certifies that it will assist the Secretary in carrying out the project." A later Federal Voting Assistance Program (2015, p. 1) report indicated that its responsibility for SERVE was ultimately determined when "in the NDAA FY 2015, Congress eliminated the requirement for FVAP to conduct the electronic voting demonstration project. With the repeal of the requirement, DoD is no longer exploring program implementation in this area." As such, the Federal Voting Assistance Program was absolved from the responsibility of being involved in the SERVE project, which was officially suspended indefinitely.

However, the Internet has been used in a small-scale capacity to promote participation in e-voting activities for overseas voters. For example, Alvarez et al. (2008) explained that Okaloosa Country, Florida "implemented the

Okaloosa Distance Balloting Pilot (ODBP), a pilot program that sought to develop a solution model for other counties with large UOCAVA populations." A total of 93 votes were cast (the 94th potential voter opted to not cast a ballot) on behalf of overseas voters that participated in the pilot from October 24, 2008 through November 2, 2008 at three different locations including Japan (21), Germany (33) and England (40), in which "encrypted ballots were transmitted through a secure virtual private network (VPN)" (Alvarez et al., 2008). The ODBP general election process at kiosks created a paper receipt for the voter (to verify the vote was cast accurately) and for government (to compare against the electronic tally), which was reported to have resulted in a 100-percent match when "officials conducted a post-election vote comparison" (Alvarez et al., 2008). However, there were critiques associated with the voting process that may have called the results into question (Mahoney, 2010). Mahoney (2010, p. 2) noted there were auditing issues as it relates to "accounting for the number of voters and ballots as well as comparison of paper records with electronic ballots; gaps and discrepancies must be explained and documented." Mahoney (2010, p. 2) continued by noting that the ODBP reflected "ballot secrecy problems" and "voting system used in the Okaloosa project did not permit auditing of the version of the voting system used in the kiosks." If overcoming potential issues associated with auditability of electronic votes cast, secrecy in the process of casting a ballot and verifiability of software being used universally in all kiosks can be maintained, then there are a number of lessons learned that may create a foundation on which future Internet voting endeavors are built. The ODBP program provided promising results associated with a small sample population size participating in the election through the Internet, and the kiosk format in which this was facilitated may provide a template for future wide-scale online U.S. elections. There have been additional promising endeavors related to the usage of the Internet to facilitate a number of components associated with online voting in federal elections for overseas voters. Section 575 of the National Defense Authorization Act of 2010 (United States Congress, 2010) is entitled "The Military and Overseas Empowerment Act (MOVE)." It requires that states, unless granted a hardship waiver by the federal government, must provide "absent uniformed services voters and overseas voters" the opportunity to request absentee ballots be sent to them either through the traditional mail services or through electronic means. The usage of the Internet to facilitate sending absentee ballots to overseas voters provides an advantage in the speed of dissemination process in which receipt of the form is expedited considerably when compared against traditional mail service. In addition, the previously created Electronic Transmission Service (ETS) would provide the means in which overseas voters could cast an official absentee ballot electronically in certain qualifying circumstances. Box 10.1 highlights information from the Department of Defense (2004) associated with defining ETS.

Box 10.1 Electronic Transmission Service (ETS)

Electronic Transmission Service (ETS). FVAP's ETS allows citizens and state and local government officials, where permitted by law, to fax election materials, such as a request for registration and/or ballot (FPCA), a blank ballot sent to the voter by the local election officials, a voted ballot returned to the local election official, and other election correspondence when conditions do not allow for timely receipt and return of these materials.

DoD (2004). Retrieved from www.dod.mil/pubs/foi/Reading_Room/
Personnel_Related/13-F-0748_Report_on_DoD_Action_to_Support_
Voting_Assistance_to_Armed_Forces.pdf.

In accordance with the Federal Voting Assistance Program (2012, p. 3), the creation of the "Electronic Transmission Service (ETS) enables local election officials to transmit and receive election materials via fax or email to/from Uniformed members and overseas citizens at no cost." The Federal Voting Assistance Program's (FVAP) Electronic Transmission Service (ETS) Manual (2012, p. 3) further indicates that if state election laws allow "local election officials should use the ETS any time he/she believes the regular absentee ballot cannot be received, voted, and returned by mail in time to be counted, provided that fax and/or email are permitted by state law or regulatory authority." Here, the federal government allows for state discretion to determine whether local election officials may use the ETS and for what functions as it relates to e-voting. This includes that states may allow for local election officials to e-mail absentee ballots and receive voted ballots through ETS. For example, the state of Indiana allows for voted absentee ballots to be returned through mail, email or fax (www.fvap.gov/uploads/FVAP/States/indiana. pdf). Indiana (2016) also provides voters the opportunity to check on the status of their absentee ballot online (https://indianavoters.in.gov/PublicSite/ Public/FT1/PublicLookupMain.aspx?Link=Registration). Although SERVE was canceled due to its questionable ability to facilitate a secure online voting environment for overseas voters and the small-scale ODBP online voting program for overseas voters led to arguably positive results, the potential for the use of the Internet to facilitate e-voting activities for voters in the future remains intriguing and promising. This relates in part to the development of the ETS, which has been used to facilitate Internet voting for overseas voters and the example of kiosk-based voting associated with ODBP, which may provide a foundation on which larger scale domestic online voting could be based.

Thus far, the application of online voting in the U.S. has had very limited use save for a handful of examples of this ideal in practice during binding elections. As U.S. online voting is still at best in its preliminary stages, the future of the role of the Internet to facilitate binding elections will be dependent on a wide range of variables which will be determined more fully in upcoming years. In relation, there are many lessons learned from domestic and global Internet voting that may help to provide guidelines for early-stage development. The feasibility of utilizing the Internet to facilitate future wide-scale binding elections in the United States will depend on better understanding the potential positives and negatives argued to be attributed to examples of online voting in practice. There are a number of potential benefits derived from facilitating voting through the Internet that have been identified within the literature and help to serve to strengthen the potential for continued expansion of e-voting's application. The use of the Internet may create a level of convenience for the voter, as online voting can be far less time consuming and can cost less than having to commute to polling stations to participate directly in the electoral process (Kenski, 2005). The proponents of online voting believe that higher levels of convenience and greater ease of access will help to increase voter participation levels in many respects. Online voting could potentially increase participation by expanding traditional boundaries of on-site voting booths at polling stations to include cyber-space in which reduced travel time may benefit citizens that are disabled, that have to traverse long distances or go through lengthy public transportation commutes, that are not located domestically at the time of the election and that have a work schedule that is not accommodating to regular hours of operation for election stations (Gibson, 2001). It is also possible that online voting may potentially "reconnect the individual to the community" and "enhance the legitimacy of the system by increasing turnout" (Kenski, 2005). Online voting is also often viewed as a more effective means in which to increase participation among young eligible voters who have a relatively high comfort level with technological innovations as the use of digital tools in their lives has generally become an everyday occurrence (Gibson, 2001; Kenski, 2005; Schaupp & Carter, 2005). Schaupp and Carter (2005) observed that college students age 18–24, who usually have lower voter turnout than citizens from other voting age demographics and are somewhat apathetic regarding this form of civic engagement, may best use the future potential of e-voting to increase online participation in elections. Schaupp and Carter (2005) noted that marketing online voting benefits such as "convenience and compatibility" can contribute to enhancing the levels of participation for the potentially apathetic college student age demographic. The advantages for future online voting designs include an enhanced level of convenience over traditional absentee ballot processes that out-of-state students would have to complete in order to vote and an effort by government to use electronic means compatible with the technologically savvy lifestyle of modern college students (Schaupp & Carter, 2005). There are arguments that online voting will be capable of lowering overall administrative costs associated with the electoral process and that online voting serves as a "natural or logical progression in voting technology" by applying readily available innovations already commonly in use (Gibson, 2001). The proponents of online voting believe that application of this means will potentially help to increase voter participation levels based on a number of significant benefits. Online voting may provide voters with a certain level of convenience when compared to voting on site at an election polling station. The opportunity to vote online from a home computer or mobile device is far more convenient than traveling to and from the polls to participate in an election. The E-Governance Era has seen the usage of technology to create virtual venues that facilitate a sense of community among digital participants. This ideal can be extended to the online voting process in which boundaries for participation are expanded to include digital means. In relation, providing electronic means that support a more convenient voting experience may increase participation in elections for tech-savvy citizens. This will potentially contribute to increasing voter participation among younger voters who are generally comfortable with, and often have a preference for, using technological innovations to facilitate a wide range of communication activities. The possibility that online voting could reduce the administrative costs of the election strengthens the argument to adopt this means based on the potential in providing fiscal benefits to government. If retention of savings can be accomplished during the development and implementation stages, then this would accommodate fiscally conservative expectations from within the budgeting environment. In addition, it is the tradition of U.S. electoral reforms to apply emerging technologies and this expectation can carry the modern voting process into the digital era by offering technologically innovative means in a supplementary capacity. Admittedly, the lack of consensus on what constitutes logic, or what could conceivably qualify as a logical progression regarding the application of technology in governance, is something of a grey area at best. An 18-year-old participating in his or her first presidential election in 2016 may view that the "logical" progression of technology for voting should include a vast array of modern digital tools in a significantly different way from a citizen collecting social security that has been participating in elections for the past 50 years. The governmental decision to use digital means to increase levels of voter participation and a citizen's decision to use those means based on preferences may be applicable to considerations associated with what would constitute logical application of available innovations. This will require contextual analysis to determine whether the requisite convergence of technical capacity, political will and social expectations are present to sustain online voting endeavors. Lastly, the application of technological innovations is historically relevant regarding the U.S. government fulfillment of duties. The development of E-Governance Era means that would support the use of the Internet for voting is indicative of government's continued efforts to use new technology in accordance with expectations of citizens to provide a more complete deliberative framework.

It would be imprudent to introduce the potential benefits for online voting without also acknowledging that this process may yield adverse consequences. Therefore, a number of potential critiques associated with online voting should be identified before considering implementation of wide-scale Internet-based voting in binding elections. Prevost and Schafner (2008, p. 526) observed, "even if voting is only a mouse click away, some citizens may still fail to log on and vote unless they are mobilized to participation in the political system." This speaks to the importance of recognizing that simply providing electronic means, such as those associated with online voting, is not a guarantee that an increased level of participation from the public will result. The usage of the Internet to facilitate binding elections may also yield circumstances that run counter to traditional expectations for this type of civic engagement. The level of insulation of the voting booth may be reduced for those participating in online elections in which citizens may "access sources of information right up to the point of choice" (Gibson, 2001, p. 583). This could possibly be used to launch last-minute Internet campaigning tactics through e-mails, pop-up ads, or web banners, which could potentially have an impulse-buy effect on citizens participating in the online voting process. The integrity of the voting booth could be significantly diminished in instances in which the environmental expectations for solitude and privacy are supplemented by a modernized digital attempt at last-minute political marketing designed to influence electoral outcomes. Simons and Jones (2012) identified possible Internet voting fallacies that include the promise of offering savings during the electoral process and the belief that higher voter turnout would be achieved. Online voting is argued to potentially reduce levels of political participation levels because it may threaten traditional civic engagement rituals and degrade important societal expectations for public sphere equality in which registered voters commute to the polls regardless of social status, which may yield greater levels of disinterest in civic engagement (Gibson, 2001). Here, the traditional expectations associated with participating in elections in which all citizens trek en masse on election day to their local polling booths is diminished somewhat if digitally savvy individuals in society participate in online voting. If online voting serves to somehow reduce overall levels of citizens participating in elections because of the potential to degrade interest in wide-scale civic engagement, then this would be counterproductive, belying the original intent of the digital endeavor. There are also considerations associated with potential negative implications of online voting as it relates to the influence of the digital divide on the electoral process. It is important to recognize that digital divide inequities may be further exacerbated when considering utilizing online voting in the event that some citizens may be further disadvantaged in this scenario because they may not have ownership of a home computer, have not had the opportunity to develop requisite skill levels associated with personal computer use and are without home Internet access (Gibson, 2001). The online voting process will potentially lower travel costs, eliminate commuting time and extend voting hours, which will provide greater benefits to those individuals who do have home computers and Internet access (Gibson, 2001). Gibson (2001, p. 568) explained that "while there is no systematic denial of the right to exercise the franchise, the barriers to voting are lowered for a particular subset of voters, creating a fundamentally unequal situation." In this circumstance, the benefits associated with online voting may not be enjoyed by all citizens due to an inequitable lowering of barriers to participation as it relates to the digital divide. Kenski (2005, p. 297) noted that "online voting and the digital divide may be damaging to the composition of the voting electorate at the group level and further distance minorities from the political process." The use of the Internet for conducting elections may intensify the digital divide problem related to demographic underrepresentation if online voting only manages to increase participation among the elite societal groups, which are argued to already maintain higher levels of civic engagement than disadvantaged citizens (Kenski, 2005). Simons and Jones (2012, p. 74) observed that because of "many successful attacks against governments, major banks, and the world's technology leaders, it should be relatively easy to entrap large numbers of voters who are not technologists." Here, there may be concerns associated with the digital divide in which citizens that may be less technically proficient can possibly be more susceptible to security threats associated with the online e-voting process. This aspect of the digital divide is focused on the wide array of individuals that fall under the umbrella of technological have-nots in society, including citizens that are eligible for Social Security who may have yet to familiarize themselves with innovations or citizens who reside in rural America in which access to innovations may be limited. The digital divide in this case may create higher levels of risk for those citizens who are less familiar with Internet functionality associated with the usage of online voting. It is important to consider the influence of the digital divide on the online voting processes. Online voting may potentially endanger a number of important democratic expectations associated with traditional voting engagement processes and may unintentionally create barriers to participation based on the digital divide affecting who is able to vote through this innovative means. It may also create increased concerns associated with preserving the security of online elections in some cases. The digital divide continues to be an influential factor in determining the usage of E-Governance Era innovations toward government actions.

There are also a number of technical-based concerns associated with the use of Internet voting in which security failings can potentially affect the outcomes of elections and can negatively influence perceptions associated with the levels of trust in government. If the potential threats associated with security risks become reality, then this may ultimately reduce levels of citizens' trust that the government processes and outcomes are legitimate. Online voting security interests includes a wide range of activities, such as eliminating concerns for the process to authenticate voter identity, maintaining secret ballot processing in accordance with democratic principles, securing the Internet voting means to preserve the integrity of the election and preventing possible outside interference that is intended to alter voter participation outcomes (Kenski, 2005). Gibson (2001) explained that there are three distinct security concerns associated with online voting: ensuring authentication (the voter casting the ballot is identified as accurate), privacy (the process is secret and no outside parties have access to ballots cast) and integrity (the ballot cast by the voter is not interfered with or altered at any point in time). As noted, there are a number of significant concerns associated with the security of Internet voting that can affect whether the electoral process and outcomes are considered to be legitimate. The security of the online voting process is essential in preventing intentional alterations of original ballots cast by citizens and for maintaining the trust of citizens that election outcomes are legitimate. A further look at how potential security failings that may occur during the online voting process can affect levels of citizen trust in government are highlighted here. Fortier (2000, p. 459) expanded on the general importance of ensuring secure technology usage by noting that "both potential and actual users of computer networking have expressed concerns about the confidentiality of the information being circulated through the technology and the security of systems they come to rely on." In relation, security failings and information breaches derived from technical miscues during online elections have significant implications for the overall integrity of democracy. There are considerations associated with whether citizens' trust in online e-voting methods perceived as failures could further degrade already questionable levels of confidence in the U.S. government (Schaupp & Carter, 2005). Citizen perceptions in this regard relate to trust in the technology being used and trust in the government that is utilizing the technology (McKnight et al., 2002; Schaupp & Carter, 2005). Schaupp and Carter (2005, p. 587) noted that a "lack of trust in the security and reliability of the technology" may serve as a barrier to the acceptance of online voting in that "before citizens will entrust such a significant portion of their civic voice to a computer-based system, they must have confidence in its ability to perform accurately and reliably." Claassen et al. (2013, p. 216) explained that it is important for the public to trust that "elections will produce fair outcomes" and a failure on this account may create a circumstance in which "voters may choose to stay home, thereby compromising the legitimacy of the government." Alvarez, Katz, and Pomares (2011, p. 200) studied the potential of e-voting methods in Argentina and Columbia to affect levels of voter confidence in the electoral process and explains that "whether e-voting can become a tool for increasing citizens' trust in elections or, on the contrary, a barrier for political participation, depends to a great extent on voters' attitudes and perceptions regarding the new voting procedures." Alvarez, Katz, and Pomares (2011) observed that contextual factors within the political environment—such as the voter's belief in the potential effectiveness of new technological devices being used in elections and the levels of voter trust in the government entities like election commissions utilizing those means—could influence public confidence in e-voting means. The online voting conducted by the Estonian government serves as a cautionary tale highlighting potential security issues that may affect election outcomes and, ultimately, reduce faith in the legitimacy of government. This includes the possibility that online elections may be subject to malicious home computer attacks designed to steal voter information for the purpose of altering votes being cast and attacks on government servers intended to alter, or miscount, votes that have been submitted by participants (Lust, 2015). The negative impact of security-related issues on online elections can be compounded by the lack of a verifiable paper trail to help ensure the integrity of the process and by the possibility that the voters whom are subjected to malicious home computer attacks altering their original vote could also be sent a phony confirmation message to further sell the election fraud (Lust, 2015). Mercuri (2002, p. 48) discussed the importance of taking preventative measures to protect against such security weaknesses by noting that "appropriate system testing" may play a critical role in the identification of existing imperfections. To help prevent negative effects associated with denial of service or malicious attacks on the electronic voting process, it is also possible to extend the election from one day to several days in order to create a larger timeframe serving as a preventative measure to guard against such unforeseen circumstances (Gibson, 2001). Before any significant efforts are taken in the United States to implement online voting on a national scale, it is important to acknowledge, and hopefully account for, the potential adverse effects that may result from doing so. The issue of security is of the utmost importance in determining the future feasibility of online voting. If ensuring that the online voting process is sufficiently secure is not possible, then the deleterious effects to the integrity of the electoral system will render this endeavor as an untenable digital means within context of deliberative democracy. Trust in the electoral process and faith in the integrity of the voting outcomes is instrumental in cementing and preserving governmental legitimacy. The preservation of both must be maintained for online voting in the U.S. system to be seriously considered as a viable option.

The role of ICTs in elections can be multifaceted so that developing an understanding of the application of a given voting technology can be dependent on elements such as determining the geographical variances in where the election process occurs. In addition, there are various perspectives associated with how to define the purpose of usage of modern technology when it is applied to the voting process. Bannister and Connolly (2012) made a distinction regarding the application of ICTs in electoral processes that can facilitate e-voting (which occurs on site through modernized e-machines) and online voting (which occurs via multiple locations through a diversity of innovative means). For Gibson (2001), there is a difference between the broad conception of "e-voting," which involves voting through any modern technological innovation means (DREs, online, etc.), regardless of location, and the sub-category of "i-voting," which involves participation in a binding election exclusively by casting a ballot online. The nature of e-voting is far from simplistic; the process involves multiple interrelated activities at each level of government in a federal system, and actualizing the broad scope of voting activities on such a large scale is multidimensional in many respects. Jin-Wook (2006) believed that e-voting can comprise diverse activities through identifiable dimensions, such as those related to casting votes through ICTS and in circumstances that "exceed the simple act of voting." In this sense, the overall nature of e-voting is considered to include actions at multiple stages throughout the electoral process and concludes when citizens eventually cast ballots through existing technologies or emerging ICTs. Here, e-voting is inclusive of the process of casting a ballot through available modern technology (either on site or online) and a number of interactive electronic events that stem from information dissemination practices for various stages throughout the election process (e.g., campaigning, conducting research on candidates, registering to vote, etc.) as indicated in Figure 10.1.

There are a number of possible benefits derived from e-voting that can contribute to improving the electoral system in a number of ways. The application of ICTs may play a role in reducing various types of monetary and non-monetary costs associated with the aforementioned dimensions of e-voting. In this sense, there is the potential that the Internet may be capable of positively affecting different types of costs associated with voting (Berinsky, 2005; Jin-Wook, 2006). Jin-Wook (2006) observed that incentives to participate in e-voting may be derived from the capacity to reduce various monetary cost considerations that independently serve as "practical and psychological" barriers associated with specifics such as registration costs, traveling to voting stations to participate in the election and lengthy wait times to vote. For example, it is suggested that the Internet may be capable of significantly reducing the fiscal costs for government in administering the actual voting process from start to finish (Jin-Wook, 2006). The ability to reduce this type of cost of voting through ICTs may be diminished somewhat if legal issues arise that will need to ultimately be settled in court and this can offset potential projected saving associated with e-voting (Jin-Wook, 2006). The applicability of potential losses include fiscal costs associated with expensive legal battles in court and non-monetary costs in which

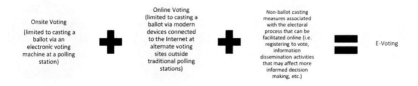

Figure 10.1 E-Voting

perceptions of governmental legitimacy are negatively affected by e-voting results being contested in the court system. In addition, the fiscal savings associated with e-voting can extend to the spectrum of activities that involve the dissemination of information that may eventually affect how citizens formulate electoral decisions. The Internet can be a more fiscally sound alternative for citizens to become better informed about political candidates and it is also a cost-effective means for political candidates to disseminate personalized information associated with their respective campaigns (Jin-Wook, 2006). Overall, fiscal savings derived from e-voting can extend to a reduction of administrative costs for government associated with facilitating the election process while also being capable of diffusing citizens' costs associated with many aspects of participation. It is also possible that campaign costs for candidates may be reduced by utilizing more cost-effective supplementary digital marketing techniques and that citizens can benefit from using a variety of electronic means to research information associated with candidates in a cost-effective manner from anywhere with an Internet connection.

E-voting may also affect non-monetary costs that have deeper deliberative democracy implications. There are potential benefits associated with e-voting related to the ability of this means to strengthen overall levels of trust in the voting process and, by association, increase levels of faith in government on behalf of citizens. Avgerou et al. (2009) discussed the potential link between the usage of ICTs to facilitate E-Government activities such as e-voting and the ability of ICTs to successfully foster higher levels of trust in government on behalf of citizens. Trust in e-voting is derived from the comfort level on a societal scale of the application of ICTs, the ease of use associated with e-machines and the ability of government to provide a highly robust security plan to ensure electoral integrity (Avgerou et al., 2009). Avgerou et al. (2009, p. 142) discussed the importance of secure e-voting machines during municipal-level elections in Brazil by remarking that "the technical trustworthiness of the entire system is ensured by a security infrastructure aimed at preventing data from being intentionally or unintentionally modified and/or deleted." In relation, it is also possible that ICTs such as the Internet may be used toward electoral reformation, which affects "cognitive costs" related to the expectations in the ability of active citizen–government participation to positively affect who votes and how frequently they engage in this type of event (Berinsky, 2005). Jin-Wook (2006) also noted that there may be higher "latent" costs incurred by political candidates who opt to ignore the importance of maintaining a digital presence during an election campaign, potentially exceeding drawbacks incurred by citizens who do not take advantage of available digital information dissemination means to educate themselves on candidates before voting. The multiple dimensions associated with the application of e-voting means, those related to casting ballots and those focused on disseminating information, and the potential costs, monetary and non-monetary, are further explored below.

The initial dimension of e-voting concerns processes associated with casting a ballot and could include the usage of various ICTs associated with any number of reforms derived from HAVA. For example, a number of e-machines have been used in federal elections including direct recording electronic (DRE) voting devices that apply innovations such as touch screen technologies for casting votes and those that facilitate digital vote counting, which is automatically tallied when ballots are cast. It also includes the future potential associated with ICTs being applied to facilitate e-voting online through the Internet. This aspect of e-voting continues to generally be lacking in a great deal of large-scale practical significance in the United States at the federal level. This may be because there are presently insufficient levels of demand from the public that would require government to acquiesce to contextual cues for wide-scale adoption of online voting. For example, it may yet be untenable to consider a wide-scale renovation of the traditional on-site voting methodology, as this process remains deeply ingrained within the public's expectations for participation in elections. There may also be considerations that the development, implementation and maintenance of technology is not yet appropriately cost effective on a national scale for federal elections and that the technology may not yet be able to meet expectations that online voting processes are sufficiently secure. The fear of the lack of security in technology used to cast votes online may have been deepened recently by the alleged hack attempts by Russia that were perpetrated during the 2016 presidential election. This includes the hack of the Democratic National Committee (DNC) and the subsequent publication of information through WikiLeaks as a possible attempt to affect election outcomes. If online information is not secure and the release of hacked information may be capable of affecting electoral outcomes, then the trust in the ability of government to secure online voting procedures at this time may be insufficient to warrant its application. Ultimately, the initial dimension of e-voting is realistically more focused on applying innovations toward modernizing voting machines used on site at polling stations within the traditional context of a voting booth in the short term and toward electronic means that may potentially facilitate widespread online voting opportunities in future election scenarios. Here, technology is used to promote deliberative democracy by facilitating active citizen participation means such as e-voting that are capable of influencing the political system. The initial dimension associated with e-voting is focused on the important role in which innovations are used by citizens to cast votes in an election while also setting the groundwork for considering citizen–government information-based interactions associated with e-voting.

It is also important to acknowledge the second dimension of e-voting in which the applications of ICTs may affect non-ballot-casting activities. This includes that ICTs can facilitate citizens obtaining pertinent information online that may provide a clearer picture associated with political candidates running for office. For example, a political candidate may incorporate electronic components to a campaign that include the development of a website, the usage of web banners and the application of e-mail serving a digital grassroots function. The review of webpages for individuals seeking election to public office may provide helpful information associated with their value-based stance on policy issues of importance, past work experiences that would be applicable to their service if elected and even a wide array of personal beliefs held by the candidate. If the individual is an incumbent seeking re-election to public office, then citizens may also able to review extensive online information associated with public voting records and legislation proposed by the elected officials during their tenure in office. Here, e-voting may provide more cost-effective means for both political candidates and citizens as it relates to efforts to facilitate mutual interactions associated with information dissemination. This provides citizens that aspire to learn more about a candidate running for office at any level of government with readily available means to pursue this interest at their convenience and at relatively minimal cost. For example, the 2016 nominee for the Republican Party (Donald J. Trump: www.donaldjtrump.com/) and the nominee for the Democratic Party (Hillary Clinton: www.hillaryclinton.com/) each maintained a website that provided information associated with their respective campaign platforms leading into the November presidential election. In addition, third-party candidates with significant ballot access such as Gary Johnson from the Libertarian Party (www.johnsonweld.com/), Jill Stein from the Green Party (www.jill2016.com/) and Darrell Castle from the Constitution Party (www.constitutionparty.com/) also maintained websites to support their respective bids to become president. In this sense, the usage of the Internet allows for a certain level of equity for political parties, which can all develop a website to support their effort to win an election to political office. The two major parties (i.e., Republican, Democrat) and all third parties in the United States (i.e., Libertarian Party, Green Party, Constitution Party, etc.) may participate in the online political marketing process during elections in a relatively equitable fashion as access to the Internet is non-exclusionary to any of the candidates running for office. In relation, there is also a degree of vertical equity as it relates to candidates running for office at the national, state and local levels, as access is also non-exclusionary in nature. Therefore, candidates running for office at the local or national level are both free to develop a website and Internet-based campaign components supporting their respective bids for public office. When considering the high advertising costs for running political ads on television, a website is a comparatively more cost-effective way in which a political candidate can connect with potential voters in the E-Governance Era. Although cost effective, it would presently be unrealistic for a political candidate to only consider utilizing digital means to disseminate information to citizens due to the digital divide and the passive nature of the Internet. This continues to highlight the importance of utilizing traditional means and digital means to accomplish tasks in the E-Governance Era, including those associated with the information dissemination aspect of e-voting. In general, ICTs can make information more readily available to citizens, who can used it to make more informed voting decisions. ICTs can support deliberative democracy expectations associated with information dissemination and can empower citizens who actively seek online information for the purpose of making more informed voting decisions. Again, creating increased levels of access to online information through ICTs does not guarantee that citizens will make efforts to use that information when making voting choices. Governmental efforts to promote citizen participation may still succumb to the persistent influence of voter apathy, regardless of the technological innovation applied to strengthen the deliberative democracy framework. However, it is important to recognize the potential of the information dissemination dimension of e-voting to play a role in the empowerment of citizens that chose to use these means. The application of innovation to facilitate a vast array of deliberative activities associated with the multiple dimensions of e-voting continues to show great promise for the future of E-Governance. The deliberative framework can be strengthened significantly by utilizing technological innovation to promote more easily disseminated information and may lead to more informed decision-making from citizens during the voting process.

There are a plethora of potential opportunities to affect costs associated with each of the respective dimensions of e-voting, including those involving casting votes and disseminating information that may affect voter behavior. As online voting has yet to be fully actualized in the modern era on a broad federal scale, the potential for this aspect of U.S. e-voting to reduce future monetary electoral costs is still largely speculative in some respects. It is plausible that aspects of e-voting are capable of reducing administrative costs for government for a wide range of activities (i.e., casting digital ballots, tallying votes electronically, etc.) and direct costs to the voters associated with registering voter information and having to miss work in order to wait in line to vote. In relation, the future of online e-voting may potentially be helpful in reducing travel costs associated with commuting to polling stations that may have otherwise provided a fiscal barrier to some citizens. This fiscal barrier could be related to any combination of actual costs a citizen may incur traveling to and from a voting location. Citizens living in rural areas of the country without access to public transportation may need to travel in their own automobile, which requires costs associated with gasoline or citizens residing in urban areas without access to an automobile may use public transportation which requires a fiscal outlay. In cases such as this, online e-voting could reduce monetary costs associated with having to travel to and from the polling station to participate in the election. A citizen may be required to incur a personal loss of income if he or she is voting during hours traditionally spent fulfilling job duties.

While the future of monetary savings derived from casting ballots online shows promise, e-voting can presently offer savings in other dimensions associated with the topic. For example, the dimension of e-voting associated with registration for elections can reflect cost savings in the modern government system to a certain degree. Presently, ICTs can be used to facilitate this dimension of e-voting to potentially offset fiscal loss associated with having to travel to a location and possibly missing time at work in order to register to vote on site in a traditional capacity. This includes that voter registration information associated with parameters for eligibility requirements, the location of voter polling places, dates for upcoming elections and printable voter registration forms are made readily accessible through online means. In relation, there are numerous available governmental websites that provide citizens with the opportunity to obtain important voter registration information and even the opportunity to register to vote online. This includes state websites, federal websites and non-government websites that have an online presence designed to help facilitate the voter registration process. If a citizen living in New Jersey was eligible to vote and was seeking to vote in the 2016 presidential election, then there would be many cost-effective online means available that could help facilitate this registration process. The state of New Jersey, as do most U.S. states, has numerous online options that provide a blend of traditional and digital means to promote voter registration. For example, a citizen residing in New Jersey can log on to The State of New Jersey Department of State website to review information through the Division of Elections to determine if he or she is presently registered to vote (https://voter.njsvrs.com/PublicAccess/servlet/com.sa ber.publicaccess.control.PublicAccessNavigationServlet?USERPROCESS=Pu blicSearch). The website also provides a link that offers information associated with voter eligibility requirements, instructions for registering to vote and even provides citizens with a printable traditional voter registration form that is able to be sent to a County Commissioner without paying for postage if mailed from within the United States (www.state.nj.us/state/elec tions/voting-information.html). A supplemental online governmental resource at the state level in New Jersey that provides guidance to citizens who are seeking to register to vote includes the Department of Motor Vehicles (www.dmv.org/nj-new-jersey/voter-registration.php). However, that same citizen could choose to obtain information and begin the voter registration process through any number of federal websites. This includes voter registration information located at federal government-oriented websites such as USA.Gov (www.usa.gov/register-to-vote), the United States Election Assistance Commission (www.eac.gov/voter_resources/register_to_vote.aspx) and the Federal Voting Assistance Program through the Department of Defense (www.fvap.gov/info/about/purpose/privacy). Lastly, there are also various non-government websites that provide voter registration information, such as the Rock the Vote campaign (www.rockthevote.com/?referrer=https:// www.google.com/) and others (https://www.facebook.com/VOTE.org/).

In addition to the capacity of ICTs applied toward e-voting to reduce monetary costs, there is also the possibility that usage may have an impact on the costs of voting that are non-monetary in nature. This includes what

Berinsky (2005) and Jin-Wook (2006) referred to as "cognitive" and "latent" costs, respectively. There are a wide variety of non-monetary costs that may be affected dependent on whether the usage of e-voting in the E-Governance Era is perceived as a success or failure. For example, citizens' perceptions of the legitimacy of e-voting actions may result from government being successful in adapting innovations to accommodate expectations within the deliberative democracy framework in the E-Governance Era. This includes the importance of maintaining the ability to consistently facilitate deliberative actions associated with e-voting in a secure setting. If security breaches occur during the application of ICTs used to facilitate e-voting procedures, then this may negatively affect perceptions associated with the overall legitimacy of democracy. A security breach of online means used for registering citizens to vote and during voting through e-machines on site at polling stations may greatly deteriorate the legitimacy of the electoral process in the eyes of the public. The legitimacy of e-voting dimensions focused on non-vote-casting endeavors becomes weakened in cases in which it is perceived that personal information is somehow not secure when registering to vote online. More importantly, the possibility that voting outcomes may come into question as being illegitimate due to security breaches may irreparably diminish citizen perceptions of legitimacy in government activities associated with e-voting. This relates to the possibility that e-machines at polling booths could potentially be hacked to alter a vote for a candidate that was not originally selected. If the future of voting is to eventually be facilitated online on a wide-scale federal level, then it is paramount that government officials take measures to preserve the integrity of the outcomes associated with all aspects of the electronic election process.

It is also important to note that there may be additional non-monetary cost considerations associated with ICTs that are applied toward various means associated with e-voting. This includes being aware of the possible role that the digital divide may play in alienating those citizens that are unable or unwilling to transition to participating in e-voting on site through e-machines or online, should this option become actualized on a broader scale in binding elections. Ultimately, voter preferences will play a role in dictating the means used by the individual participating in elections. The likely continued existence of the digital divide reinforces the importance of remaining wary of considerations to incorporate an electoral system in the immediate future that is wholly electronic, further justifying that diversity in deliberative means be maintained. A modern E-Governance Era electoral system that fails to successfully coordinate the integration of traditional means with digital means may incur non-monetary costs, such as potentially yielding lower levels of participation by those citizens that are without necessary measures to accommodate their voter preferences. The results associated with elections that are lacking in a more universally appealing voting system capable of simultaneously supporting traditional and digital means may be perceived as being incongruent with the actual will of the overall public regarding preferences for elected officials in office and, by association, with the resulting government actions taken by those elected officials. In relation, technical disenfranchisement resulting from an electoral system that fails to recognize the effects of the digital divide may potentially negatively affect levels of citizen trust in government. Failure to use a voting schema that is representative of diverse means capable of accommodating multiple electoral preferences of citizens can adversely impact perceptions associated with governmental legitimacy. The perception that government actions, short-term electoral results and long-term governmental behaviors, derivative of a voting system with a possible representativeness deficiency that is unable to accommodate a diverse range of user preferences could be subject to criticism of legitimacy and may potentially garner lower levels of citizen faith in government.

In sum, the dimensions of e-voting include activities associated with the process of casting a vote during an election and non-vote casting measures that may promote more informed voting decisions on behalf of citizens participating in elections. E-voting efforts in the United States serve as an example in which technological innovation is presently applicable toward facilitating a number of electoral activities, and also set a foundation in which future e-voting designs will require continued reflection. This includes ballot-casting e-voting means that occurs presently through modern voting machine technologies on site at polling stations and the potential of utilizing online voting to facilitate binding elections at all levels of government in the federal system in the future. In addition, there are a number of non-ballot-casting elements of e-voting activities (i.e., information dissemination, registering to vote, etc.) that are capable of affecting voter participation and voter behavior in upcoming elections. In addition, monetary and non-monetary concerns associated with each of the aforementioned dimensions of e-voting require attention. The technological advancements in the E-Governance Era have affected changes to the processes of applying innovations to improve performance of governmental duties and have played a role in shifting societal expectations associated with how to better facilitate a wide array of those government actions. Here, the usage of innovation may affect monetary costs associated with e-voting activities related to registering eligible citizens to vote, government's administration of the electoral process and the means in which election-centric information is disseminated from government to citizens. There are significant concerns associated with the impact of e-voting on non-monetary related topics associated with citizen-participation levels and in citizens' faith in government to adequately perform electoral duties. For example, the proficiency of government to accurately tally votes cast by a citizen on site through secure e-machines continues to be of importance. The future of developing secure Internet e-voting processes facilitated through computers, handheld devices or public kiosks will be crucial to ensure accuracy in voting results and to assist in cultivating perceptions of legitimate government actions enacted by public officials placed in office via online e-voting participation. Also, the potential usage of a blend of traditional means and digital means provide future challenges to e-voting in the E-Governance Era that must ultimately be addressed during wide-scale federal elections in the United States. The future of voting reforms will likely require government to attend to unparalleled complexities associated with constructing an electoral schema that is able to adequately accommodate citizen preferences by providing choices in which to participate in a traditional fashion or digital fashion. E-voting in the E-Governance Era can potentially affect citizen participation levels within the deliberative democracy framework, alter citizen perceptions associated with the legitimacy in government and influence system outcomes in the form of government actions derived from electoral results.

As noted, there are a number of potential benefits associated with applying innovations toward facilitating the dimensions of e-voting that involve vote-casting measures or non-vote-casting measures that may contribute to strengthening the overall deliberative framework. However, there are also critiques associated with the usage of modern technological innovations to facilitate e-voting dimensions during elections that should not be ignored. This includes the possible non-monetary-oriented security concerns regarding the integrity of casting a ballot or with facilitating the transfer of personal information of citizens during non-ballot casting endeavors like registering to vote that may affect trust in government. The preservation of the legitimacy of the electoral process in the E-Governance Era has an added degree of difficulty in which security concerns associated with the usage of technology in e-voting endeavors applies unprecedented levels of innovations toward the fulfillment of this task. Here, on-site voting through modernized e-machines used presently in elections and online voting, should this option become viable, applies various forms of technology that are subject to uniquely contemporary security concerns.

In relation, there are arguments that the possibility of online voting is presently untenable on a wide scale due to a variety of E-Governance Era security risks. Simons and Jones (2012, p. 71) argued against claims that elections held through the Internet are inevitable, as "secure Internet voting is unachievable for the foreseeable future" partly because e-voting through computers is presently flawed based on instances in which "elections can be stolen by inserting malware into code on large numbers of machines." This includes security risks that can threaten the integrity of online computer-based e-voting means, which may be subjected to intentional attempts to manipulate votes. In relation, a security concern associated with the future of online voting includes cyber-attack activities, such as phishing, that could potentially have significant negative repercussions on electoral processes and outcomes. The Department of Homeland Security (2016) defined *phishing* as "an attempt by an individual or group to solicit personal information from unsuspecting users by employing social engineering techniques. Phishing e-mails are crafted to appear as is if they have been sent from a legitimate organization or known individual. These e-mails often attempt to entice users to click on a link that will take the user to a fraudulent website that appears legitimate." Akinyelu and Adewumi (2014, p. 1) explained that "phishing is an act that attempts to electronically obtain delicate or confidential information from users (usually for the purpose of theft) by creating a replica website of a legitimate organization. Phishing is usually perpetrated with the aid of an electronic device (such as iPads and computer) and a computer network." James (2005, p. 2) stated that "the term *phishing* comes from the fact that cyber-attackers are fishing for data; the ph is derived from the sophisticated techniques they employ, to distinguish their activities from the more simplistic fishing." Hong (2012) noted that "phishing is a kind of social-engineering attack in which criminals use spoofed e-mail messages to trick people into sharing sensitive information or installing malware on their computers." Bergholz et al. (2010) discussed that phishing efforts to obtain various types of personal information may be facilitated though activities that are either "malware based" or through various other designs that are focused on deception. Bergholz et al. (2010) explained that malware-based phishing disseminates "malicious software" when misleading e-mails are opened by the user or through "exploiting security holes in the computer software" that grants the phisher access to targeted information. Hong (2012) observed that phishing methods have expanded from e-mails to also include communication means such as voice-over IP (VOIP), short message service (SMS), instant messaging (IM), social networking and massively multiplayer online (MMO) gaming platforms. Deceptive phishing techniques include "mimicry" (Bergholz et al., 2010), which fabricates official looking e-mails, websites and/or logos in which the design is intended to give the sender the appearance of authenticity. The deception is based partly on the belief that the phishing message, be it visual or text based, has been sent from a "trusted brand" (Hong, 2012). In relation, deceptive phishing techniques include the practice of "social engineering," which is essentially crafting a believable story to trick the user into participating in revealing critical information (Jakobsson & Myers, 2007; Bergholz et al., 2010; Jensen, 2011; Pyzik, 2015). Jensen (2011) preferred the use of the term *digital forgery* over phishing partly as a means to redirect the focus of the conversation to recognize the rhetorical capacity of electronic designs like "websites" and "logos" used during the deceiver–deceived relationship dynamic. Phishing has also grown in scope from vague, unspecific broad attacks sent *en masse* to a more specifically engineered "spearfishing" effort that have a more situationally relevant design (Hong, 2012). These types of attacks have a more contextual component to them in which a believable story is coupled with some level of personalized information to further strengthen the level of deception. This type of cyber-attack can include contextually relevant information to make the phishing attempt more believable so that it appears as if a person (i.e., family member, friend, coworker, etc.) or entity (i.e., employer, government agency, etc.) that is trusted by the receiver is involved. Phishing can target specific individuals or entire organizations in the public sector and private sector in order to gain access to critical personal identity information, corporate trade secrets and even national security–related intelligence (Hong, 2012). The general end-game associated with phishing schemes is often to obtain information used to generate illicitly gained funds. Jensen (2011) explained that "the exigent problem that drives phishing research is the economic losses that result for successful phishing solicitations." However, finances are not the only variety of losses that could be incurred as a result of phishing. The success of phishing endeavors may result in fiscal losses of individuals or organizations while also creating a potential "loss of reputation and reduced customer trust" (Bergholz et al., 2010). This relates directly to the negative repercussions associated with government failure to create a voting environment which is not secured against possible cyber-attacks such as phishing that may diminish trust in the legitimacy of elections.

Conceptually, there is a shared responsibility for preventing phishing schemes that is both organizational and individual in nature. In addition, the focus of such preventative measures exceeds simply being that of solving a technical quandary and delves into understanding the human element that is involved in an attempt at deception in the sender–receiver relationship. The organizational responsibility for combating phishing scams reflects a combination of developing more effective technical tools and education programs that allow for individuals to identify, and hopefully avoid, this form of cyber-attack (Hong, 2012). Wright and Marett (2010, p. 297) echoed the importance of developing means to combat phishing, including offering a combination of "technological tools, such as phishing toolbars and email filters" and making efforts to educate "the Web user" that serves as "the last line of defense." However, it is also important to note that efforts to develop technical advancements and educational programs are not surefire means "if the person behind the keyboard falls for a phish" (Hong, 2012). This speaks to the human element associated with phishing scams that cannot simply be discounted when addressing security concerns (Jensen, 2011). Wright and Marett (2010, p. 276) focused on the human element of phishing dynamics between the "deceiver" and "receiver" from the perspective of seeking to understand "what behavioral factors influence one's decision to respond to phishers" rooted in literature of "deceptive communication research." Jensen (2011) observed the "social dimensions" of phishing, which involves the intended recipient's perceptions of messages purposefully constructed with the intention to deceive in an interactive scenario. Jensen (2011, p. 175, 180) argued against "ignoring the rhetorical dimensions of phishing" while observing that this dynamic includes purposeful efforts that provide a "juxtaposition of image and text" designed to deceive. Phishing is reflective of a purposefully deceptive effort in which the sender constructs a message, visual and/or textual, to convince the intended recipient to engage in interactions designed initially to grant access to important personalized information. This aspect of phishing is reflective of a communicative function in which purposefully constructed persuasive arguments serve as a form of narrative within the deliberative democracy framework. Box 10.2 highlights how Barthes and Duisit (1975, p. 237) explained narrative constructs

---

Box 10.2 Narrative Constructs

Among the vehicles of narrative are articulated language, whether oral or written, pictures, still or moving, gestures and an ordered mixture of all those substances; Narrative is present in myth, legend, fables, tales, short stories, epics, history, tragedy, drame (suspense drama), comedy, pantomime, paintings, stained glass windows, movies, local news and conversation.

Here, the construction of phishing messages, a form of narrative that can be text and image based, serves as an argument designed to persuade the targeted recipient of a contextual message allowing the deceiver to obtain personalized information intended for use to achieve nefarious goals. This phishing dynamic between sender and receiver is represented in Figure 10.2.

Providing individuals with the tools to thwart phishing schemes requires a combination of the development of innovation means capable of identifying the threat on behalf of an organization and actively maintaining educational programs designed to promote awareness of the purposes of such technology-based safeguards available to the users. There is also the importance of recognizing the role that the human element may play in contributing to the overall understanding of the relationship dynamics between the sender (who is attempting to deceive) and intended receiver (the potential deceived) during a targeted phishing attack. For example, deceivers are individuals that intentionally construct technology-based phishing schemes designed to persuade the individual user into electronic-based engagements that will result in granting access to sensitive information. The phishing constructs, text and/or image based, are designed by the sender(s) and the intended target of this brand of electronic criminality is perpetrated against the unsuspecting recipient(s). The technical means serve as the digital bridge between the deceiver and the potentially deceived. These technical means are

Figure 10.2 Phishing Dynamics

reflective of contextual constructs that have a persuasive function insofar as they are designed to convince the user into taking various actions that will result in the transfer of sensitive information. The recognition of the presence of contextual electronic arguments inherent within phishing schemes, designed to persuade individuals to engage in interactions potentially resulting in breaches of information, can contribute to developing a broader understanding of the sender–receiver relationship dynamic.

On the micro level, the technical components of phishing ploys are the means in which one person (the deceiver) attempts to electronically perpetrate a criminal act against other individuals (the potential deceived). On the macro level, this concept is also applicable when large public sector or private sector entities are the target of cyber-attacks such as those designed for phishing purposes. This includes large-scale phishing attacks that may be perpetrated against government agencies that have critical national security information by potential symmetrical enemies, such as other governments, or asymmetrical enemies, such as terrorist organizations. The advancements in technology in the E-Governance Era has led to an increased application of electronic tools by government in the fulfillment of various public sector activities, but has also brought with it a unique set of innovation-based concerns. This is especially true as it relates to the usage of ICTs toward deliberative actions associated with the each of the dimensions of e-voting. The nature of election fraud in the E-Governance Era has shifted somewhat in that innovations used to facilitate the dimensions of e-voting may create new methods for stealing votes, altering overall election outcomes and disenfranchising citizens through technological duplicity. As noted, voter fraud could be facilitated on site at election booths in which e-machines are subject to software hacks capable of affecting the outcomes. Voter fraud considerations are also relevant for e-voting—fraud could be facilitated in an online capacity in which multiple security concerns may diminish the potential for wide-scale application in U.S. federal elections. Logically, cyber-attacks such as phishing scams can be used to threaten the safety of information regarding the identity of voters and even potentially affect the outcomes of an online election. The faith of citizens in government as a "trusted brand" (Hong, 2012) can be diminished if official electoral entities are falsely represented through digital deception associated with phishing attempts that successfully affects e-voting processes and/or outcomes. Most importantly in the context of digital deliberative democracy framework, there are greater ramifications if the possibility that election outcomes are altered through phishing designs. The phishing schemes that discloses voter identification information could be used to cast a vote on behalf of citizens without their knowledge. This also includes falsely indicating to the citizen that a vote has been cast through false websites which appear legitimate, when it has not been tallied during the election process. These examples of technical disenfranchisement can negatively affect levels of trust in e-voting election outcomes and the reputation of government in general. E-Governance

Era e-voting concerns stemming from the application of advancements in modern technology serve as a cautionary tale as it relates to maintaining citizens' trust in the ability of government to adequately facilitate participative means within a deliberative democracy.

References

Akinyelu, A. A., & Adewumi, A. O. (2014) Classification of phishing email using random forest machine learning technique. *Journal of Applied Mathematics*, 1–6. doi: 10.1155/2014/425731.

Alvarez, M., Katz, G., & Pomares, J. (2011) The impact of new technologies on voter confidence in Latin America: Evidence from e-voting experiments in Argentina and Colombia. *Journal of Information Technology & Politics*, 8(2): 199–217. doi: 10.1080/19331681.2011.559739.

Alvaraz, M., Hall, Thad E., Gimble, K., & Griepentrog, B. (2008) The 2008 Okaloosa distance balloting pilot project. Fors Marsh Group, LLC. Retrieved from www.fvap.gov/uploads/FVAP/OkaloosaPilotProject_20151228.pdf.

Avgerou, C., Ganzaroli, A., Poulymenakou, A., & Reinhard, N. (2009) Interpreting the trustworthiness of government mediated by information and communication technology: Lessons from electronic voting in Brazil. *Information Technology for Development*, 15(2): 133–148. doi: 10.1002/itdj.20120.

Bannister, F., & Connolly, R. (2012) Forward to the past: Lessons for the future of e-government from the story so far. *Information Polity: The International Journal of Government & Democracy in the Information Age*, 17(3/4): 211–226.

Barthes, R., & Duisit, L. (1975) An introduction to the structural analysis of narrative. *New Literary History: A Journal of Theory and Interpretation*, 6(2): 237–272.

Bergholz, A., De Beer, J., Glahn, S., Moens, M., Paaß, G., & Strobel, S. (2010) New filtering approaches for phishing email. *Journal of Computer Security*, 18(1): 7–35. doi: 10.3233/JCS-2010-0371.

Berinsky, A. J. (2005) The perverse consequences of electoral reform in the United States. *American Politics Research*, 33(4): 471.

Claassen, R., Magleby, D., Monson, J., & Patterson, K. (2013) Voter confidence and the election-day voting experience. *Political Behavior*, 35(2): 215–235. doi: 10.1007/s11109-012-9202-4.

Fortier, F. (2000) Virtual communities, real struggles: Seeking alternatives for democratic networking. In M. Gurstein (ed.), *Community informatics: Enabling communities with information and communications technologies* (pp. 446–469). Hershey, PA: IGI Global.

Gibson, R. (2001) Elections online: Assessing Internet voting in light of the Arizona democratic primary. *Political Science Quarterly*, 116(4): 561–583.

Hong, J. (2012) The state of phishing attacks. *Communications of the ACM*, 55(1): 74–81. doi: 10.1145/2063176.2063197.

Indiana Statewide Voter Registration System. (2016) Retrieved from https://indiana voters.in.gov/PublicSite/Public/FT1/PublicLookupMain.aspx?Link=Registration.

Jakobsson, M., & Myers, S. (eds). (2007) *Phishing and countermeasures: Understanding the increasing problem of electronic identity theft*. Hoboken, NJ: Wiley.

James, L. (2005) *Phishing exposed*. Rockland, MA: Syngress.

Jefferson, D., Rubin, A., Simons, B., & Wagner, D. (2004) *A security analysis of the Secure Electronic Registration and Voting Experiment (SERVE)*. Retrieved from https://people.eecs.berkeley.edu/~daw/papers/servereport.pdf.

Jensen, K. (2011) A matter of concern: Kenneth Burke, phishing, and the rhetoric of national insecurity. *Rhetoric Review*, 30(2): 170–190. doi: 10.1080/07350198.2011.552378.

Jin-Wook, C. (2006) Deliberative democracy, rational participation and e-voting in South Korea. *Asian Journal of Political Science*, 14(1): 64–81. 10.1080/02185370600832547.

Kenski, K. (2005) To i-vote or not to i-vote?: Opinions about Internet voting from Arizona voters. *Social Science Computer Review*, 23(3): 293–303. doi: 10.1177/0894439305275851.

Krishnan, K. P. (2014) E-voting leveraging cloud computing for better corporate governance in India. *Annamalai International Journal of Business Studies & Research*, 6(1): 10–14.

Lust, A. (2015) Online voting: Boon or bane for democracy? *Information Polity: The International Journal of Government & Democracy in the Information Age*, 20(4): 313–323. doi: 10.3233/IP-150373.

Mahoney, M. (2010) Comment of pilot project testing and certification. Retrieved from www.eac.gov/assets/1/AssetManager/Martha%20Mahoney%20-%20Comment%20on%20Pilot%20Project%20Testing%20and%20Certification.pdf.

McKnight, D. H., Choudhury, V., & Kacmar, C. (2002) Developing and validating trust measures for e-commerce: An integrative typology. *Information Systems Research*, 13(3): 334–359.

Mercuri, R. (2002) A better ballot box? New electronic voting systems pose risks as well as solutions. *IEEE Spectrum*, 39(10): 46–50.

Prevost, A. K., & Schaffner, B. F. (2008) Digital divide or just another absentee ballot? Evaluating Internet voting in the 2004 Michigan democratic primary. *American Politics Research*, 36(4): 510–529.

Pyzik, K. (2015) Shutting the door on social engineering. *Internal Auditor*, 72(5): 20–21.

Schaupp, L. C., & Carter, L. (2005) E-voting: From apathy to adoption. *Journal of Enterprise Information Management*, 18(5): 586–601. Retrieved from http://search.proquest.com/docview/220020269?accountid=32521.

Simons, B., & Jones, D. W. (2012) Internet voting in the U.S. *Communications of the ACM*, 55(10): 68–77. doi: 10.1145/2347736.2347754.

Solop, F. I. (2001) Digital democracy comes of age: Internet voting and the 2000 Arizona democratic primary election. *PS: Political Science & Politics*, 34(2): 289–293. doi: 10.1017/S104909650100052X.

United States Congress. (2004) Public Law 108–375 108th Congress: Ronald W. Reagan National Defense Authorization Act for Fiscal Year 2005. Retrieved from www.gpo.gov/fdsys/pkg/PLAW-108publ375/pdf/PLAW-108publ375.pdf.

United States Congress. (2010) National Defense Authorization Act of 2010: Section 575 The Military and Overseas Empowerment Act (MOVE). Retrieved from www.justice.gov/sites/default/files/crt/legacy/2011/01/06/MOVE_Act.pdf.

United States Department of Defense. (2004) Report of DoD Actions to Support Voting Assistance to Armed Forces Outside the U.S. As Required by Section 568 of the Ronald W. Reagan National Defense Authorization Act for Fiscal Year 2005. Retrieved from www.dod.mil/pubs/foi/Reading_Room/Personnel_Related/13-F-0748_Report_on_DoD_Action_to_Support_Voting_Assistance_to_Armed_Forces.pdf.

United States Department of Homeland Security. (2016) How do I?: Report cyber incidents. Retrieved from www.dhs.gov/how-do-i/report-cyber-incidents.

United States Department of Justice. (2010) Fact sheet: MOVE act. Retrieved from www.justice.gov/opa/pr/fact-sheet-move-act.

United States Federal Voting Assistance Program. (2012) Electronic transmission service manual. Retrieved from www.fvap.gov/uploads/FVAP/EO/etsmanualfor leos.pdf.

United States Federal Voting Assistance Program. (2015) Review of the FVAP work related to remote electronic voting for the UOCAVA population. Retrieved from www.fvap.gov/uploads/FVAP/Reports/FVAP_EVDP_20151229_final.pdf.

United States Federal Voting Assistance Program. (2016) Indiana. Retrieved from www.fvap.gov/vao/vag/chapter2/indiana.

United States Government Accountability Office. (2007) Elections: Action plans needed to fully address challenges in electronic absentee voting initiatives for military and overseas citizens. Retrieved from www.gao.gov/new.items/d07774.pdf.

Wright, R. T., & Marett, K. (2010) The influence of experiential and dispositional factors in phishing: An empirical investigation of the deceived. *Journal of Management Information Systems*, 27(1): 273–303. doi: 10.2753/MIS0742–1222270111.

Index

Page numbers in bold refer to tables. Page numbers in italic refer to figures.